T R A V E L E R ' S

VIETNAM
LAOS & CAMBODIA
C O M P A N I O N

The Traveler's Companions
ARGENTINA • AUSTRALIA • BALI • CALIFORNIA • CANADA • CHINA • COSTA RICA •
CUBA • EASTERN CANADA • ECUADOR • FLORIDA • HAWAII • HONG KONG • INDIA •
INDONESIA • JAPAN • KENYA • MALAYSIA & SINGAPORE • MEDITERRANEAN FRANCE •
MEXICO • NEPAL • NEW ENGLAND • NEW ZEALAND • PERU • PHILIPPINES • PORTUGAL •
RUSSIA • SOUTH AFRICA • SOUTHERN ENGLAND • SPAIN • THAILAND • TURKEY •
VENEZUELA • VIETNAM, LAOS AND CAMBODIA • WESTERN CANADA

Traveler's Vietnam, Laos and Cambodia Companion

First published 1998
Second Edition 2002
The Globe Pequot Press
246 Goose Lane, PO Box 480
Guilford, CT 06437 USA
www.globe-pequot.com

© 2002 by The Globe Pequot Press, Guilford CT, USA

ISBN: 0-7627-2334-3

Created, edited and produced by
Allan Amsel Publishing, 53, rue Beaudouin
27700 Les Andelys, France.
E-mail: AAmsel@aol.com

Editor in Chief: Allan Amsel
Editor: Anne Trager
Picture editor and book designer: Roberto Rossi

Based on an original text by Derek Maitland

Printed by Samwha Printing Co. Ltd., Seoul, South Korea

TRAVELER'S
VIETNAM
LAOS & CAMBODIA
COMPANION

by Chris Taylor

photographed by Alain Evrard

Second Edition

The
Globe
Pequot
Press

GUILFORD
CONNECTICUT

Contents

MAPS

Vietnam, Laos & Cambodia	8-9
Hanoi	106
Northern Vietnam	123
Central Vietnam	130
Saigon (Ho Chi Minh City)	158
Southern Vietnam	178
Phnom Penh	194
Cambodia	205
Central Vientiane	228
Laos	237

TOP SPOTS   11
Discover a Temple City   11
Ride the *Reunification Express*   12
Haggle in a Country Market   13
Ponder the Mystery of the Plain of Jars   15
Explore the Tonkinese Alps   15
Witness a Cultural Revival   17
Be a "Tunnel Rat"   18
Mosey down the Mekong   19
Admire Banteay Srei   20
Ride the Perfume River   22

YOUR CHOICE   25
The Great Outdoors   25
Sporting Spree   30
The Open Road   32
Backpacking   33
Living It Up   38
Family Fun   41
Cultural Kicks   41
Shop till You Drop   47
Festive Flings   50
Short Breaks   53
Galloping Gourmet   54
Special Interests   58
Taking a Tour   59

WELCOME TO INDOCHINA   63

INDOCHINA AND ITS PEOPLE   69
The Ancient Hindu Kingdoms   70
The Chinese Impact   70
Arrival of the Mountain People   72
Birth of the Khmer Empire   75
Enter the Thais   76
The French Connection   78
The Seeds of Revolt   79
Independence and the First Indochina War   80
The Second Indochina War and
the Americans   83
The Khmer Rouge Horror   85
Vietnam Invades Cambodia   86
The Aftermath   86
Indochina Today   86
Indochina's People   88
The Economy   89
Politics   91
Religion   95
Geography   98

NORTHERN AND CENTRAL VIETNAM   **101**

Hanoi   103
  General Information • Getting Around •
  What to See and Do • Shopping •
  Where to Stay • Where to Eat •
  Nightlife • How to Get There •
  Around Hanoi
Hai Phong   121
  What to See and Do • Where to Stay •
  Where to Eat • How to Get There
Ha Long Bay   123
  Where to Stay and Eat •
  How to Get There
Dien Bien Phu   124
Lai Chau   125
Sa Pa   125
Bac Ha   126
Heading South   127
Hue   127
  General Information • What to See
  and Do • Where to Stay • Where to Eat •
  How to Get There • Around Hue
Da Nang   140
  What to See and Do • Where to Stay •
  Where to Eat • How to Get There •
  Around Da Nang
Hoi An (Fai Fo)   144
  What to See and Do • Where to Stay •
  Where to Eat • How to Get There
Qui Nhon   148
  What to See and Do • Where to Stay
  and Eat • How to Get There

Nha Trang   149
  What to See and Do • Where to Stay •
  Where to Eat • Around Nha Trang •
  How to Get There
Da Lat   152
  What to See and Do • Where to Stay •
  Where to Eat • Around Da Lat •
  How to Get There

SOUTHERN VIETNAM   **157**

Saigon (Ho Chi Minh City)   158
  General Information • Getting Around •
  What to See and Do • Where to Stay •
  Where to Eat • Nightlife •
  How to Get There
Around Saigon   176
  Phan Thiet • Vung Tau • Tay Ninh •
  Cu Chi Tunnels
The Mekong Delta   179
  My Tho • Can Tho • Long Xuyen •
  Chau Doc
The Islands   186
  Phu Quoc • Con Dau Islands

CAMBODIA   **189**

Phnom Penh   191
  General Information • Getting Around •
  What to See and Do • Where to Stay •
  Where to Eat • Nightlife •
  How to Get There •
Around Phnom Penh   206
  The Killing Fields • Odong • Ta Promh
  Tonle Bati • Phnom Chiso (Surya Parvata) •
  Koh Dach • Sihanoukville (Kompong Saom)

Siem Reap	209
General Information • What to See and Do • Where to Stay • Where to Eat • How to Get There	
LAOS	**221**
Vientiane	223
General Information • Getting Around • What to See and Do • Shopping • Environs • Where to Stay • Where to Eat • How to Get There	
Luang Prabang	237
General Information • What to See and Do • Where to Stay • Where to Eat • Environs • How to Get There	
North of Luang Prabang	248
Luang Nam Tha • Muang Sing • Muang Xay	
Xieng Khoang (Plain of Jars)	250
Where to Stay and Eat	
Pakse and the South	252
Pakse • Champassak and Wat Phu • Si Phan Don — The 4,000 Islands • Thatlo Resort • How to Get There	
TRAVELERS' TIPS	**259**
Getting There	261
Flights to Indochina • Overland to Indochina	
Arriving and Leaving	263
Visas • Customs • Departure Taxes	
Embassies and Consulates	264
Foreign Representation in Indochina • Indochinese Representation Abroad	
Tourist Information	265
Getting Around	265
By Air • By Road • By Boat • By Rail	
Accommodation	266
Restaurants	268
Basics	268
Business and Banking Hours • Currency • Electricity • National Holidays • Time • Tipping	
Communication and Media	270
Telephones, Fax and Internet • Media	
Etiquette	271
Health	272
Security	272
Women Alone	272
Gay and Lesbian Travelers	273
Disabled Travelers	273
When to Go	273
What to Take	274
Language Basics	274
Recommended Web Sites	276
Recommended Reading	276
QUICK REFERENCE A–Z GUIDE	**279**
to Places and Topics of Interest	

BANGLADESH

MYANMA

TRAVELER'S
VIETNAM
LAOS & CAMBODIA
COMPANION

N

BANGLADESH
CHINA
TAIWAN
INDIA
MYANMAR
LAOS
THAILAND
VIETNAM
CAMBODIA
PHILIPPINES
N
MALAYSIA
SINGAPORE   BORNEO
SUMATRA

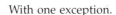

TOP SPOTS

With one exception.

The decision to leave the temple of Ta Phrom the way it was first discovered was controversial. One restorer lashed out suggesting it was motivated simply by the need to give bourgeois tourists the "exhilaration" of being latter-day Mouhots. Perhaps. Yet, wandering around the jungly precincts of Ta Phrom is one of the highlights of any Angkor visit — as if one had stumbled into the real-life inspiration for an *Indiana Jones* film set.

This is a temple that is best visited twice — once with a guide and once alone. (Unlike other temples in the Angkor complex, some of which are best seen at dusk or sunrise, the time of day is less important.) Ta Phrom is a labyrinth of tight passageways and narrow enclosures, many of them choked with the creeping root systems of massive trees, or blocked by fallen piles of masonry. A guide can lead the way to some of the best sections from which to view and photograph the jungle's attack on the temple. Wandering alone, on the other hand, really does evoke the feeling of having made a remarkable discovery — the remnants of a lost civilization in the jungle.

Less immediately impressive than either Angkor Wat itself or the eerie multi-faced Bayon, the twelfth-century Ta Phrom was nevertheless once one of

Discover a Temple City

When the French explorer Henri Mouhot came across the temple complex of Angkor wat and described his findings in a book, complete with pen and ink sketches, in 1868, he brought a long-forgotten wonder to world attention. At that time Angkor had been left to the jungle for so many centuries that it was in danger of being swallowed up completely, its mostly sandstone structure eroded by the elements and bat droppings and its form at the mercy of the muscular embrace of the jungle's roots and creepers. Restoration work began in the 1920s and was seriously underway by the 1960s. Interrupted by the madness of the Khmer Rouge era, it is proceeding once again.

OPPOSITE: Figures from the Lao version of the Hindu epic *Ramayana* decorate temple doors in Luang Prabang. ABOVE: Monks make an alms round at the Wat Phu festival in Champassak.

the most important temples in the entire Angkor complex. It claimed a congregation of close to 100,000 and a small army of attendant officials and dancers. Today it is marked by a haunting stillness, shrouded in shadow by the centuries-old trees, only the occasional shaft of sunlight breaking through and highlighting a bas relief that evokes the days when brocaded dancers performed in its courtyards.

Ride the
Reunification Express

Train aficionados can't afford to miss Vietnam's *Thong Nhat*, or *Reunification Express*, which spans the 2,012 km (1,250 miles) that separates Saigon and Hanoi. The journey can take an epic 48 hours or a slightly less grueling 36 hours, depending on the service — making something of a mockery of the appellation "express." Be that as it may, it is not a journey anyone forgets in a hurry.

The *Express* recommenced operations on December 31, 1976. Originally built by the French in the late 1930s, it was

bombed incessantly during the war, to nearly total destruction. Re-launching the railway was the culmination of months of restoration involving the repair of 158 stations, over 1,330 bridges, nearly 30 tunnels and 1,370 shunts. The single track was one of the first projects undertaken after the 1975 reunification.

While service has improved over the years, riding in the train remains an adventure, a chance to see the country in comfort yet still experience the everyday life of the Vietnamese. Every station-stop is a tumult of noise and action, as hawkers crowd to the barred train windows selling freshly boiled eggs, bottles of drinks, tea and coffee, exotic-looking fruit, bowls of steaming noodles and mysterious packets of food. As night falls, people in the cheaper hard seats start hanging up their hammocks, until the carriages and passageways are festooned with a maze of swinging bodies, comfortably ensconced in folds of dark green spun polyester. Several concessions have been made to tourism — namely the price, which is more than double what the Vietnamese pay: but in Vietnam, this is the norm.

As in China, travel classes include hard seat (best avoided) and soft seat, and hard sleeper (a wooden rack in a cabin of six) and soft sleeper, which is recommended as the most comfortable way to experience the train journey. If you are not traveling in a party of four, trust luck and the goodwill of the booking staff for your travel companions — they tend to group foreigners together.

Although food is available on the train, it is recommended that travelers bring some goodies of their own. The cooler winter months, when it is possible to snuggle in under the warm blankets, are probably the best time to travel. Even the soft-sleeper carriages are not air conditioned, which means that in the height of summer, train travel can be a sweaty experience.

For anyone who finds the distance and time involved a little daunting, it is perfectly possible to take just one or two legs of the journey or to break the trip along the way with a stopover. Hanoi to Hue is a pleasant overnight ride, arriving around midday, while the Hue to Da Nang sector provides a picturesque five-hour ride through luscious countryside.

Haggle in a Country Market

Despite the assault of malls and supermarkets, the traditional market continues to hold its own throughout Asia. Nowhere is this more the case than in Indochina, where modern shopping complexes are either thin on the ground or non-existent.

For many Westerners, visiting a country market is an opportunity to see and photograph some local color and perhaps to get some bargain on fabrics or souvenirs. But for locals the market is the equivalent of a department store, a bar, a coffee shop and restaurant all rolled into one. Going to market is less about snatching some bargains and heading home than about catching up on the gossip and having some fun while shopping for essentials — or perhaps selling them.

And herein lies the key to haggling. Successful bargaining relies on forging a relationship. The hard-nosed business-

OPPOSITE: The sparkling white stupas of Wat Botum, Phnom Penh. ABOVE: Rudimentary food stalls sell delicious food in northern Vietnam.

person with an eagle eye for the best price may well find the best price elusive if he or she is not prepared to have a little fun and do a little play-acting along the way.

The number-one rule is: do it with a smile. In other words, think "game" rather than "competition sport." The language barrier needn't be a barrier at all: finger counting, facial expressions, pen and paper (everybody knows Arabic numerals), not to mention the ubiquitous calculator, can all play a part in clinching a deal for anyone who cares to leap into the fray.

The market streets of Sa Pa in northern Vietnam are a good place to put newly gleaned skills to use, where traditionally dressed tribal women (don't let those sweet smiles deceive you into thinking they are softies) sell hand-embroidered costumes and handicrafts. Bac Ha, also in northern Vietnam, is another. It is best on Sundays, when the lower reaches of the small town swarm with tribal villagers, known, in a loose translation, as the "Variegated" or "Flower" Hmong because of their colorful costumes.

Another excellent market to hone haggling skills and shop for souvenirs is the Central Market in Phnom Penh. Known locally as the Psar Thmei ("new

market"), it's a fascinating place to get lost in for an hour or two. Almost definitive of Asian all-in-one marketplaces, it sells everything from local fabrics to fresh vegetables — with a lot of surprises in between. The popular tourist item here is the *krama*, a checkered scarf that in Cambodia serves a host of purposes; everything from, well, a scarf to a towel.

Not that all markets are about haggling for goodies to take home. Many are worth visiting simply to soak up the lively atmosphere. In northwestern Laos for example, close to the Chinese border, is the tiny village of Muang Sing, a Mecca for hundreds of surrounding tribal villages. Wearing their tribal best, villagers converge on the market each morning to sell their wares. Many come on foot, but the lucky ones come proudly bundled into a wagon attached to a communally owned tractor.

Visitors who have no time to venture into rural areas can enjoy a similar spectacle in Laos's Luang Prabang morning produce market — though be warned, this is no place for animal lovers, and particularly dog lovers.

In Central Vietnam, Hue's morning market sprawls on either side of the

Perfume River. Sampans piloted by cone-hatted women converge at the stone steps leading to the market. Later the same women can be seen making their way through the crowds bearing great baskets of vegetables, or perhaps a squealing pig or two tucked under their arms.

Even more colorful is the bustling floating market in Phung Hiep, a small market town 35 km (20 miles) from Can Tho, also in the Delta. Floating markets are a dying breed in Asia, and where they survive they have often been turned into tourist traps. But this one — a riot of small sampans piled with fresh produce, each negotiating its way delicately through the crowded maze of craft — is the real article.

Ponder the Mystery of the Plain of Jars

Hundreds of giant stone jars — the largest over three-and-a-half meters (12 ft) high and the smallest roughly half a meter (20 inches) — lie as if randomly tossed upon the arid plains of Laos's Xieng Khoang Province. These antique jars have captured the imagination of all who visit the stark, bomb-scarred plains of northeastern Laos. The Plain of Jars is a "marvel … a mystery … a site unique in all the world, due to its archeological value, its cultural specificity, the unknowns that it hides within," according to Mr. Frederico Mayor, leader of a February 1998 UNESCO delegation that allocated US$50,000 towards the site's rehabilitation.

The origins of the jars? Speculation runs high, yet these enigmatic creations remain a mystery. Carved from non-indigenous limestone, no one knows how the jars, some weighing as much as seven tons, were transported here. Strangely, despite the many momentous battles that have occurred here — the most recent being the Vietnam War, when they were literally rained with bombs — the jars remain virtually unscathed. When the first Western archeologist, Madeleine Colani, discovered the jars in the mid-

1930s she concluded they were funerary urns, because jewelry, beads and bronze artifacts were found in their vicinity, although today no trace of such items remain. Adding to the mystery, similar jars are also scattered over a remote and almost inaccessible plain on the Indonesian island of Sulawesi.

Clustered in several sites, the jars are most accessible at Thong Hai Vin, about half an hour's drive from the town of Phonsavan. Two other sites can also be visited, though the roads are atrocious.

To visit the Plain of Jars, most visitors fly to Phonsavan via Vientiane or Luang Prabang, making it possible to take in Indochina's number-one mystery as part of a loop of the country. It is not, however, an expedition for the fainthearted — accommodation is basic and traveling in the area can be quite rough.

Explore the Tonkinese Alps

Vietnam's highest peak, Mount Fansipan, rises 3,142 m (10,309 ft) above rugged mountain highlands near the Chinese border, towering over the old French colonial hill station of Sa Pa. An old trading town in the center of a region populated with hill tribes, Sa Pa's streets fill daily — particularly on Saturday — with villagers coming to the market with their produce and, more frequently now, tribal clothing and handmade souvenirs for the growing number of tourists.

Panoramas of Mount Fansipan are best viewed from the Victoria Hotel, Sa Pa's French-run resort, one of a few resorts found outside the capital cities. Guests can spend evenings around open log fires sipping French wine and dining on cheese soufflés and hearty *pot au feu*.

Few travelers actually hike to the summit of Mount Fansipan — the stiff climb takes three to six days up and down. However, practically everybody who visits the hill station of Sa Pa walks

The mystery of Laos' giant stone jars remains unexplained.

in the surrounding countryside, enjoying the cool climate, farmlands and hill-tribe villages. One of the more popular walks is to the Hmong village of Cat Cat, less than an hour west of Sa Pa. A small huddle of wooden homes set among bamboo groves, it is a picturesque destination with a nearby waterfall. Guided hikes to hill-tribe villages farther afield are readily available in Sa Pa, and enterprising locals are constantly developing new trekking routes. The small hotels around the bazaar on the main street offer tours and rent jeeps (or battered old Russian four-wheel drives).

October to May are the best months for exploring, when the air is coolest and the rainy season has passed. The winter months from December to March can be very cold, and mist can sometimes obscure the views. Springtime (April to May), on the other hand, brings plum blossoms and magnificent views across the mountains.

While tours to Sa Pa can be booked in Hanoi, they are quite unnecessary. Trains depart each evening around 9 PM from Hanoi Station, arriving at the Chinese border town of Lao Cai at around 7 AM. From the station counter, you can buy a tourist bus ticket to Sa Pa for a nominal sum and embark on the panoramic 45-minute drive through the mountains to the village.

Witness a Cultural Revival

Setting: Phnom Penh's School of Fine Arts. Time: every morning, from around 7 AM. Dancers: Khmer youth. Role: embodying heavenly nymphs, or *apsaras*, of Hindu mythology. To be there is to witness classical Khmer dance, part of the royal tradition, returning to life in a nation's budding cultural revival.

In Year Zero (1975), when the Khmer Rouge tried to radically restructure Cambodia into a peasant-dominated agrarian economy, almost all of the country's intelligentsia, craftspeople and artists were brutally killed. For

those few who have survived, fortunate enough to have fled the country or to have avoided detection, the huge task now awaits of educating the latest generation in cultural traditions that all but died. Today it is once again possible to see young girls learning the graceful moves of Khmer classical dance, which echo the celestial nymphs depicted in carvings in the many galleries and temples of Angkor Wat.

This is no performance for the benefit of tourists, but a window into the country's culture. Classes consist of about 40 students whose ages range from five or six to sixteen. Most of the students are girls, although some boys also take part.

It is best to arrive at the school a little after 7 AM and politely request the gate sentry for permission to enter. Some of the classes take place in an open-sided pavilion, making it easy to discretely observe the proceedings without bothering the teachers or the students.

OPPOSITE: A Red Zao woman, a member of one of the Sa Pa region's many minority groups. ABOVE: Banteay Srei is well known for its finely executed sandstone carvings, like this delicate apsara.

Dance is just one of Cambodia's arts that is being resuscitated: in parts of the country you may be lucky enough to stumble upon a rural performance of masked theatre or a shadow puppet show that incorporates stories from the classic Indian epic, the *Ramayana*. The Ministry of Culture and Fine Arts, Street 180, is sometimes able to organize special dance and music performances by students of the School of Fine Arts, though it is easier to make such arrangements through one of Phnom Penh's better hotels.

Classical Khmer dance performances are also held in Siem Reap at the Performance House in the Grand Hotel d'Angkor on a regular basis. Otherwise, the best place to witness classical dance is during the Ramayana Festival held each November full moon at Angkor Wat. Classical dancers from Indonesia, Myanmar, Laos and Thailand are invited to participate in this celebration of dance and the arts.

Be a "Tunnel Rat"

Imagine a network of tunnels more than 200 km (124 miles) in length, complete with schools, hospitals, weapons factories, living quarters and military command centers. This was the "underground city" of Cu Chi, just 35 km (22 miles) from Saigon. At their height the tunnels housed some 12,000 people. The Viet Cong planned the Tet Offensive here, which was to change the course of the Vietnam War.

The tunnels were scooped out by hand, the hard clay spirited away and hidden in nearby bomb craters. Stake-filled traps were hidden in the paths leading to tunnel entrances. Baffled vents dissipated the cooking smoke that might have revealed their presence.

In these times of peace, two sections of the Cu Chi Tunnels — at Ben Binh and Ben Duoc — have been preserved

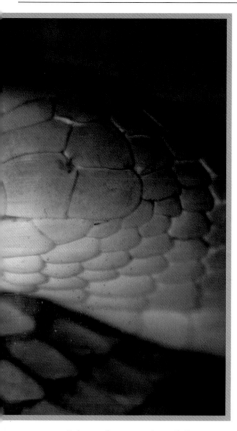

Anyone who feels vaguely cheated by the fact that the tunnels that are open to tourists today are not exactly the real thing are likely to feel different once they clamber underground. This is definitely not an experience recommended for the claustrophobic. It is an eerie feeling, stooped and groping the way forwards, to imagine the lives of the many thousands who lived in such conditions for years, only emerging above ground in the darkness to tend carefully hidden crops.

Although widened for easier access, the tunnels at Ben Binh are the genuine article, part of a massive network, the full extent of which can be seen on a map at the visitor's center next to the tunnels. The tunnels at Ben Duoc, on the other hand, are a reconstruction, but nonetheless interesting for all that. Some avail themselves of the opportunity here to fire off a few rounds (at a price of course) with an AK47 — a hideously noisy instrument of destruction — at an attached shooting range, though it is hard not to feel that this is the crasser extreme of Vietnam War tourism.

Mosey down the Mekong

For 4,200 km (2,600 miles), much of which is navigable, the mighty Mekong journeys to the sea. The river is the border between parts of Thailand and Laos, before entering Cambodia and finally the Vietnam delta, forming what was once one of the great highways of Southeast Asia.

River traffic has thinned in recent years, as roads gradually improve throughout Indochina, but today tourism may be bringing the river's revival. All three Indochinese nations see the attraction for tourists of floating on one of Asia's most famous rivers.

One doesn't need to be an intrepid explorer to enjoy the Mekong, and even a short ride can evoke a feeling for this

as memorials to the tenacity of the Vietnamese who first opposed the French colonials and later the American-backed southern regime. Together they comprise perhaps the oddest tourist attraction in all of Southeast Asia.

Access to the tunnels was via trapdoors so well concealed that even those that opened into the United States military base of Dong Du — allowing Viet Cong troops to make surprise attacks — escaped detection. Today a favorite game among the guides who take tourists to the sites is to have them rummage around in the undergrowth looking for the trapdoor that leads down into a renovated — read widened to accommodate bulky Westerners — section of the tunnels. It is a challenge that few can resist, and no one, it is said, rises to: it comes as a genuine surprise to find that the trapdoor has been under everybody's noses all along.

Although a little unappetizing, in the Mekong Delta snake wine is believed to impart strength and vigor.

Vientiane or Luang Prabang. Costs are minimal, as are the facilities.

The memorable three-hour ride from Pakse to Champassak in southern Laos, the gateway to the pre-Angkor Wat Phu, is by far the most enjoyable way to reach the ancient complex, which is then only a four-kilometer (two-and-a-half-mile) cyclo or taxi ride away. Visitors can jump in with the locals on a public river ferry for a few kip, or pay more and charter a boat for a few dollars. For those who prefer an extra feeling of security, tour operators organize trips for groups.

Admire Banteay Srei

Fabled Angkor Wat is undoubtedly the cultural highpoint of any tour of Indochina, but Banteay Srei, the pink "Citadel of Women," 32 km (20 miles) from the main Angkor Wat complex, is one of those little-known treats that reward travelers with a sense of having escaped the beaten trail and seen something truly unique. Featuring intricate, exquisitely executed pink sandstone carvings and depictions of heavenly deities and celestial nymphs, or *apsaras*, it is commonly regarded as one of the artistic highpoints of the Angkor legacy.

The temple is studded with the finest stone relief work, every inch of the surface covered with details of trailing flower tendrils interlocked with leaves, geometric patterns and intricately executed flutings. Scenes from the classic Indian epic *Ramayana* are illustrated in detail, one depicting the much despised and feared Rahwana making off, spear in hand, with the beautiful Sita, wife of the good King Rama. Stolid temple guards holding clubs stand guard over the entrances.

Founded in 987, during the reign of King Rajendravarman, Banteay Srei was

massive river. In Laos, one need not even make prior arrangements to take a river trip. Increasing numbers of budget travelers, for instance, enter Laos from northern Thailand at Huay Xai. From here, high-speed long-tail boats hurtle down the Mekong to the old royal capital of Luang Prabang. If this mode of transportation seems a little too adventurous (travelers are required to wear safety helmets, and ear-plugs are not a bad idea either), tour operators such as Diethelm (see TAKING A TOUR, page 59 in YOUR CHOICE) conduct up-market river cruises between Huay Xai and Luang Prabang.

An easy river daytrip out of Luang Prabang runs north to Pak Ou Buddha Caves, a ride of an hour or two with a stop at a Hmong village along the way. Boats can be rented at the boat jetty or through an organized tour easily arranged at most hotel front desks.

Visitors with a taste for basic travel can take a three-day downstream or four-day upstream river cargo boat from Vientiane to Luang Prabang. Although not a tour option at this stage, the trip can be arranged by making inquiries at the boat jetty in either

ABOVE: This stone temple guard stands watch over the ruins of Banteay Srei temple. OPPOSITE: Craft and produce of all descriptions are sold at the bustling floating market of Cai Rang in the Mekong Delta.

built on a much smaller scale than Angkor Wat, but in some ways this makes it easier to appreciate. Where Angkor is a multi-level complex, Banteay Srei is a far simpler, one-level concern, its main entrance lined with what were once giant stone standing lingams, many of which have since fallen into disrepair.

Inaccessible since the 1970s due to Khmer Rouge activity, the temple finally reopened in 1997, making it a must-see on the temple-tour circuit. Because of

the distance from Angkor, only the most dedicated visitors make it here, but the road to Banteay Srei provides a pleasant, if bumpy, drive through the rural Cambodia of ricefields and simple, stilted houses. The site is best visited in the cool of the early morning, before the heat of the day, or in the late afternoon. Tours are easily arranged in Siem Reap, from your hotel tour desk. Consider incorporating Banteay Srei into a tour of Angkor.

Ride the Perfume River

Scattered among farms and rice fields, ruins of an imperial past dot the landscape along Vietnam's Perfume River (Huong Giang), named for a scented shrub that grows along its banks. And what better way to explore the tombs and pagodas of the country's former rulers than by boat?

The Perfume River flows through Hue, one of Vietnam's most romantic cities and once home to Vietnam's most powerful emperors. The Nguyen Dynasty (1802–1945) was the first single court to rule both the north (Annam) and the

south (Viet Thuong), and thus brought into being the country we now know as Vietnam.

Unfortunately, much of this dynasty's historical legacy — its palaces and mausoleums — was all but leveled in the Tet Offensive of 1968. Ongoing restoration work proceeds on some of the more important structures, but the pace is slow. While some visitors find the imperial tombs surrounding Hue something of a disappointment, others enjoy touring these crumbling ruins for their setting in this bucolic Vietnamese landscape.

All boat trips on the Perfume River take in the Mausoleum of Khai Dinh, who ruled from 1916 to 1925. Here dragons and guardian beasts protect the inner courtyard where Khai Dinh himself can be seen in a curious, and somewhat surreal, East-meets-West atmosphere. It's a pleasant journey from here to the Mausoleum of Minh Mang (1820–40), the most impressive of the surviving tombs. Three ceremonial gates lead to granite staircases that in turn take the visitor to a temple and three bridges, the central marble one being, in its time, the sole preserve of the emperor himself.

Standard boat tours wind up late in the afternoon at the seven-story Thien Mu Pagoda. This nineteenth-century reconstruction of a pagoda first founded in 1601 provides a perfect vantage point from which to watch the sun set over the river.

Ready-made tours of the river abound in Hue, but it is also possible to rent a covered sampan and proceed at your own pace. To do so, check with your hotel or try at the boat depot adjacent to the Century Riverside Hotel at 49 Le Loi Street, where boats are available for US$30 to US$40 for the day. Simple food is available at food stalls near some of the tombs, or better yet, have your hotel prepare a picnic basket and then stop somewhere along the river for lunch. All of Hue's better hotels can arrange evening cruises on royal barges that serve imperial Hue cuisine.

OPPOSITE TOP: A pleasure pavilion looks across the placid waters at Tu Duc tombs, Hue. OPPOSITE BOTTOM: At the Thien Mu Pagoda, offerings are placed before effigies of the Buddha to pay respects. ABOVE: Luscious fresh produce on sale at Hue's Central Market.

YOUR CHOICE

and souvenir shops, and few local tourists ever make it to the national park on the other side of the island.

Another impediment to exploring Indochina's outdoors is the fact that so much of it is still littered with unexploded land mines, which continue to cause dreadful casualties, especially among children and farmers. While areas are being cleared, the work is by no means completed, and probably will not be for decades. Laos's Xieng Khoang Province (and the Plain of Jars) and the areas around Angkor Wat in Cambodia are now considered safe to visit, though it is still advisable to stick to well-marked paths, and caution is required in areas that are far from the normal tourist trails. The best course of action in such areas is to hire a local guide.

Nevertheless, Indochina is not without its areas of great natural beauty, and national parks have been established — many of them can be visited by tours or individually by those with their own transportation. Accommodation and other tourist facilities in such places tend to be basic, but are gradually improving as local authorities realize that foreigners are willing to spend money on experiencing Indochina's natural beauty.

The Great Outdoors

In Indochina, the Great Outdoors — from trekking or enjoying a walk in the rainforest — remains a little-developed tourist concept. In a region where the majority of the population depends on a rural subsistence economy entailing daily hours of backbreaking labor, the Great Outdoors is perceived as something to be tamed rather than to be explored during leisure hours.

At outdoor attractions such as Central Vietnam's Valley of Love in Da Lat, local tourists rush to have their pictures taken against kitsch concrete statues, and take pony rides wearing cowboy hats. On Vietnam's remote Cat Ba Island, the small township is crowded with karaoke bars

OPPOSITE: A waterfall by the That Lo resort, Boloven plateau, southern Laos. ABOVE: The placid blue waters of Nha Trang's beaches attract vacationers from around the world.

WATERFALLS

With so many rugged and untouched mountain ranges, Laos is blessed with an abundance of fine waterfalls, and some particularly spectacular ones. In fact, waterfalls tend to feature so heavily on tourist schedules that it is easy to tire of them after a while. Some originate in the deep jungle-covered mountains of the **Boloven Plateau**, falling near the Se Kong River, an area toured by Diethelm (see TAKING A TOUR, page 59) on their southern Laos circuit. Near Paksong, it is possible to visit the 130-m (425-ft) **Tad Phan Falls** and the 10-m (33-ft) **That Lo Falls**, where the pleasant bungalows at the Tatlo Resort ((031) 212725 overlook the falls.

Others such as the **Kuang Xi Falls**, 30 km (19 miles) south of Luang Prabang, make an easy daytrip by motorcycle or jumbo from the That Luang Market. In Vietnam's Central Highlands, close to Buon Ma Thuot, are the **Dray Sap Waterfall**, 25 km (15 miles) out of town on a good road, and the **Krong Bong**

Waterfall, 45 km (28 miles) from town past the village of Lak.

NATIONAL PARKS

While Indochina has designated national parks, most are not yet accessible or have minimal facilities. Illegal logging continues to encroach on primary forest, and in Vietnam the years of war brought vast ecological devastation. Still, the picture is not all dismal. Flying from Vientiane to Luang Prabang in Laos, one sees nothing but mile after mile of primary forest covering steep and rugged mountain ridges, with the very occasional clearing for a small tribal village.

VIETNAM

With 87 national parks, Vietnam would appear to be making a bold effort to protect its environment. The statistics tell a different story. Only 29 percent of the country's forested land remains, and more forests are disappearing, with the current crop of clearings being made for coffee plantations in the Central Highlands. Eight primeval forest areas have been classified as national parks — these are Cuc Phuong, Cat Ba Island, Ba VI, Ba Be Lakes, Bach Ma, Nam Cat Thien, Con Dau Island and Phu Quoc Island. Especen Tourist offers tours to several of these national parks (see TAKING A TOUR, page 59).

Hiking is also an option in the **Hoang Liem Nature Reserve**, near the tribal trading town and French colonial hill station of Sa Pa in the far north of Vietnam, close to the Chinese border. The reserve contains Vietnam's highest peak, the 3,142-m (10,309-ft) Mount Fansipan (see EXPLORE THE TONKINESE ALPS, page 15 in TOP SPOTS). Guides can be found in Sa Pa, and organized tours can be organized in Hanoi.

Also accessible from Hanoi is the **Cat Ba Archipelago**. Beautiful beaches and grottoes mark the main island's coastline, while thick forest covers much of this 570-hectare (1,400-acre) national park. Access is via Vietnam's Ha Long Bay, 80 km (50 miles) east of

the mainland town of Hai Phong. The archipelago's 366 islands and islets spread across the bay. Hornbills, reptiles and mammals including wild cats, gibbons, boar, monkeys and deer inhabit the pristine forests. Mangrove forests and freshwater swamps are home to a variety of water birds. The main town is something of a tourist trap, with hotels, shops and karaoke bars catering to local tourists. A 30-minute boat journey away, however, is pristine forest. Guides are recommended to explore the park properly, and they are easily hired in town. Fast boats and a slower ferry (which takes around four hours) go out to the main island from Hai Phong's Cat Ba ferry terminal. Hai

Phong is accessible by train from Hanoi — the recommended way to travel.

Ba Be Lake (pronounced "bar bay") is a clear-water lake filled with rare fish and abundant colonies of aquatic bird species. It is surrounded by limestone karsts and is one of Vietnam's more attractive national parks, covering an area of 23,340 hectares (577,670 acres). Trails lead through the park, and to the villages of several minority groups. Ba Be is a full day's trip from Hanoi, so at least three days are required for a visit.

OPPOSITE: Small chalets sit by a sparkling river and waterfall at the That Lo Resort in southern Laos. ABOVE: The crumbling ruins of Cham towers stand proudly by the roadside south of Nha Trang in central Vietnam.

It can be incorporated into a tour of the north or as a trip on its own. Especen Tourist and Saigon Tourist (see TAKING A TOUR, page 59) handle tours, and there is simple accommodation within the park confines. Independent arrivals will find guides and transport awaiting them.

The 25,000-hectare (61,770-acre) **Cuc Phuong National Park**, 140 km (90 miles) southwest of Hanoi, is easier to visit, taking around three hours, and is one of Vietnam's few remaining examples of primeval tropical forest. The park is home to 2,000 different plant species, including rare trees, and 64 animal species, including yellow monkeys and flying lizards. The chances of seeing these rare creatures are fairly slim. If organized in advance with park staff, it is possible, however, to visit the **Endangered Primate Rescue Center**, which is overseen by a German zoologist. The monkeys here have mostly been rescued from poachers who cater to a lucrative market in China. Accommodation is available within the park.

In central Vietnam, about 45 km (28 miles) south of Hue, is **Bach Ma National Park**. Established to protect a corridor of forest that stretches from the Lao border to the South China Sea, it is home to nine species of primates and also to the Sao La antelope, which was only discovered in 1992 — sightings of Sao La antelope are, of course, rare. The

French used this area as a hill resort, and some of the French mansions have been restored and established as guesthouses, which make good bases to explore some of the park's trails — the Rhododendron Trail and the Five Lakes Trail are particularly popular.

In the south, **Nam Cat Thien National Park** lies about 150 km (95 miles) north of Saigon, adjoining the provinces of Dong Nai, Song Be and Lam Dong in the Central Vietnam Highlands. The reserve covers an area of some 10,000 hectares (24,700 acres), the natural habitat of unusual Asian species such as the nearly extinct Asian rhinoceros and the Indochinese tiger, along with pythons, crocodiles, elephants and flying squirrels.

The reserve is accessed from the main Da Lat road north of Saigon, and guides and simple accommodation are available within the park confines.

In southern Vietnam's Dong Thap Province, the 7,500-hectare (18,500-acre) **Tram Chim Reserve** in the Mekong Delta is the domain of nearly 150 species of birds, including 15 rare species. Red headed cranes, lotus ponds and storks can be seen there.

Also located within the vast Mekong Delta is the **Tam Nong Reserve**. Covering around 750 hectares (1,850 acres), the reserve is home to nearly 150 species of birds, including flamingoes and thousands of storks during the wet season (May through July).

CAMBODIA

In 1993, the king of Cambodia, His Majesty Norodom Sihanouk, issued "The Creation and Designation of Protected Areas" decree, which established 23 protected areas covering 3.4 million hectares (over 8.4 million acres), including national parks and wildlife sanctuaries. Meanwhile, although much hope is pinned on tourism as part of Cambodia's recovery, development of its national parks has been slow. Currently the most accessible park is the **Kirirom National Park** in the southern province

OPPOSITE: Boys playing in the river at Siem Reap for their afternoon bath. ABOVE: Wild horses are herded along a road on the Boloven plateau in South Laos.

of Kompong Speu. It has a visitor's center and provides the opportunity to see Cambodia's highest mountain — the 1,771-m (5,810-ft) Mount Oral. The park is also rich in wildlife, including elephants, monkeys, snakes, barking deer and the occasional leopard and tiger.

LAOS

The Lao Government, wishing to "avoid the negative environmental impact which often results from tourism," has established good conservation policies for their abundant wilderness areas, and in 1993, established legal protection for 17 areas, mostly in the south. Known as NBCAs, or National Biodiversity Conservation Areas, they cover a total of 24,600 sq km (nearly 9,500 sq miles): around one tenth of the country's total area. While such moves are laudable, with 50 percent of Laos covered by primary forest, much of this resource remains threatened by avaricious Thai logging concerns.

Laos's rainforest is inhabited by wildlife such as the leopard cat, Javan mongoose, Malayan sun bear, Saola ox, gibbon, langur, goat-antelope (a newly

discovered species of deer antelope) and a species of ox (vu quang).

The place that is being held up as a "model eco-tourism resort" is the Thatlo Resort ((031) 212725 at Saravan in southern Laos, a pleasant two hour's drive from Pakse. Situated on the foothills of the Boloven Plateau, the resort consists of simple chalets overlooking the Se Set River and waterfalls in open jungle. Nearby are tribal villages, which can be visited on elephant back; the elephants can be rented at the resort.

Sporting Spree

Thailand or Malaysia may be better destinations for action sports such as paragliding, water skiing, or even windsurfing, Vietnam does offer some adventure sports. **Canoeing** among the massive limestone karst formations and 3,000 islands that rise almost perpendicular from the green waters of Ha Long Bay is popular. Arrangements can be organized through Sea Canoe International ((66-76) 212252 FAX (66-76) 212172 E-MAIL webinfo@seacanoe.com

WEB SITE http://seacanoe.com, PO Box 276, Phuket 83000, Thailand.

In the quickly developing resort of Nha Trang in the south central region, the offshore islands offer a variety of **scuba diving** opportunities. Several dive companies have sprung up in town, taking divers to the surrounding islands. Vietravel ((058) 811375 FAX (058) 811374, 88 Tran Phu Street, Nha Trang, runs dive trips to a nearby island about 60 km (37 miles) away, where they have a guesthouse. Ana Mandara Resort ((058) 829928 has a dive shop at 86 Tran Phu Street. Also recommended is the Blue Diving Club ((058) 825390 FAX (058) 824214 at the Coconut Grove Resort, 40 Tran Phu Street. In Da Nang, the Furama Resort ((0511) 847888, 68 Ho Xuan Huong, Bac My An, offers scuba diving, with a dive shop operating from the beachfront hotel at China Beach.

Visitors to the highland resort town of Da Lat, just an hour or two from Nha Trang, will see one of Vietnam's most beautiful **golf** courses and the first championship course in the country, the Da Lat Palace Golf Club ((08) 823-0227 FAX (08) 822-2347. The cool weather and early morning mist covering the greens makes playing on this course an almost mystical experience for any golfer; a visit is highly recommended. Guests of the Sofital Da Lat Palace Hotels and the Da Lat Novotel have automatic access to the club. Another golf club to try in Vietnam is the Ocean Dunes Golf Club ((08) 824-3749 in Phan Thiet, adjacent to the Novotel Phan Thiet Hotel and near a beautiful beach.

One of Vietnam's great adventures, and one of the best ways to see the country firsthand, is to take to the road by bicycle. Several companies offer escorted Vietnam **cycling** tours. Intrepid Travel (see TAKING A TOUR, page 59) offers a 14-day, low-impact, back-road tour from Hanoi to Saigon, with a maximum of 10 people per group. Participants bring their own bicycle and have days off for relaxation. They are followed by a backup vehicle and cover the Hue–Hanoi sector by train.

OPPOSITE: A minority woman tends her farm in Vietnam's central highlands. ABOVE: Elephant-riding through the jungle, from the That Lo Resort in southern Laos.

31

The Open Road

While not without some fabulous scenery, Indochina is hardly a place visitors come away from with fond memories of the open road. Driving ranges from erratic to appalling and the roads are generally in a state of terrible disrepair. As in China, self-driving is not an option, though it is possible to rent motorcycles in certain parts of Vietnam and Cambodia. Those wishing to get around under their own steam will have to rent a car with a driver, and this is probably not such a bad thing — local drivers at least are accustomed to local driving techniques. Essentially, however, the rule of thumb in Indochina is that travelers only resort to road travel when other forms of transportation are unavailable.

In Cambodia, for example, almost everyone who elects to travel overland from Phnom Penh to Siem Reap does so by boat — it's considerably faster and more comfortable than by road. Those who don't take the boat tend to fly. In Vietnam, those wishing to get from Hanoi to Saigon in a hurry either fly or take the train. In Laos, travelers uniformly journey by boat wherever they are available, to avoid the travails of Laos's particularly bad roads.

But there are some exceptions. In Laos the route from Vientiane to Luang Prabang, not so long ago too dangerous to traverse, has been upgraded and provides an interesting glimpse of the countryside, cutting through the jungle-covered mountain ranges of central Laos.

Indochina's big drive is the epic journey along Vietnam's National Highway 1, which connects Hanoi to Saigon. Vietnam's main artery is in good condition and, for the most part, remains uncrowded. While heavy truck traffic is increasing, there are still plenty of stretches where the only "vehicle" in sight will be a lone oxcart. For much of the way, the road passes directly through farmlands and small villages; it also offers some splendid views of Vietnam's breathtaking and unexploited coastline.

From the somewhat arid plains of southern Vietnam, the road heads north past inviting beaches before hitting the mountains at the Huy Van Pass, followed by the spectacular descent into the greener vistas of northern Vietnam.

The best way to travel Highway 1 is with stopovers en-route. Most travelers making their way north from Saigon, for example, spend a night or two at the beach resort of Nha Trang or at the quieter beach of Doc Lic — about an hour's drive (40 km or 25 miles) north of Nha Trang. The well-preserved traditional town of Hoi An — a delightful mix of Chinese, Japanese and Vietnamese influences — is a deservedly popular stopover between Nha Trang and Hue, the ancient Vietnamese imperial city, which many travelers find themselves lingering in longer than they had planned. Less enjoyable, the Hue–Hanoi has less to see en-route, making the train a good option for this last (or first, if you are traveling south) leg. National Highway 1 can be covered by rental car, motorcycle, bicycle or the less expensive Open Tour Bus service (see BACKPACKING, below).

Another popular Vietnamese road trip is the northwest mountain road that draws a giant loop from Hanoi, west to Hoa Bin then to Son La and out to the historic Dien Bien Phu. Road conditions, however, are not nearly as good on this route as on Highway 1.

From Dien Bien Phu, the road proceeds across to Lai Chau then down to Sa Pa and the Chinese border town of Lao Cai, and up to Bac Ha before returning to Lao Cai and back to Hanoi. Although you can easily drive this loop as a five- or six-day tour, it is better to set aside a couple of extra days for exploring. Time the trip to be in Sa Pa on Saturday for market day and then in Bac Ha for its spectacular Sunday market, when all the tribal folk from surrounding mountains come to town dressed in their Sunday best. The trip is best made by jeep or motorcycle, as the mountain roads in particular are in bad shape. Hotels on

this route are for the most part very basic, with the exception of the Victoria Hotel in Sa Pa.

In the South, the Mekong Delta can be explored by car, and in fact many tours offer just that, but most travelers sensibly travel by boat.

Backpacking

After Thailand, Indochina has emerged as Southeast Asia's top backpacking destination. Indeed, in Indochina, backpacking is the norm rather than the exception, and in Laos, where mainstream tourism is still so new, the well-heeled and penurious are often found sharing the same transportation, and sometimes even the same accommodation.

VIETNAM

Vietnam has the most established backpacker trails, and the Vietnamese, never slow to recognize a business opportunity, have jumped into the breach to provide budget travelers with every conceivable service they could need. In fact, local entrepreneurs have such a grip on the backpacker market

that it is difficult not to feel at times that budget travel in Vietnam is simply organized tourism under another name.

Perhaps the best example of this is the so-called "Open Tour Bus" service that links Saigon and Hanoi, taking in some of Vietnam's most popular backpacker destinations en-route. While it's easy to be cynical about "independent travelers" massed in air-conditioned buses and being ferried from one destination to the next, it is in all fairness an excellent service that provides first-time visitors an opportunity to see the best of the country in relative comfort and without having the bother of constantly making transportation arrangements. The most popular stopovers en route are Hue, Hoi An, Nha Trang and Da Lat. It is possible to buy a ticket for just one (or more) sectors, or alternatively passengers can disembark anywhere along the way and then take local transportation to the next embarkation point. Bookings are required only a day or less in advance, which makes it very convenient. Tickets

ABOVE: Hue river ferries are used by local women en route to market. OVERLEAF: Vung Tau beach is a quiet place for a swim on week days.

for the bus can be bought at backpacker cafés and travel agencies in Hanoi or Saigon, or in downtown Hue, Da Lat, Nha Trang or Hoi An.

The only complaint that travelers tend to have about the service is that the operators push their customers to stay at hotels or guesthouses on their pay list. Some of these are good value; others are not. Feel free to take a taxi or a cyclo to a hotel of your own choice after disembarking the bus.

On the accommodation front, Vietnam is for the most part a bargain. In many of the most popular backpacker destinations, it's still possible to get a bed in a shared room for two or three dollars. Even in destinations where rock-bottom

guesthouse accommodation is not available, it is usually possible to find a room for between US$5 and US$10, meaning that costs over the long haul should average out somewhere between US$5 and US$10, depending mostly on just what you are prepared to put up with.

But the best bargains are on the food front. It's possible to eat on the streets and in markets for less than a dollar, and the travelers' cafés that have proliferated throughout Vietnam offer all the familiar backpacker favorites along with local cuisine of varying authenticity.

LAOS
It is tempting to say that the budget travel industry in Laos is still in its

infancy, but the scene there is changing so rapidly that such a statement is unlikely to have currency for much longer. The word has got around, and Laos has emerged as *the* place for independent budget travelers to prove their mettle in Southeast Asia. As a result, Laos already has a well-beaten backpacker trail, and all the usual amenities are springing up to cater to their needs.

True, the transportation infrastructure is probably the least developed in all of Southeast Asia. Those traveling independently on a budget will find public buses few and far between, and in some cases non-existent — trucks with rows of seats in the back take the place of buses in more remote destinations. But for many budget travelers this simply adds to the adventure of travel in Laos.

There are little grounds for complaint on other fronts. Laos has no shortage of inexpensive accommodation, not only in popular backpacker destinations but also in destinations farther afield. Dining, too, costs next to nothing, providing you do not opt to splurge too often in the tourist-class restaurants in Vientiane and Luang Prabang.

CAMBODIA

Cambodia is not as popular with the backpacker set as Laos and Vietnam, though it does have a certain cachet. The problem is twofold: first, despite the great improvements in public order that have been achieved over the last few years, there is still a perception that Cambodia is dangerous; and, second, Cambodia's dollar economy makes it more expensive than neighboring Laos and Vietnam.

The dangers of traveling in Cambodia are overrated, providing you stick to the now well-trodden trail that connects Siem Reap and Sihanoukville to Phom Penh. But Cambodia is certainly not as cheap as other destinations around the region. A good example is the speedboat service to Siem Reap, which at US$25 is around two or three times more

expensive than what a comparable service would cost in Laos or Vietnam. Many travelers too find the entry price of Cambodia's chief attraction, Angkor Wat, expensive at US$20 for a day pass, and US$40 for a three-day pass.

It is possible, however, to save on other aspects of travel in Cambodia. In all the most popular backpacker destinations there are now family-run guesthouses offering rooms for as little as two or three dollars, and many of them offer equally inexpensive meals.

OPPOSITE: Pedicabs and bicycles are popular forms of transport in Hoi An, Central Vietnam. ABOVE: Colonial buildings still stand in the center of the small town of Siem Reap. BELOW: A three-wheeled bus awaits passengers in southern Laos.

Living It Up

Despite the tourism boom of the last decade, Indochina, particularly Laos and Cambodia, still lags behind neighboring countries such as Thailand and Malaysia when it comes to providing luxury for travelers. This is not to say that Indochina is only a backpacker destination, but merely that outside the major tourist destinations it is unrealistic to expect luxury amenities, and the best way to ensure a reasonable degree of comfort is to book a tour.

One interesting option for those looking to explore the region in style is to take a **Legends of Indochina** tour (WEB SITE www.legends-of-indochina.com). These are offered by a grouping of some of the region's best hotels and can be booked through most tour operators. Despite the name, the tours are not restricted to Indochina alone, and it is a measure of the region's still developing status that travel for the Indochina itineraries is almost exclusively by air, the region's roads and rail networks remaining primitive.

Surprisingly, opportunities for **luxury river cruises** are still scarce. An exception is a luxury speedboat available in Vietnam's Mekong Delta through the Victoria Hotels group (WEB SITE www.victoriahotels-asia .com/english), which has luxury hotels in the Delta towns of Can Tho and Chau Doc. The *Victoria Sprite*, which can take up to 10 people, and the *Victoria Princess*, which can take up to 28 people, link Saigon with group's delta hotels and can also be hired to continue on to Phnom Penh.

The best treat awaiting travelers in Indochina, however, is the profusion of refurbished colonial-era hotels that can be found in the region. At their best they provide guests with international luxury standards and an ambiance that is evocative of the days when French colonials governed the region.

Singling out any one of these hotels as the best is a near impossibility, but

certainly representative of just how well modern amenities can be melded with colonial nostalgia is the five-star **Sofitel Dalat Palace Hotel** in Da Lat. Renovated in a joint venture and managed by Sofitel, the exclusiveness of the property is heightened by it having just 43 rooms and suites. Guests also have access to an international-standard 18-hole golf course.

In Hanoi, the **Sofitel Metropole**, housed in a turn-of-the-century French building, is a fine luxury accommodation choice. Formerly the Thong Ngat Hotel and renovated by the Accor group, it was one of the first of Vietnam's colonial-era hotels to be brought into

the modern era. It combines Old World charm with international tourist and business facilities.

Cambodia has some marvelous hotels, but two stand out from the crowd and deserve special mention. In its heyday, Phnom Penh's old **Hotel Le Royal** played host to "globetrotters and adventurers, writers and journalists, royalty and dignitaries" from around the world. Later, in the early 1970s, it served as a base for journalists as the Khmer Rouge rose to power and the country plunged into chaos — part of the film *The Killing Fields* was set here. Today Le Royal has been restored to its former grandeur by the Raffles group

and is easily one of the most evocative and luxurious hotels in the region.

Rivaling Le Royal is the **Grand Hotel D'Angkor** in Siem Reap, which first flung open its doors in 1929 for the "wave of travelers for whom the Angkor Temples were an obligatory stopover." It too has been renovated by the Raffles group, and the results are faultless. Apart from amenities such as a 35-m (115-ft) swimming pool, the hotel also features some delightful touches, such as the library and map room, which houses Angkor-related literary and cartographic

Phnom Penh's Le Royal Hotel is arguably the best address in town.

references. A terrace garden hosts nightly cultural performances.

Vietnam has been slow to cash in on the potential of its stunning coastline, but in the beachside town on Nha Trang, in southern Vietnam, the **Ana Mandara Resort** offers luxury resort accommodation that rivals resorts in more popular beach destinations such as nearby Thailand. Set on the beachfront among luxuriant gardens, tastefully furnished chalets have been built to resemble a traditional Vietnamese village.

Several restaurants in the region deserve special mention as venues in which to enjoy the high life. In Hanoi the Sofitel Metropole's **Le Beaulieu Continental Restaurant** has been charming and intoxicating diners for more than a century. For classic French cuisine in surroundings evocative of Vietnam's colonial past, there is no other restaurant in the region to compare with it.

Hue, in central Vietnam, is the place to sample imperial Hue cuisine, which comes in courses of nibbles, many of them to be wrapped by the dinner in fresh, leafy vegetables. The best places to

try this cuisine are the hotel restaurants around town. Chief among them is the **Huong Giang Hotel**, whose Royal Restaurant tantalizes its diners with dishes that were once fit only for a king.

Saigon is the dining capital of Vietnam, and it offers a diversity of restaurants, some as notable for their atmosphere as they are for the offerings from the kitchen. **La Bibliothèque** is a Saigon institution run by Madame Nguyen Phuoc Dai in her villa close to Notre Dame Cathedral. Guests enjoy their meals in what was once her library, and the books are still there, creating the sensation of dining in the home of a Vietnamese aristocrat.

Meanwhile, in Luang Prabang, Laos, a visit to **Indochina Spirit** is highly recommended. Housed in a delightful villa and littered with bric-a-brac and objets d'art, it also features classical live Lao music in the evenings. Its forte is Thai cuisine, but it also has some Lao specialties that are worth sampling. Despite the luxurious appearance of the restaurant, it is a very inexpensive evening out, even with a bottle of French wine thrown in.

Family Fun

Indochina is not Asia's best family destination. It is, of course, possible to visit the region with children, but at times the adventurous nature of Indochina travel may be trying. On the positive side, Vietnamese, Cambodians and Laos love children and delight in playing with and looking after them. To find a suitable person to look after or entertain the kids for a few hours is no problem at all. This means also that families traveling with children will find that traveling together, even to remote parts of these countries, can bring another dimension to travel and help to make many new friends.

On the down side, if the children get ill, pick up stomach bugs or the like, reliable medical facilities are only available in the cities of Hanoi, Saigon, Phnom Penh and Vientiane. In the event of a serious accident or illness, it will be necessary to fly to Bangkok or your home country. As a basic precaution, bring medication for diarrhea, mosquito repellant and other necessities. Bottled water is readily available all over Indochina, as are canned soft drinks.

Another drawback of traveling with children in Indochina is that so many of the region's attractions, no matter how fascinating to adults, are of limited interest to children. Tours of wats and museums celebrating local resistance to colonialism are likely to bore the average child.

Cultural Kicks

In a region where most tourist attractions are cultural, just exploring Indochina can be a cultural kick in itself. Dance and drama, museums and music, wats, temples and palaces abound, especially in Laos and Cambodia, where history has left a rich legacy of statuary, royal regalia and Buddhas that would be worth a king's ransom on the open market — indeed, much of it, unfortunately, has already done so.

DANCE
One of the most enjoyable experiences Indochina can offer is a traditional dance performance. Cambodia and Laos, which both have royal dance traditions that share similarities with those of Thailand, offer a more exotic spectacle than the Chinese-influenced dance of Vietnam. In both countries, the elaborately costumed court dances share the same Indian influences that can be seen in Thai and Javanese dance. In Cambodia, dancers are stitched into body-hugging, heavily brocaded garments and wear jeweled headgear. Subtle gestures of the face and hands tell a story, which is usually drawn from the classic Indian *Ramayana*. In fact, every year a *Ramayana* festival is held on the November full moon at Angkor Wat — a splendid three-day festival where invitees from Laos, Malaysia, Java and Thailand try to outperform each other with magnificent versions of this ancient Indian tale of the triumph of good over evil.

In addition to this mainstream classical dance — generally of royal origins — are the folk dancing traditions of the many ethnic minorities scattered across the region. However, opportunities to see such dances are rare, unless you travel to remote regions and are lucky

OPPOSITE : Saigon's quirky Maxim's Restaurant offers an eclectic menu and a taste of old Saigon. ABOVE: Hammocks are enjoyed by all ages along the Mekong Delta.

enough to arrive at a minority village during a traditional festival. Mainstream classical dance performances are not as plentiful as one might expect anywhere in the region, particularly in Cambodia, where turbulent years of war and the emergence of clean-the-slate Communist party interrupted such traditions.

Today it is tourism that is bringing them back to life, and the best chance visitors have to see classical dance is in the five-star tourist hotels. The Villa Santi in Luang Prabang, for example, has regular shows of traditional Lao dance and music in its colorful garden restaurant, and the Hotel Lane Xang in Vientiane is another venue for seeing traditional dance.

In Cambodia, the impressively renovated Grand Hotel d'Angkor in Siem Reap features nightly performances by local dance troupes, and the highly regarded National Cambodian Dance Company occasionally stages performances in the forecourts of Angkor Wat.

MUSIC
A range of unexpected instruments can be found in Vietnam's musical tradition. In the north, many stylistic aspects of the country's music and dance can be traced back to an early Chinese influence, with a similar five-note pentatonic scale and orchestras of up to 40 musicians playing the sort of instruments you would see in

These instruments provide the basis of folk, classical, chamber and theatrical music, all of which are performed, sometimes accompanied by dance, in the municipal opera houses of Hanoi and Saigon, at conservatories and cultural centers, and at special hotel cultural shows — details are listed in the NIGHTLIFE sections of the relevant destination chapters.

Western music also resounds from municipal halls, dance clubs and bars throughout Vietnam. Ballroom dancing is very popular — a bizarre anachronism maybe, but pursued by hundreds of couples in special dance halls complete with ear-splitting, amplified music and five-piece orchestras. At one end of the musical spectrum, you can eat to the music of Chopin at the Piano Bar in Hanoi, or enjoy a student chamber recital at a conservatory right alongside the Citadel in Hue; and at the other, drop into clubs in Hanoi or Saigon for some rock and pop.

In Laos and Cambodia, traditional music shares a common heritage with Thai music, using gamelan-like instruments, gongs and lilting hill tribe bamboo flutes. The best opportunities to hear it are at dance performances.

PUPPETRY
Vietnam's inimitable wooden water puppets began as a village tradition performed on the local pond, usually near a small temple or shrine. Today, performances are available in the big cities to entertain the tourists. In Hanoi, a puppet performance can be seen at the **Municipal Water Puppet Theater**, where a troupe founded by Ho Chi Minh performs nightly.

In Cambodia the ancient art of shadow puppetry still lingers, though performances, to the accompaniment of folk music, are mostly the preserve of country weddings and festivals, and only very fortunate Western visitors get to see them.

China. But the moody, melodic base of Vietnamese music is provided by an instrument very much its own — the *danbau*, a single-string zither with a willowy tuning rod at one end, which, caressed by the musician's fingers, controls the tone and pitch of each note. In addition to reed flutes, gongs and mandolin-type stringed instruments, Vietnamese musicians also play a bamboo xylophone, which hangs like a curtain before the musician. Another bamboo instrument provides bass accompaniment: the musician claps his hands at the mouths of thick, graduated tubes very much like the pipes of an organ; the resulting pulses of air produce low, resonant sounds.

Traditional opera in New Saigon is a colorful mix of Chinese and Vietnamese influences.

MUSEUMS

At their worst, Indochina's museums tend to be jingoistic, one-sided celebrations of the region's various victories over their colonial oppressors. At their best, they provide a fascinating insight into Indochinese history.

One of the most interesting is the **Vietnam Museum of Ethnology** on the western outskirts of Hanoi. With foreign support, the museum has put together a compelling series of exhibits showcasing the cultural traditions and ethnological backgrounds of Vietnam's 54 minority groups. Hanoi's **Fine Arts Museum** is also worth a visit, featuring some fine statuary, though it is some disappointment when you consider the breadth of Vietnam's artistic achievement over its long history.

Of Hanoi's war museums, the most worthwhile are the **Army Museum**, whose exhibits of weaponry and scale models cover the entire Vietnam conflict, from the French defeat at Dien Bien Phu to the 1975 fall of Saigon.

On the road south from Hanoi, nearly everybody stops off at Da Nang to visit the **Cham Museum**, which houses the best of the surviving statuary from the Cham era.

For those who do not have an overwhelming interest in the Vietnam War, consider leaving the obligatory war museum excursion for Saigon, where the **War Remnants Museum** is a major tourist attraction. The exhibits here depicting American war atrocities leave nobody unmoved. Even if the overall effect is somewhat one-sided, it is nevertheless an essential stop.

Also recommended in Saigon is the **History Museum**, which takes visitors on a journey from the Bronze Age to the present, and the **Reunification Palace**, housed in the former Presidential Palace and home of President Nguyen Van Thieu, which contains some excellent examples of Vietnamese art. Lastly, while in Saigon, try and find the time to call into the city's **Fine Arts Museum**, which contains not only some very interesting Vietnamese

revolutionary art but also some priceless exhibits of Funan art.

Cambodia's most important museum is the **National Museum** in central Phnom Penh, adjacent to the Royal Palace. The building itself is — if a little tatty — beautifully designed in Khmer style, and is filled with precious stone statues from Angkor Wat and other significant Khmer sites across the country. Apart from Angkor Wat itself, it is the best place in the world to get a sense of just how great was the ancient Khmer artistic accomplishment.

OPPOSITE: A tribal boy wears a traditional headdress in northern Laos. ABOVE: Monks relax alongside a stone lion outside Wat Xieng Thong in Luang Prabang. BELOW: Carol Cassidy's Vientiane studio creates handlooms that sell to the elite.

The **Lao Revolutionary Museum**, in Vientiane, Laos, has become a fixture on the city's sightseeing circuit. Housed in a beautiful French-era building, the exhibits here follow the leftist Pathet Lao's struggle for power, with pictures and some weaponry. Of more cultural interest, however, is the **Royal Palace Museum** in Luang Prabang, once the palace of the royal family. This ornately decorated palace is filled with precious Buddha images and the possessions of Laos's last king. If you visit only one museum in Laos it should be this one.

Shop till You Drop

Glitzy shopping malls with the latest designer fashions are not what Indochina is about — save all that for a side trip to Singapore, Hong Kong or Bangkok. As in China, the socialist revolution stifled or deliberately obliterated much of the past in Vietnam and Cambodia, and only to a slightly lesser extent Laos, and many art and craft traditions have only began to recover in recent years.

Nevertheless, tourism is leading to a lively resurgence of crafts production all over the region. Beautifully produced handicrafts, gems, silverware, ceramics, textiles, lacquer ware, antiques and, in Vietnam, exciting new art works from emerging and established artists are available in abundance.

Vietnam has a wealth of good buys. The pale green Celadon ceramics so beloved of collectors are still being made in Hanoi using traditional methods. Where treasured old pieces can fetch hundreds of dollars on the international market, new pieces are very reasonably priced, selling for US$10 to US$20. **Celadon Green**, at 29 Dong Du Street in Saigon, offers a wide range of pieces from bowls and cups and tea pots to plates, jars and urns.

The lacquered idols and statues found in temples, where centuries of incense smoke have added a patina of preciousness, are now being manufactured again, and although they lack the telling wear of age, some are beautiful. For a good selection try **Antika** ((04) 828-3583, at the Camelia Hotel, 13 Luong Ngoc Quyen in Hanoi; **Quang Minh** ((04) 825-1497 at 40 Hang Be, Hanoi; or **Heritage** on Dong Khoi Street in Saigon.

Handmade glassware can be found at **East Meets West**, 24 Le Loi Street, District 1, Saigon. Glassware and exuberant hand-painted ceramic tea sets sell for around US$20 aside numerous other Vietnamese-crafted goodies at **The Home Zone**, 41 Dinh Tien Hoang, District 1, Saigon.

Elegant platters made of lacquer-covered bamboo, some finished in gold leaf, others in earthen shades of terracotta, are made in small villages outside Hanoi. Sizes range from small to enormous, and the platters make an elegant design statement in a modern room. Several of the gift shops near Hoan Kiem Lake sell them, but check each piece before buying. There is no quality control, and some pieces will have flaws. **Heritage** ((08) 823-5438, 53 Dong Khoi Street, Saigon, sells quality pieces.

Although many of its tribal cultures have been all but obliterated in Vietnam, a new cultural awareness seems to have surfaced in the cities at least, and tribal textiles and costumes are suddenly coming into vogue — no doubt also assisted by the rising tide of non-governmental organizations. Shops in both Hanoi and Saigon are selling tribal textiles, whole outfits and colorfully assembled models for tourist wear. Shops sponsored by non-governmental organizations in Hanoi are selling tourist-type, handloomed textiles which, being made especially for the tourist market, are pretty but worth little as collection pieces. Shops to try in Hanoi include **Quang Minh — The Culture of Vietnam Ethnic Groups** ((04) 825-1947, a little shop with many interesting things

A Lao woman displays a handloomed woven skirt in a village on the Boloven plateau in southern Laos.

at 40 Hang Be Street in Hanoi's Old Quarter. A second shop with the same name is located at 44 Hang Gai Street ℂ (04) 828-0509, also in the Old Quarter. The **Pan Flute** ℂ (04) 826-0493, at 42 Hang Bac in the Old Quarter, sells minority clothes and accessories, while **Annam Crafts** ℂ (04) 863-4551, at 3 Dinh Liet Street, sells traditional Vietnamese textiles and handicrafts.

For the real quality textiles, it is necessary to head to **Laos**, where hand-woven textiles are part of the lifestyle. All Lao women wear them as a matter of course — and by government decree, an effective way to keep the home industries turning. The diversity of weaves and patterns is nothing short of extraordinary, although increasingly patterns are becoming standardized as the government tries to introduce a "national" mentality rather than a regional one.

Hand-spun silks and cottons are the main materials used. The best are hand dyed using traditional natural dyes from plants and trees, whose colors are so rich and yet subtle they appear almost luminescent. Many pieces feature intriguing animistic patterns and motifs, portraying the beliefs of the hill-tribe artists who created them.

Even the modern article, which purists tend to scorn because they are chemically dyed, can be beautiful. A visit to the weaving village of Ban Phanom, just four kilometers (two and a half miles) outside Luang Prabang, will convince you that, while the dyes have changed, the workmanship and creativity haven't deteriorated.

As the vogue increases, so do the prices. It is not unusual to see a good example of an old hand-woven piece sell for US$1,000 — an already-established market price. Check the morning market in Vientiane for an absorbing delve into the world of textiles.

Laos is also a good place to find some examples of superb, finely wrought, authentic tribal basketware, as well as attractive new designs. Antique Chinese ceramics and porcelain can also be found in antique shops in both Luang Prabang and Vientiane.

In Laos the tourist market is quite well catered to, including some very attractive antique shops in Luang

Prabang and textile stalls too numerous to mention. Shops and galleries worth visiting include **Doris Jewelry** ((021) 218800 EXTENSION 1169 run by Vivian Wang, in the glittering (and air conditioned) Lao Hotel Plaza, 63 Samsenthai Road. Her superb collection of textiles and antiques are worth spending on. The Lao Women's Union's **The Art of Silk** ((021) 214308 has a marvelous collection of antique textiles in the upstairs museum, while downstairs there are plenty of nice pieces for sale. **Kanchana** in That Dam District, 102 Samsenthai Road, has some beautiful antique pieces and many well-crafted modern pieces that incorporate traditional designs in tone-on-tone colors. **Satri Laos Silk** ((021) 543874, 79/4 Setthathirat Road, Wat Mixay, is also worth visiting. The studio of internationally known American Carol Cassidy — a weaver who bills herself as having single-handedly "rejuvenated the Laos silk industry" — can be visited at her **Laos Textiles** studio ((021) 212123 just off Setthathirat Road, where visitors can view her modern pieces using traditional Laos designs. Not to be missed is Vientiane's **Thanon Thalat Sao**, Morning Market (which actually stays open all day). It is crammed with textile stalls and some local handicrafts of varying quality. The number of stalls selling antique pieces (and imitation antique pieces) is expanding rapidly as demand escalates.

Cambodia is a little short on quality crafts, the country's top craftspeople having fled the country or been lost to the Khmer Rouge purges. The most exciting place to head for is the **Russian Market**, on Street 182 near Street 111 in Phnom Penh. Within the dim interior are antiques, textiles and an abundance of newer handicrafts in small stalls interspersed with other stalls selling food, produce, fruit, tools and hardware and piles of rice and spices — it all adds to the color. Also to be found in the Russian Market, and in other markets around town, are several stalls selling marvelous blue and white china with exuberant floral designs.

Hand-painted cups, saucers, plates and bowls are piled high, nesting in straw holders like some strange birds. Although we are not talking Wedgwood quality here, the rough execution is eminently pleasing, as is the price. A whole dinner set could be bought for less than US$20, but transportation could cost a little more.

Cambodia is best known for its quality textiles, especially the fine old silk *ikats* that are becoming increasingly difficult to find. One place to look is the **Khmer Handicraft Promotion Society** ((023) 362463, 18 Street 302, which has a good selection of fabrics, along with other handicrafts.

In the dozens of stalls around Phnom Penh's **Central Market** are piles and piles of new handloomed silks and cottons. While lacking the luster of the old ones, they are still very attractive and quite collectible. Hand-woven silk or cotton Khmer headwear — the distinctive red-and-white or blue-and-white checkered scarves worn by most rural Cambodians and the Khmer Rouge — sell for a few dollars and make fine gifts and souvenirs. Beware when buying, some are handwoven with polyester, which is not quite the same thing.

OPPOSITE: A Saigon painter in his Dong Khoi street studio. ABOVE: A boy in Central Vietnam sells trinkets on Lang Co beach.

Festive Flings

Festivals play an important role in the lives of the people of Indochina, and there are important festivals on somewhere nearly every month of the year, many centered on a religious event or agricultural ritual. Many of the festivities rely on the lunar calendar, shifting dates with the full moon. Readers may want to refer to Paula Burch's Lunisolar Calendar WEB SITE www .flash.net/~pburch/lunarcal.html, which can give the lunar dates and corresponding Gregorian dates for the coming year.

JANUARY
New Year is celebrated across Indochina as a national holiday on January 1. January 7 is Cambodia's **National Day**, which commemorates the fall of the Khmer Rouge. In mid-January, Laos observes **Boun Khoun Khao**, a harvest festival in which village ceremonies give thanks to the spirits of the land.

Falling sometime during December and January in Laos is **Boun Pha Wet**, a festival celebrated in temples with recitations of the *Jataka*, the story of Buddha's life. Monks are ordained at this time. The actual dates vary from village to village to enable villagers to visit their friends and relatives during celebrations.

FEBRUARY
Magha Puja is held on the full moon of the third lunar month (usually early February), and is celebrated with particular fervor at Wat Phu in southern Laos. During this massive celebration, crowds descend on the ancient wat to make offerings to the spirits and to give alms to parading monks. Bullfights and boat races are part of the festivities.

Tet, the Lunar New Year, is celebrated by the Chinese and Vietnamese communities all over Indochina. Firecrackers are generally banned these days, especially in the larger towns, making it a less noisy occasion than previously, though often tapes of firecrackers are played at ear-splitting volumes. Vietnam shuts down for five days for Tet, and lesser celebrations occur in Laos and Cambodia.

In mid-February in Vietnam, the **Lim Festival**, which features traditional folk-singing, is held 30 km (19 miles) outside Hanoi in Lim Village in Bac Ninh Province. People from 49 villages, dressed in local costume, converge on the tiny town.

MARCH/APRIL
Cambodia honors **Women's Day** on March 8 with parades and floats in the main towns.

The **Boun Pi Mai**, Laos's New Year, held in mid-April, is best witnessed in Luang Prabang, where the three days are

set aside for temple offerings, elephant parades and other activities to welcome the new year. A tip: wear old clothes and watch out for water fights; visitors receive no mercy from the water buckets. Boun Pi Mai is a national holiday in Laos. Cambodia's **Bonn Chaul Chhnam** celebrates the new year in mid-April with a national holiday.

MAY
Cambodia, Laos and Vietnam all recognize **Labor Day** as a national holiday on May 1, and on May 6, Cambodian rural communities celebrate **Bonn Dak Ben** and **Pchoum Ben**, the Royal Plowing Ceremony, which is an ancient Brahman

ritual marking the beginning of the rice planting season. May 9 is Cambodia's **Genocide Day**, held in memory of victims of the Khmer Rouge.

In Laos on the May full moon is **Boun Visahhabousa** (**Vesak** or **Waicak**), when the country commemorates the birth, death and enlightenment of the Buddha. Chanting and candlelit processions are held in the wats. Vietnam also celebrates Vesak Day, as does Cambodia. In Laos, **Boun Bang Fai** (Rocket Festival) — a pre-Buddhist rain and fertility rite — coincides with Vesak Day and is celebrated

The devout make offerings to Buddhist monks at the Wat Phu festival in southern Laos.

along with Vesak on the full moon. One of the best and most enjoyable festivals, it includes dancing, music and parades of giant wooden phalluses. In the villages, bamboo rockets are shot into the clouds to bring down the rain.

May 19 is **Ho Chi Minh's Birthday**, which is a national holiday in Vietnam.

JULY/AUGUST/SEPTEMBER

In Laos, the **Boun Khao Phansaa** is celebrated on the July full moon, marking the beginning of Buddhist Lent — a quiet time when monks remain in the monastery. Many ordinations occur in wats at this time.

In Laos, the August **Boun Kao Padap Dinh** is the time for making offerings to the dead and cremations. It is not necessarily a sad time at all.

September 2 is Vietnam's **National Day**, commemorating the 1945 Independence Proclamation by Ho Chi Minh.

OCTOBER/NOVEMBER/DECEMBER

On the October full moon, Laos celebrates **Boun Awk Phansaa**, marking the end of the three-month monks' retreat, with the **Lai Hua Fai** (Festival of Lights). Lit candles are floated in small banana leaf boats on rivers and lakes. It is held in conjunction with the **Boun Nam Water Festival** and **Boun Suang Heua** (boat races), when longboat races are held in towns with rivers or lakes, especially Vientiane and Luang Prabang. In Cambodia, the **Boun Kathen** is a 29-day festival when town and country inhabitants bring new robes to the wats for the monks.

Cambodia celebrates His Majesty the King's Birthday on October 30 and November 1, with festivities including parades and fireworks on the river near the palace.

The popular **Boun That Luang** November full moon festival at Wat That Luang in Vientiane represents the biggest festival of the year. Monks gather at Vientiane's largest wat to receive alms on the first day. Parades between Wat That Luang and Wat Si Muang, fireworks and a massive

candlelit circumnavigation of Wat That Luang accompany a carnival.

Cambodia's **Independence Day** is November 9. On November 25 and 26 longboats race and fireworks pop during Cambodia's **Water Festival**. On the days around the November full moon in Siem Reap, the **Ramayana Festival** is held at Angkor Wat with three days of classical dance.

Speeches, parades and festivities honor the power of the people on **Lao National Day**, December 2. This joyous public holiday is celebrated across the country.

Short Breaks

Top of the getaway list in Southeast Asia is the charming royal city of **Luang Prabang**, which is directly accessible by Bangkok Airways from Bangkok, Thailand, or by a short flight from Vientiane. The Indochinese equivalent of Bali's Ubud, Luang Prabang is quickly becoming recognized among artists and the romantically inclined as a place to be. A UNESCO World Heritage Site, the small town sits at the confluence of the Nam Khan and the Mekong Rivers. With its palm trees and golden spires, its uncrowded streets lined with colonial

OPPOSITE: A giant Naga head stands amongst the stupas in Phnom Penh's Royal Palace.
ABOVE: Monks outside the gilded doors of a chapel at Wat Xieng Thong in Luang Prabang.

entertainment, including excursions to nearby islands, diving and other water sports. A long, sandy beach fronts the town, and numerous old colonial-style hotels are still standing even as high-rise hotels are taking over.

But Indochina's premier short break is easily **Angkor Wat**, accessible by direct flights from several Asian destinations, and overland by bus from Bangkok. The nearby town of Siem Reap has evolved from a sleepy backwater with nothing in the way of amenities into a bustling town that offers a wide range of accommodation, dining and nightlife. Meanwhile, Angkor itself is a cultural attraction without parallel in Southeast Asia — even a quick two-day visit that allows for at least one dawn visit to the Bayon and a dusk visit to Angkor Wat is an experience that will stay with you for the rest of your life.

Galloping Gourmet

The proletarian revolution that followed the war reduced the cuisines of Vietnam and, particularly, Cambodia to the level of basic sustenance. Cuisine was considered a bourgeois decadence. This philosophy, compounded with the austerity and social leveling the Communists brought in, spelled disaster for food lovers. However, the return of tourism and the demand for something more than boiled rice and vegetables has revived the region's restaurant industry, and Vietnamese cuisine, especially, is as good as it ever was.

VIETNAMESE CUISINE
Vietnamese cooking, a cuisine with a strong Chinese influence, is somewhat less varied than its northern neighbor — covering probably 500 different dishes compared with some 2,000 in the Chinese culinary compendium. It distinguishes itself by its use of fresh vegetables such as lettuce, mint, basil and other herbs, rolled around snacks or added to soup-based dishes.

architecture, its ancient wats punctuated by the bright saffron robes of wandering monks and its big, red Mekong sunsets, Luang Prabang is a romantic setting guaranteed to charm. Add to this a few charming boutique hotels and some decent restaurants, not of the Michelin-star variety but pleasant enough, and you have all the ingredients for an inspired short stay.

Vietnam's capital, with its leafy tree lined streets and dun-colored colonial buildings, also has a sedate charm that invites wandering. Days can be spent exploring the many museums and markets at a leisurely pace, amply provided by the bicycles and cyclos that still pedal the streets. **Hanoi** is particularly pleasant in winter when cold temperatures make it necessary to rug up in warm clothes, and the atmosphere takes on a disconcerting "Europe in Asia" feel.

For a beach-resort holiday, **Nha Trang** ranks as a surfer's paradise, or possibly the Pattaya of Indochina, minus the bar girls. Nha Trang offers plenty of

Indochinese food centers on the ubiquitous noodle soups, *pho*. The most popular are *pho bo* (beef noodles) and *pho ga* (chicken noodles), and great steaming bowls of these soups are both heartwarming and nourishing — the comfort food of Indochina.

Besides language and architecture, the French left behind a wonderful legacy of bread baking, and Indochina is one of the few places, if not the only place, in Asia where you can find decent bread. Every morning, street stalls in all the main towns and even country villages are piled with fragrant fresh bread, ready to eat, accompanied by pâtés or fresh fried eggs and cups of fragrant coffee. Ironically, possibly as a move to please their customers, some hotels are serving softer, processed breads rather than the crusty, French-style baguettes of the streets; fortunately, there are still a minority who maintain tradition. Crisp baguettes are especially good in Saigon with loads of fresh Vietnamese butter and Da Lat strawberry preserves. One of the most pleasant

places to enjoy this delicious breakfast, accompanied with a cup of fragrant *café filtre* and fresh fried eggs (not the factory variety), is at the Roof Garden of Saigon's Rex Hotel in the cool of the early morning, or at the Givral Café facing the Opera.

It's another delight altogether to experience Indochinese coffee. Although freeze-dried Nescafé is flooding the region — considered to be quite the sophisticated thing to offer — you can still get the traditional beverage in most cafés and restaurants. On the streets, the locally grown coffee is filtered onto an inch or so of sweetened condensed milk, then stirred into a mixture the color and texture of mud. It's unusual, but it provides a deliciously powerful kick-start to any day.

Vietnam's tasty street food can be enjoyed across the country. One of the most well-known and ubiquitous dishes is *cha gio*, or fried spring rolls. Paper-

OPPOSITE: Small sweet raspberry-like fruits are eaten with salt in Da Lat. BELOW: A woman selling bread outside her house in Luang Prabang.

thin, rice-flour wrappers contain a mix of shrimp, minced pork, bean sprouts, cellophane noodles and vegetables; they appear in various forms throughout Vietnam. The rolls are wrapped in salad greens and dipped in fish sauce before being eaten with chopsticks (foreigners are allowed to eat with their fingers).

Cold, white rice noodles known as *bun* are served in a variety of ways. A favorite among many travelers is *bun cha* — freshly barbecued slices of pork or pork patties served with a delicious, slightly spicy dipping sauce, *bun* and salad. Other varieties include *bun bo*, which comes served in a large bowl with *bun*, chopped spring roll, beef slices, bean sprouts, fried garlic, and a spicy sour sauce. It is quite possible to eat this delicious meal for days on end without ever tiring of it.

Hanoi has some of the best street food in Asia. In the heart of the Old Quarter, women sit at tiny tables on the pavement huddled over a charcoal fire, cooking their specialty — the one dish they know how to make well. Some of these roadside restaurants will serve up piles of freshly cooked red crabs, but beware of the tourist markup.

A unique Hanoi specialty that dates back to the city's early days is *cha ca vong*, a dish available at only one traditional restaurant in the Old Quarter, called Cha Ca La Vong. The restaurant serves nothing else: fish is cooked at the table over a charcoal brazier with oil, spices (mostly turmeric) and dill, served with a plate of greens to toss into the pan.

Another interesting feature of Vietnamese and Indochinese food is the fermented sauce known in Vietnam as *nuoc nam* — a pungent and flavorsome mix of certain fish varieties fermented with salt for periods of up to 12 months. It becomes quite delicious when mixed with chilies, lime juice, sugar and garlic, giving new meaning to simple rice (*com*) dishes. Another delicious dip comes with freshly steamed crab: a simple mixture of black pepper and salt (more often monosodium glutamate) and lime juice, which gives a tangy bite to any seafood.

LAO CUISINE
Across the border in Laos, the cuisine shares similarities with Thai food, especially in the liberal use of fresh

ingredients, lime juice, plentiful hot chilies, coriander and flavorsome fermented fish concoctions.

Unlike the Vietnamese love for noodles, the Lao staple is sticky rice (*khao niaw*), which is rolled into ping-pong-sized balls and consumed in vast quantities along with small portions taken from side dishes. A generous mixture of spices go into Lao cooking, including lime juice, lemongrass, chilies, galangal root (a cousin of the ginger plant), marjoram, basil, coriander, ginger and tamarind.

One of the best dishes in the fairly limited Lao repertoire is *laap*, a fresh mix of minced meat (beef, *sin ngua*, or chicken, *kai*), spices, lime juice, garlic, vegetables (*phak*) and chilies, served with sticky rice in individual bamboo containers and accompanied by a salad of lettuce, mint and other greens.

Another delicious staple reminiscent of Thai food is *tam som*, a spicy salad of sliced green papaya, chilies, lime juice, garlic and condiments all pounded together and served with sticky rice.

Luang Prabang has its own special cuisine, which includes watercress salads and a kind of fried river-seaweed

wafer decorated with sesame seeds known as *khai paen* — an acquired taste, but certainly interesting. Chinese- and Vietnamese-influenced foods are also popular and easy to find in Laos. The noodle soup known as *pho*, Vietnamese-style fried spring rolls known as *yaw jeun*, and Thai-style marinated and grilled chicken are also popular and quite delicious.

Perhaps the hardest of all Lao condiments for foreigners to become accustomed to is a coarse, fermented fish paste called *paa daek* that is found on restaurant tables. The best that can be said of its aroma is "unpleasant to the uninitiated," though stronger words have been heard.

KHMER CUISINE

Khmer cuisine is probably the least known in all Asia. Its main influences are Thai and Chinese, with the result that for many trying it for the first time it is like a milder version of Thai cuisine.

OPPOSITE: Smoke from cooking fires adds a touch of romance to a Luang Prabang evening scene.
ABOVE: This French pasty shop in Hanoi has served the likes of actress Catherine Deneuve.

The horror of the Khmer Rouge years was a major interruption to the nation's culinary tradition, but it has bounced back in recent years and it is now possible to enjoy the best in Khmer food in Phnom Penh and Siem Reap.

Fish from the Tonle Sap lake is a major ingredient in Khmer food, and is usually eaten grilled, steamed or in soup. Soups feature heavily in the local diet, with some inexpensive restaurants serving nothing but — hot and sour flavors, not unlike neighboring Thailand's *tom yam*, are often used in the soups.

Special Interests

ARCHITECTURE

The convergence of indigenous architectural styles with French colonial and later Stalinist-inspired architecture makes Indochina a fascinating place to explore. The Chinese-influenced Vietnamese imperial architecture can best be seen in Hue at the tombs of the Nguyen Dynasty, which are scattered across the surrounding countryside. In Hanoi the stately lines of the Vietnamese Temple of Literature mingle with classical French architecture. Fortunately, much of Hanoi's newer development has been engineered outside the city center, thereby retaining a degree of architectural integrity rare in an Asian city. Grand French neoclassical buildings can be found lining the riverfront of the old port city of Hai Phong, while Da Lat has been nicknamed Little France, so numerous are its colonial buildings. Vientiane, Phnom Penh and even to a lesser degree Saigon (its older buildings and temples linger on but are well hidden behind the new high-rises), all have fine colonial buildings to be proud of.

The ancient Chinese/Japanese trading port of Vietnam's Hoi An is a great architectural find. The narrow streets are lined with over 500 nineteenth-century and earlier Chinese and Japanese buildings. Deep-set Chinese houses (to epth of at least 35 m or 115 ft) stand next to pagodas and temples. Ancient clan houses have been converted to bars, while others fulfill their original function. The town is also home to the Japanese Covered Bridge, which once connected the Japanese quarter to the Chinese quarter.

Architecturally, Indochina's jewel is Cambodia's temple city of Angkor. The sprawling complex of temples, with their relief friezes and stunning statuary, is one of the wonders of the East.

PAINTING

Gradual liberalization in Vietnam has seen an explosion of artistic talent. Painters who went underground or turned to propaganda art during the dark years were suddenly free to paint again. The French colonialists had started the School of Arts of the Far East early in the twentieth century, giving young Vietnamese students a thorough grounding in contemporary and classical art. Today many artists are fusing such Western influences with Vietnam's own folk-art traditions, giving birth to work that is attracting international attention. Needless to say there is plenty of fluff mixed in with the true talent, but an exploration of the better galleries in Hanoi and Saigon will yield satisfying results. Check with the locally printed guides for current exhibitions in both cities.

HANDLOOM TEXTILES

The absorbing world of handloomed textiles is particularly important in Laos where every woman has an intimate appreciation of weaving and is expected to wear a handloom skirt (*sinh*) as part of her daily wardrobe, and where it would be unthinkable for a women to enter a government office wearing anything else. Even in the streets of Vientiane, it is very unusual to see women wearing trousers or factory-made dresses.

A growing number of collectors are taking an interest in the distinct regional patterns and styles of Lao textiles. Most of the cloth is woven from silk, and a visit to a market will reveal skeins of creamy-colored undyed silks, as well as richly hued pre-dyed skeins hanging from the walls.

Laos and Cambodia are both known for the superb weft silk *ikats*, whose weft threads are dyed with the patterns before weaving. For complex patterns made

with five or six colors and natural vegetable dyes, it can take months just to prepare the yarns for weaving. Cambodian and southern Lao *ikats* are probably the finest and most detailed in the world.

Small surprise then that prices have escalated rapidly in recent years. Those willing to spend time hunting around can still pick up some marvelous bargains, although even the bargains will cost a lot more than a few pennies.

An excellent book to help through the complexities of Lao handlooms is Mary Connor's *Lao Textiles and Traditions* published by Oxford University Press in 1996.

Taking a Tour

Taking a tour through Indochina does simplify what can otherwise be a logistically complicated trip — with so many border crossings and permutations of itinerary possible for the three countries,

OPPOSITE: A stall on Nha Trang beach is crowded with snacks and beer. ABOVE: The well-tended gates of Phnom Penh's Royal Palace signify order and riches.

a good organized tour can solve a lot of potential problems. That said, travel in the region has become much easier in recent years, and there are also a huge number of local tour operators, making it equally possible to fly into the region on your own and then pick and choose from the inexpensive local tours that are on offer in Vietnam, Laos and Cambodia.

AUSTRALIA

Adventure World ((02) 9956-7766, 76 Walker Street, North Sydney, has the most comprehensive package tours to Indochina of any Australian operator, and also offers specialized tours. Also recommended is **Intrepid Travel** ((03) 9473-2626 FAX (613) 9419-5878 E-MAIL info

@intrepidtravel.com, 11 Spring Street, Fitzroy, Melbourne 3065.

Australia's most well established tour operator is **Flight Centers International** — Sydney ((02) 9267-2999 Bathurst Street; **Melbourne** ((03) 9600-0799 TOLL-FREE 1800-679943, Level 7, 343 Little Collins Street; **Brisbane** ((07) 3229 5917 TOLL-FREE 1800-500204, Level 13, 157 Ann Street.

UNITED STATES

Abercrombie & Kent International ((630) 954-2944 TOLL-FREE (800) 323-7308 FAX (630) 954-3324 E-MAIL info@abercrombie kent.com, 1520 Kensington Road, Oak Brook, Illinois 60523, is one of the big names of package tourism, and offers an extensive range of Indochina tours.

For a specialist Indochina tour operator, try **Vietnam Indochina Tours** ((360) 570-2096 FAX (360) 570-2097 E-MAIL indochinatours@olywa.net, 207 Decatur Street, NW Olympia, Washington 98502.

CANADA
Pacific Rim Travel Corporation ((250) 380-4888 TOLL FREE (800) 663-1559 FAX (250) 380-7917 E-MAIL pacrimtc@pinc .com, Glentana Road, Victoria, British Columbia V9A 7B2, organizes several Indochina tours.

UNITED KINGDOM
Voyages Jules Verne is probably Europe's biggest and most experienced Asian tour operator, with offices throughout the Asia region to help smooth out accommodation and itinerary problems. They offer a broad range of Indochina tours. For brochures and detailed information, their London office is **Travel Promotions Ltd**. ((020) 7616-1000 FAX (020) 7723-8629 E-MAIL sales@vjv.co.uk, 21 Dorset Square, London NW1 6QJ.

Regent Holidays ((0117) 921-1711, 15 John Street, Bristol, is another tour operator that covers Indochina, but they're aimed at individual travelers. For those who want the comfort of knowing everything is organized but don't want the group-tour experience, Regent is the recommended operator.

Swiss-based **Kuoni Travel** has tours of all kinds. They have many offices around the region, including one in the United Kingdom ((01306) 740500 FAX (01306) 744222, Kuoni House, Dorking, Surrey, RH5 4AZ, England. Their head office is in Zurich ((01) 277-4444 FAX (01) 272-0071, Neue Hard No. 7, CH-8037.

LOCAL TOUR OPERATORS
Bangkok is the base for **Diethelm Travel** ((66-2) 255-9150 FAX (66-2) 256-0248 WEB SITE www.diethelm-travel.com, Kian Gwan Building II, 140 Wireless Road, Bangkok 10500, one of the world's most experienced Indochina tour operators. Although expensive, they have excellent knowledge of the three countries.

Many international operators have offices in Indochina. **Exotissimo** has an office in Hanoi ((04) 828-2150 FAX (04) 928-0056 at 26 Tran Nuat Duat Street and in Saigon ((08) 825 1723 FAX (08) 829 5800 at 2bis Dinh Tien Hoang Street, District 1. The well-run and recommended **Especen Tourist** ((04) 826-6856 FAX (04) 826-9612 is at 79 Hang Trung, Hanoi.

Saigon Tourist ((08) 829-8129 FAX (08) 822-4987 is at 49 Le Thanh Tan. This giant government agency owns hotels all over Vietnam and has a wide selection of specialty and tailor-made tours to suit all tastes. **Global Holidays** ((08) 822-8453 FAX (08) 822-8545, 106 Nguyen Hue Street, District 1, Saigon, is an Australian-owned and managed concern.

In Laos, **Inter Laos Tourism** ((021) 214832 or (021) 214232 FAX (021) 216306 or (021) 214232, at Setthathirat Road (Nam Phu Circle), Vientiane, is a good agency to book local tours with. **Sodetour** ((021) 216314 or (021) 213478 FAX (021) 216313 or (021) 215123, has its head office in Vientiane at 114 Quai Fa Ngum. They have other offices in Pakse and Luang Prabang.

Lane Xang Travel ((021) 212469 or (021) 213198 FAX (021) 215804 or (021) 214509 at Pang Kham Road also offers a wide range of tours.

In Cambodia, **Apsara Tours** ((023) 426562 or (023) 722019 FAX (023) 426705 can be found at Street 8, RV Vinnavaut Oum, Phnom Penh, but the best operator in town is the local office of **Diethelm Travel (Cambodia)** ((023) 426648 FAX (023) 426676, 8 240 Street, Phnom Penh.

Hand-woven baskets on sale in the Phnom Penh market.

Welcome
to
Indochina

The word Indochina conjures up images of the French-administered Far East, but today the French are long gone — even if some influences linger on — and Indochina is less a place than three very different countries, each with its own traditions and national consciousness. Nevertheless, geographically they make a great deal of sense to tour as a "package," and the differences among the three countries make such a tour only the more enjoyable.

What do they share? Perhaps above all a turbulent and often violent history of more

Western powers have only heightened the sense of tragedy. Military triumph has won Indochina the political and cultural independence that its three territories have been seeking for centuries, but at a tremendous cost: in each case, victory placed them under hard-line revolutionary socialist rule, resulting in nearly two decades of social purges, isolation, austerity and virtual economic collapse.

Only now are these unique cultures, overshadowed for so many years by conflict, emerging from their Communist restraints

than 2,000 years. For much of that time, the three countries that make up the region — Vietnam, Laos and Cambodia — have been engaged in almost continuous internecine wars and struggles to survive in the shadow of their powerful neighbors, China, Siam (Thailand) and Myanmar (Burma).

Centuries of conflict have given them a tenacity perhaps most dramatically evident in their heroic, if devastating, recent struggles — against the French, who colonized Indochina from the late 1800s, and against the Americans, who decided in the early 1960s that the toppling dominoes of Communist expansion could be halted in the region's jungles, mountains and fecund rice plains. The victories scored against both of these

and enjoying cultural renewal. Across the region, previously off-limit areas are being opened, land mines cleared from troubled areas, and tourist facilities upgraded in response to the tourism boom of recent years.

True, the region still has a long way to go, but the relatively slow pace of modernization and the low-grade impact of globalization make Indochina an adventure for travelers in a way no longer found in many surrounding countries. While tour groups will experience the usual kid-glove treatment, and independent travelers will certainly experience the odd difficulty or, at

LEFT: Tending the rice fields in Vietnam's Mekong Delta. ABOVE: A beach vendor in Quy Nhon, Vietnam.

the very least, some discomfort, the sights, sounds and experiences that await in this exciting region more than compensate for any minor discomfort.

A great pilgrimage is already under way — perhaps greater than the initial rush to visit "forbidden" China when it first re-opened its doors in 1979. The number of visitors to Vietnam has grown from around 600,000 in 1993 to an estimated more than two million in 2001. Meanwhile, the word is out, and quiet unassuming Laos is being "discovered" by some 500,000 visitors a year — and few fail to be charmed by what they find there. Even Cambodia, whose tourist potential has long been stymied by an image of lawlessness, has seen its tourist arrivals grow to some 350,000 per year, helped no doubt by the initiation of direct international flights to Siem Reap, which offers access to the region's premiere tourist attraction: Angkor Wat.

Throughout much of Indochina, the architectural legacy of the French era is being restored — examples include the old Municipal Theater, more commonly known as the Opera House, in Hanoi; the elegant central Post Office in Saigon, with its main hall reminiscent of a cavernous Victorian railway station; and a fading but stately mansion that is now the home of the Lao Revolutionary Museum in Vientiane. In Luang Prabang, Laos, the weatherworn but picturesque terraces and old public buildings of the former royal capital nestle among the golden spires of Buddhist wats as though a sleepy French provincial town has been spirited into the Far East.

For many travelers, however, it is less the legacy of colonialism than the legacy of war that makes Indochina such a compelling destination. There is no shortage of reminders — rusted, stripped helicopter gunships, some left where they crashed in the countryside, others mounted outside the war museums; spent shells and over-grown craters; "tunnel-rat" tours; and, of course, the sobering reminders of the geno-cide that the war inspired in Cambodia. From the air, it is still possible to make out the craters left by countless B-52 bombing raids over the Plain of Jars in Laos or over Da Nang in Central Vietnam. Flying into key airports throughout the region, the concrete shelters and hangars that once housed American warplanes can still be seen. Then there are the war cripples and amputees, thousands of them, especially in Vietnam and Cambodia.

Yet, despite these reminders of a savage conflict that set the region's development back by decades, Indochina today is bounc-ing back. Once again the world is being offered an opportunity to glimpse the region's rich history and culture — magnifi-cent Hindu and Buddhist temples and rel-ics like fabled Angkor Wat in Cambodia, the Cham ruins in Vietnam, and the region's oldest Buddhist landmark, Wat Phu in Laos; evocative traditional dance and, particularly in Vietnam, unique musical instruments. Not that the attractions are cultural alone. Vietnam is home to dramatic natural scen-ery such as the offshore karst formations of Ha Long Bay and the superb (and mostly undeveloped) beaches that run the length of its long coastline. In Laos, the enigmatic Plain of Jars, off-limits for decades, has been accessible for some years now, as is most of the rest of the country. Meanwhile, Viet-nam's Central Highlands and vast Mekong Delta region, is home to some of the most splendid natural scenery in all of Asia.

All this amounts to a compelling desti-nation that is made all the more enjoyable by its hospitable, charming and friendly people. Bear in mind, however, that it is changing fast. Laos may still exist in some-thing of a time-warp, but Vietnam and even Cambodia are responding to new eco-nomic freedoms and foreign investment with traffic jams, advertising hoardings and building projects that are changing the faces of the cities there. For the time be-ing, it is still possible to describe the region, in the usual cliché, as resembling "Thai-land 20 years ago," but it probably won't be so for all that much longer. All the more reason to visit now.

TOP: A hill-tribe village on the Ha Giang River, Vietnam. BOTTOM: Sunrise at Dien Bang near Da Nang.

Indochina and Its People

While archeological evidence points to very early human settlements in Indochina, the known history of the region does not begin until around 1,200 BC, when wet rice cultivation started in the Red River delta. Known as the Dong Son culture, the legacy of this early civilization is its bronze drums.

THE ANCIENT HINDU KINGDOMS

By the time of the birth of Christ, the first of two great cultural influences was beginning to give shape to Indochina. Hindu influence, which was to sweep the region from India to Indonesia, established the kingdom of Funan in what is now southern Vietnam and eastern Cambodia. From the first to sixth centuries AD, absorbed into the vast trading empire that India had created, Funan literally put the Indochina peninsula on the map, establishing far-flung trading contacts with India, China, Indonesia, Persia and the Mediterranean. In one of those discoveries that makes any historian's heart leap, archaeologists unearthed a gold Roman medallion in Vietnam's Kien Giang Province, where Funan's capital was located, dated to AD 152 and inscribed with the bust of Emperor Antoninus Pius, the successor of Hadrian. This early internationalism, and the colonial era that came much later, has a significant resonance in Vietnam's economic renaissance today: the south, particularly, has a long tradition of trade and cultural exchange with the rest of the world.

During Funan's heyday, another Indianized domain, the Hindu kingdom of Champa, arose to the north, in the coastal area around what is now Da Nang. While Funan has left an important commercial legacy, Champa bequeathed to Vietnam its most illustrious cultural relics — the Cham ruins, remains of 15 temple towers at My Son near Da Nang, and a collection of stone images and sculptures now found in the city's Cham Museum.

By the eighth century, the Champa Kingdom dominated much of today's central Vietnam, extending its rule as far south as Phan Rang. But it was constantly at war with southward-migrating Viets, who in turn were engaged in a long-running struggle for survival against imperial China.

THE CHINESE IMPACT

The people known as the Viet probably came from eastern China, an area now covered by the provinces of Jiangsu, Zhejiang and Fujian. By the third century BC they had established a kingdom called Nan Yue ("southern Viet") on the southern fringes of China and extending as far as the Red River Delta in contemporary Vietnam.

In 101 BC the Chinese emperor Wu Di struck back, conquering the Nan Yue kingdom and taking control of northern Vietnam. The conquest triggered a fierce resistance among the Vietnamese, the first of tense relations still witnessed between the two countries today. While relations between Hanoi and Beijing are now normalized, they fought

a short but bitter border war as recently as 1979 and have yet to settle their rival territorial claims to offshore oil deposits around the Spratley Islands in the South China Sea.

The first most memorable battle against Chinese central rule was fought in the year AD 40 by the Trung Sisters, two high-born Viets who led a rebellion that re-established sovereignty over the Red River Delta. Three years later the Chinese counter-attacked, grabbed the region back, and the two vanquished queens committed suicide; but they've gone down in history as Vietnam's most revered heroines, and even today you'll find key streets named Hai Ba Trung in Hanoi, Saigon and other major cities.

For more than 800 years, right up to the tenth century, the Chinese maintained and strengthened their grip on today's northern Vietnam, naming it Annam ("pacified south"). There were various Vietnamese rebellions during this period, but it took the collapse of the Tang Dynasty and China's preoccupation with power struggles in other parts of its realm to give the Vietnamese the advantage in the field. In 938 the Chinese were finally routed in a revolt led by Ngo Quyen. A thousand years of Chinese imperial rule came to an end, and Ngo established the first of 12 dynasties that were to maintain Vietnamese sovereignty and independence, despite various internal conflicts, until it fell under French domination in the mid-1800s.

Statues of mandarins guard the Khai Dinh imperial tomb in Hue, Vietnam.

However, for much of this time, Vietnamese sovereignty applied only to the northern region of today's Vietnam. The state of Champa continued to dominate central Vietnam and part of the south right up until the eighteenth century, creating a cultural division between north and south that has been most vividly emphasized in modern times by the 1954 partition of the country and the Vietnam War, and is even quite evident today. As for Funan, it simply disappeared into the maw of the Khmer empire, based in Cambodia, which controlled the Mekong Delta until this vast, rich rice bowl was brought under Vietnamese suzerainty in the seventeenth century.

Nor did the landmark battle of 938 see the last of northern invaders. In the thirteenth century the Mongol Yuan Dynasty, heirs of Kublai Khan's savage conquest, invaded northern Vietnam twice in a bid to get their hands on Champa. They were soundly defeated on both counts, and two more great warriors joined the ranks of Vietnam's resistance heroes — Tran Hung Dao, whose statue stands today high on a pedestal in Saigon's "Hero Square," and Emperor Ly Thai Tho, better known as Lei Loi, whose name has joined that of the Trung Sisters on several main streets throughout Vietnam.

ARRIVAL OF THE MOUNTAIN PEOPLE

Just as Chinese pressure to keep its empire intact welded Vietnamese nationhood, so it led to the formation of neighboring Laos. Although there was a human presence in this largely mountainous wilderness some 10,000 years ago, it was around the eighth century that the first of two major migrations by Tai-Kadai tribes from southern China began trickling through the steep hills, finally reaching the fecund Mekong River valley, where some settled and some continued on into what is now northeast Thailand. Five hundred years later another migration began, this one fleeing Mongol troops sent into China's Guangxi and Yunnan

This well-preserved Cham tower at Po Nagar, near Nha Trang in southern Vietnam dates from the sixth century.

Provinces to bring troublesome non-Han populations to heel.

While the Thais settled throughout northern Laos and Thailand, they clung together in separate tribal groups, each with its own leader. However, in the mid-thirteenth century the clans in northern Thailand organized themselves in rebellion against the Khmers, and in doing so established the kingdom of Sukhothai. In a series of pacts with Thai warlords in Chiang Mai and Phayao, Sukhothai rule was able to extend right across the Mekong to include Wieng

of Champa, which unnerved his ministers so much they deposed him and booted him into exile.

Fa Ngum's successors consolidated what was now a powerful kingdom and the embryo of the Lao nation. But when one king, Setthathirat, went missing in 1571 after a military foray into Cambodia — thought to have been slain by unpacified hill tribes in southern Laos — Lane Xang fell into 60 years of chaos, during which the Burmese, from the north, took the opportunity to pick bits of the kingdom off for themselves. Finally,

Chan (City of the Moon), whose name the French later romanized into Vientiane.

Thwarted in northern Thailand, the Khmers now gave their backing to the man who could well be called the father of Lao nationhood — Chao Fa Ngum, a warlord from Muang Sawa (later known as Luang Prabang). Fa Ngum seized Wieng Chan from the Thais and then marched on into Thailand itself; in 1353 he established the kingdom of Lane Xang (Ten Thousand Elephants) embracing the Khorat Plateau of northeast Thailand and much of what is the state of Laos today. Fa Ngum didn't stop there — he pushed Lane Xang's borders eastward to the Annamite Mountains of Vietnam and even threatened the kingdom

a new iron leader, King Suliya Vongsa, arose out of the turmoil in 1637 and, in the ensuing six decades — the longest reign of any Lao monarch — pulled the warring Lao factions back together, re-established firm centralized rule and made Lane Xang more powerful than it had ever been before. This was the kingdom's golden era. Yet when King Vonsa died in 1694 with no son to succeed him, this first Lao nation was split into three warring kingdoms — Lane Xang, Xieng Khoang and Champassak. More than that, the Laos found themselves caught in a deadly pincer, with the Thais of Siam on one side and the Vietnamese on the other, each intent on claiming this strategic mountain domain as a vassal state.

BIRTH OF THE KHMER EMPIRE

From the first to the sixth century, much of what is now Cambodia was part of the Hindu kingdom of Funan, and shared brisk trade and cultural intercourse with the outside world. But in the middle of the sixth century the reign of the Khmers began — an age of explosive expansion characterized by conquest and great cultural innovation.

In the middle of the sixth century a tribal force called the Kambujas from the

effort was made in 802 by Prince Jayavarman II, who declared independence from his mountain stronghold at Phnom Kulen, the first capital of Cambodia. The Javanese were unable to bring the Cambodians to heel and watched the rapid growth of a great imperial power under Jayavarman. More importantly, he established a dynasty in which successive kings built upon the firm centralized administration that he'd set up. The result was the Khmer Empire, which by the twelfth century had brought a large part of Vietnam, Laos and Thailand

middle Mekong region established a new kingdom called Chenla. This state then turned its attention east, to the rich Mekong Delta area and began to absorb Funan. Two centuries later, Chenla broke up into rival northern and southern kingdoms. Civil wars spread in the south as leaders fought for power, weakening the region so much that it attracted invasion and annexation by Hindu forces from Java's powerful Sailendra Kingdom.

It took two attempts to sever Cambodia from Javanese rule, which was all-powerful in the region at the time. The first try by a Khmer prince ended short when the Sailendra ruler mounted an expedition to Cambodia and beheaded him. The second

under its control and had even subjugated the kingdom of Champa.

But this move against Champa was rash and ill-fated: Cham armies struck back in 1177, destroyed Angkor and very nearly wiped out the Khmer Empire with it. Had a Khmer strongman not stepped into the breach, Cambodia would not possess one of the great cultural wonders of the world today. The empire's savior was King Jayavarman VII, who ascended to the throne in 1181 and immediately began restoring Khmer stability, sovereignty and power. But his fame rests in the new symbol of Khmer

OPPOSITE: A Van Kiew tribal village in the Cam Lo Valley, central Vietnam. ABOVE: A young fisherwoman in Da Nang.

power that he built — Angkor Thom. Many people today think of Angkor as Angkor Wat, built by Suryavarman II (1113–50) — a single, particularly spectacular temple ruin, albeit one of the most important on earth. But what Jayavarman VII built was a huge new capital, Angkor Thom, with a population of more than one million, an intricate network of canals, dams and irrigation systems, and Angkor's most celebrated monuments, the awesome Bayon Temple, the Baphuon and the Terrace of Elephants.

Reinvigorated by all this grandeur, the Khmers embarked on another period of conquest and avenged their humiliation by the Chams by driving deep into Champa and ultimately destroying this proud central Vietnamese state. But then, as with the Lane Xang empire of Laos, Khmer power waned after the death of its iron man. With the loss of Jayavarman VII, Angkor gradually fell into decline and the Khmer state weakened in the face of an onslaught by the rising new power of Southeast Asia — the Thais.

ENTER THE THAIS

By the end of the sixteenth century, both Cambodia and Laos were virtually fighting for their lives, threatened and squeezed by the Thais and the Vietnamese. Both states remain trapped to some extent in the same vice today, with Vietnam and Thailand competing for cultural, political and economic dominance. In Laos, the death of King Suliya Vongsa in 1694 and the collapse of the Lane Xang state eventually led to Vietnamese control of Wieng Chan (Vientiane) and the middle Mekong region, as well as Thai control of Champassak to the south, a rich agricultural plain near modern-day Pakse. It was when the Thais began confronting the Vietnamese in Wieng Chan, exacting tribute alongside their rivals, that Lao subservience ended.

The area's warlord, Prince Anou, boldly declared war on the Thais, with disastrous results: the Siamese destroyed Wieng Chan, then marched on Luang Prabang and Champassak, and by the closing years of the eighteenth century had occupied and virtually depopulated most of the country, forcibly resettling the Laos in northeastern Thailand.

In Cambodia, Siamese attacks began in the thirteenth century after the death of Jayavarman VII, but it took the Thais more than 200 years to secure the prize they were after — the vast treasure house and seat of Khmer power, Angkor. It was in the mid-fifteenth century that they finally overran the temple city, forcing the Khmers to move their capital to the vicinity of what is now Phnom Penh. The Khmers fought back, and at one stage managed to push their forces to the Siamese capital of Ayutthaya; but in 1594 the Thais conquered Phnom Penh, and the great age of Khmer power and prestige was finally brought to an end.

Equally significant, the Khmer collapse introduced a completely new political and military element into the Indochina arena,

and one that would have a profound effect on the region. Pressed by the Thais, and with Phnom Penh about to fall, the Cambodians became the first Indochinese to call upon Western powers for help. The request went out to the Portuguese and Spanish, the first Europeans to explore Asia; but when a Spanish expedition from Manila finally came to the rescue it was too late — the Thais had already conquered Phnom Penh.

Instead of turning on the Thais, or returning to Manila, the Spanish decided to stick around. They then became so deeply embroiled in Thai–Cambodian intrigues that the Khmers eventually had to do a complete turnabout and enlist Thai help to get rid of them. In 1599 the entire Spanish garrison in Phnom Penh was massacred, and a Thai puppet monarch put in power. From that point on the once-powerful Khmer state was ruled by a succession of beleaguered monarchs who were under such intense pressure from rivals that they had to seek Thai or Vietnamese help to stay in power.

These were costly alliances: the Vietnamese began their takeover of the southern Mekong Delta region — once a Khmer domain — in return for their assistance, and the Thais grabbed control of Battambang and Siem Reap Provinces. They latched onto the Khmer royal family, too, actually crowning one Khmer monarch in their own capital Bangkok and then installing him in power at Odong, a temple city close to

The temple ruins of Angkor Wat — the sacred city had a population of over one million in its heyday.

Phnom Penh. Indeed, the Khmer state — and modern Cambodia — might not have prevailed at all, had it not been for the intervention of the foreign power that has had the most abiding contemporary influence on Indochina — the French.

THE FRENCH CONNECTION

The French colonial experience in Indochina followed the tradition of European colonialism across the globe — exploration, followed by trade, followed by missionaries, then

culminating in military action to protect the merchants and evangelists from the inevitable cultural backlash.

Although Portuguese, Dutch and French traders and missionaries had been active in Vietnam since the sixteenth century, the French were the first to establish a military presence there. It started with a local revolt that destabilized a relatively peaceful balance of power between dynastic northern Vietnam and the kingdom of Champa in central south. In 1765, the Tay Son rebellion, led by three brothers from a wealthy trading family and aimed at stamping out corruption and poor administration, put an end to the status quo. Within eight years, the Tay Son rebels had overrun southern Vietnam,

killing 10,000 Chinese residents of Cholon (Saigon's Chinese quarter) in the process; then they went on and conquered the north.

The emperor installed in the north by the Tay Son rebels turned out to be ineffective, calling in 200,000 Chinese troops to help him maintain power. Nguyen Hue, one of the rebel brothers, responded by proclaiming himself emperor and raising an army to kick the Chinese out — which he did in 1789, routing them in a battle near Hanoi and earning himself a revered place in Vietnam's military hall of fame.

Meanwhile, as Nguyen Hue was saving the north, a prince named Nguyen Anh, usurped by the Tay Son rebellion, was plotting revenge in the south. After getting nowhere with the Thais, Nguyen Anh made elaborate overtures to the French for military assistance, even sending his four-year-old son to the court of King Louis XVI as a gesture of good faith. With the help of two warships and 400 French mercenaries, Nguyen Anh crushed the Tay Son, captured Hanoi, proclaimed himself Emperor Gia Long and set about rebuilding the war-ravaged country. More significantly, he united Vietnam — north and south — for the first time.

Emperor Gia Long consolidated and developed Vietnamese nationhood during his reign, from 1802 to 1819, but neither he nor his two successors, Minh Mang (1820–41) and Thieau Tri (1841–47), were visionary or progressive leaders. Supported by traditionalists, they ruled Vietnam with a whip in one hand and the rigid precepts of Chinese Confucianism in the other. They didn't like foreign missionaries, whom they regarded as a threat to the Confucian state. When they began executing Vietnamese Catholics and expelling Jesuit scholars and priests, they triggered a gathering clamor in France for intervention to stop the repression. And when several foreign missionaries were put to death in 1858, the French — who had helped put the Nguyen Dynasty in power, after all — finally stepped in, attacking Da Nang with a force of 14 ships, and then moving south to capture Saigon.

As with most colonial expeditions, once the French toe was in the bath there was no stepping out. Spurred by Vietnamese resistance on the one hand and efforts to open the country to trade and evangelism on the other, the French waded deeper and deeper into the region, first subduing the south then seizing the Red River Delta and Hanoi, and finally imposing a Treaty of Protectorate on the imperial court in Hue. By 1887, the colonial takeover of Vietnam was complete — and, as subsequent events have shown, the seeds of the first Indochina war were already sown.

It was not just Vietnam that had come under French rule; by this time Laos and Cambodia were also part of what the French

As harsh and unpalatable as it may now seem in this post-colonial age, French rule brought some benefits to Indochina. Colonial administration, though paying lip service to a series of puppet monarchs in each country, brought modernized government to the region and an infrastructure of roads, railways, communications and institutions, much of which has lasted through to the present day. The French also put a stop to expansionism in the region, and this gave Cambodia and Laos their first real sense of security for centuries. While French military power kept

proclaimed the Indochinese Union. In Laos, the French had been welcomed as allies against the Thais, and their legation in Luang Prabang became the launching point of a campaign to push the Siamese out of the country. By 1907, the Thais had pulled back across the Mekong River and Laos was a full French protectorate.

Cambodia's absorption into the union was inevitable, linked economically to Vietnam's Mekong Delta and providing a buffer, with Laos, against the kingdom of Siam. In 1863 the French persuaded the Cambodian monarch, King Norodom, to sign a treaty of protectorate, and 11 years later he was coerced into another agreement, giving the French full colonial power.

the Thais at bay to the west, Vietnam's imperialist ambitions were also thwarted.

THE SEEDS OF REVOLT

It's probably because of this protection that both Laos and Cambodia gave the French very little trouble during what could be called the idyllic years of colonial rule. Resistance was minimal, and occasional rebellions were directed mainly at corrupt or harsh native officials rather than the French. But both countries paid the price of foreign

OPPOSITE: A ceramic bas-relief at Wat Phnom in Phnom Penh records the ceding of Battambang province to Cambodia in the 1907 Franco–Siamese treaty. ABOVE: French colonial architecture in Hanoi.

occupation — their cultures and traditional institutions were submerged by the weight of French administration, education, religion and undeniable sense of superiority. While newly emerging middle classes welcomed French ways, an underlying vein of anger and resistance obviously existed, ultimately exploding with brutal fury in April 1975 in the Khmer Rouge pogrom, directed at virtually everything foreign, sophisticated or even educated in Cambodia.

Vietnam was a much different kettle of fish. From the very beginning of French rule there was fierce and often widespread resistance — not surprising when set against the tremendous battles that had been fought through the centuries to keep China at bay. As in the other Indochina states, there were Vietnamese who came to terms with and even flourished in the transplanted French culture — particularly the ruling elite, bureaucrats, merchants and sections of the armed forces and police — but much of the vastly agrarian population found itself laboring under the yoke of a system set up to exploit the country and its people economically.

In times of rebellion, and there were many intrigues and uprisings, French reprisal was often brutal. The guillotine was brought in to deal with extremists. Examples of these awful contraptions are on show today in the grounds of the War Museum in Saigon and in the Hoa Lo Prison Museum in Hanoi.

From the turn of the last century right up until World War II, the French found themselves in almost continual struggle against nationalist movements. The Japanese victory over Russia in 1905 and the 1911 to 1912 republican revolution in China heartened the dissidents. The rise of an urban proletariat and a growing corps of students who'd been free to study in France and other Western nations eventually produced the one political force with the manifesto, dedication and organization capable of leading the nationalist cause: the Communists under Ho Chi Minh.

After organizing strikes, unrest and uprisings against the French for more than two decades — and coming under increasingly fierce French reaction — the Vietnamese Communists found the opportunity they'd been waiting for when the Japanese occupied Vietnam and Indochina in World War II. Working with the Viet Minh — the name of these nationalist guerrillas taken from the League for the Independence of Vietnam (*Viet Nam Doc Lap Dong Minh Hoi*) — they were the only force to seriously resist Japanese rule. In 1944, the Viet Minh were receiving financial and military aid from the Americans. Ho Chi Minh thought he would get United States blessing for full independence after the war, but the Americans neglected an opportunity that would have saved both nations from the savagery of the Vietnam War years later. In September 1945, with the Japanese defeated, the Viet Minh controlled so much of Vietnam that Ho Chi Minh was able to declare independence and proclaim the establishment of the Democratic Republic of Vietnam. What happened then was an act of almost obscene political cynicism on the part of the victorious Western powers.

The Chinese were given the task of disarming the Japanese north of the 17th parallel in Vietnam, and the British were assigned to the south. The Chinese went on a rampage in the north, and Ho Chi Minh had to accept French help, of all things, to halt their pillaging. In the south, the British not only used defeated Japanese forces to help maintain public order, it was soon clear that their main task was to help the French regain colonial power. The Americans stood by and did nothing.

INDEPENDENCE AND THE FIRST INDOCHINA WAR

Within weeks, the French were ruling Vietnam again, but by now the lust for independence was too strong. In early 1947, some weeks after a vicious French attack on opposition elements in Hai Phong, serious fighting broke out in Hanoi and the first Indochina war began.

It took the Viet Minh eight years to drive the French out of Vietnam for good, and the character and strategy of the combat was virtually a preview of the second, far more destructive, war to come. The French received massive American military aid. The

Saigon's most enduring landmark; the Notre Dame Cathedral.

Viet Minh fought a war of attrition, a guerrilla campaign, which combined shrewd military and political action — their political agenda based on growing disenchantment in France itself and opposition to the war. When victory finally came at Dien Bien Phu in May 1954 — the Viet Minh pouring in the thousands from trenches and emplacements after laying siege to the French positions for nearly two months — it was an ignominious end to the French empire in Indochina: the 10,000 or more soldiers and Legionnaires who surrendered were not just

In Cambodia, another now-familiar figure had strode onto the national stage — Prince Norodom Sihanouk, proclaimed king by the Vichy French during the Japanese occupation, and still in power when the country gained full independence along with Laos in 1953. Although Sihanouk later abdicated, allowing his father to become king, he virtually ruled Cambodia until the monarch died in 1960, as prime minister and head of the all-powerful People's Socialist Community party. After his father's death he made himself chief-of-state. Although a

demoralized, but starving and virtually abandoned by their compatriots back home.

It seems astonishing today that the French fought so fiercely to retain Vietnam when they'd already divested themselves of the rest of Indochina by the time they made their last stand at Dien Bien Phu. Laos had been granted full independence in 1953 against the background of complex political maneuvering that threw up two nationalist figures who were to have a significant impact on the country's future course — Prince Souvanna Phouma, a neutralist leader, and the leftist Prince Souvanna Vong, who sought support from the Vietnamese Communists for a revolution under the banner of the Laos Patriotic Front, or Pathet Lao.

self-proclaimed neutralist, Sihanouk's conceited, self-centered policies — in which he treated Cambodia and its people as his personal property — created the seedbed, as we shall see, for left-wing revolution in Cambodia and the dark agony it ultimately suffered under the Khmer Rouge.

The full independence of Vietnam, Laos and Cambodia was officially ratified by the Geneva Accords of July 1954. But while these agreements left Laos and Cambodia intact, they divided Vietnam at the 17th parallel, with Ho Chi Minh's despotic Communists ruling the north and an equally despotic, United States-backed anti-Communist Ngo Dinh Diem controlling the south.

One of Diem's first official acts was to renege on the Geneva Accords, refusing to take part in nationwide elections that had been dictated in the agreements. He held a referendum instead, asking voters whether he should continue to rule the south. Amid claims of rabid vote-rigging, he won a resounding "yes" and proclaimed himself president of the Republic of Vietnam. The United States and most of its European and Asian allies immediately recognized his regime, underscoring the 17th parallel as the line that had been drawn against further Communist expansion in the region.

THE SECOND INDOCHINA WAR AND THE AMERICANS

With Diem's rise to power, the die was cast for American involvement in Vietnam, and for the inevitable war. Diem soon proved so corrupt, repressive and politically paranoid that he became an embarrassment to Washington and was overthrown and murdered in a United States-backed coup in 1963. But by now, Hanoi had launched its military campaign to liberate the south and reunite the country; Washington's bid to halt the toppling dominoes of Communist expansion had become a crusade, with Vietnam its chief battleground; more than 16,000 United States military advisers, sent in by the Kennedy administration, were already trying to prop up a southern political infrastructure that was to remain every bit as repressive and corrupt as the Diem regime.

A year later, Kennedy was dead, two United States warships had come under what they claimed was an "unprovoked" attack in the Gulf of Tonkin off North Vietnam, and President Lyndon Johnson had launched a massive bombing reprisal against the north. The Vietnam War — the second Indochina War — had begun.

The war lasted 11 years, and the terrible cost to both sides — the Americans and the Vietnamese — has been evident since the last shot was fired, and will be debated for decades to come. Its savagery deeply undermined the American public's faith in its own ideals and institutions, and spawned a high-level political philosophy, espoused by a succession of presidents — Johnson,

Nixon and, later, Ronald Reagan — that anything goes if it means containing Communism. Defeat cost America its belief in its own righteousness and invincibility, much of its global prestige and its supremacy in Asia, not to mention 58,000 servicemen killed in action and almost double that number — though this figure is not uncontroversial — who have committed suicide, possibly for war-related reasons, at home since.

For Vietnam, victory — as heroic as it was — cost an estimated four million civilian lives, along with hundreds of thousands of military casualties in the North and South. And while it re-established national sovereignty and pride, it put the Communists in power, with the political and social repression and "cleansing" inevitable under hard-line, embittered revolutionary rule. More than that, it closed Indochina's doors to the rest of the world for some 15 years, during which a series of copybook Marxist social and economic experiments virtually bankrupted the three economies. In Vietnam's case, the American trading and financial embargo imposed after the fall of the south in 1975 denied it access to desperately needed World Bank, IMF (International Monetary Fund) and ADB (Asian Development Bank) loans for reconstruction and development. If there is an epitaph to be written on the Vietnam War, it is the war that nobody really won.

We can look back today with terrible fascination at the litany of events, misconceptions and mistakes that made the second Indochina war such a global trauma. The American bombing campaign against North Vietnam, which began in 1963 and continued throughout the war, pitted high-technology against a well-organized agricultural society with relatively little industrial capacity, but which was able to repair roads, bridges, dams and dikes as fast as they were damaged. When the first United States Marines were deployed in Da Nang in March 1965 — spearheading President Johnson's massive build-up of American forces in South Vietnam — the stage was already set for the ultimate failure of mecha-

Young soldiers at the Liberation Day parade, Da Nang.

nized, main-force warfare against an elusive, highly mobile guerrilla enemy.

The United States and ARVN (Army of the Republic of Vietnam) rural pacification program, aimed at isolating the Communist Viet Cong guerrillas and destroying their infrastructure, simply led to the wholesale uprooting of thousands of rural families from their ancestral homes and left them to languish in armed resettlement camps. The strategy of search-and-destroy, an attempt to hunt down and eliminate Viet Cong and infiltrating North Vietnamese

uted to the discreditable caliber of leadership that Washington supported, namely presidents Nguyen Cao Ky and Nguyen Van Thieu, who are alleged to have used the pacification scheme more against their rivals than against the Communists. The key political blunder that the American military hierarchy made was in assuring an already uneasy American public back home that the war was practically won — that the "light at the end of the tunnel" could be seen — as early in the conflict as 1967. The Communist Tet Offensive of January 1968, however costly

units, generally floundered in confusion — for who was to say with certainty who were Viet Cong and who were government loyalists in a population that all looked the same? Moreover, a CIA-operated covert war called the Phoenix Program, which employed intimidation, terror, torture and assassination in a bid to fight the Communists on their own terms — and which virtually governed the pacification program throughout the conflict — became so badly corrupted and out of hand that it victimized and alienated millions of neutral Vietnamese.

The Americans lost the political war, too. Much of the failure of the Phoenix Program — as infamous as it was — has been attrib-

it proved in Communist lives, blew open the credibility gap between the Pentagon and the public, cut the heart out of American support for the war and turned the United States anti-war movement into a national cause. From that point on, the American involvement in Vietnam was more a prolonged tactical retreat.

Perhaps the most disastrous step taken by the Americans was President Richard Nixon's invasion of eastern Cambodia in April 1970, an offensive aimed at destroying Viet Cong border sanctuaries and easing pressure on the United States in the Paris peace negotiations. Up until that time, Cambodia and Laos had been sidelines to the main conflict in Vietnam — though Laos had sustained an American bombing campaign estimated to be among the heaviest in history.

At the start of the American build-up in Vietnam in 1963, Laos had been in turmoil, with three political factions, including the leftist Pathet Lao under Prince Souvanna Vong and Prince Souvanna Phouma's neutralists, jockeying for power. In 1964, after a series of failed attempts to form coalition governments, Souvanna Vong pulled out of what he regarded as a rigged match and took his guerrilla forces into the mountains. American military advisers moved in to support the government, a massive bombing operation was unleashed against Pathet Lao bases and infiltration routes, and the CIA raised an army of specially trained Hmong hill tribe warriors and Thais for covert operations.

THE KHMER ROUGE HORROR

In Cambodia, United States involvement came about partly as a result of Prince Sihanouk's struggle to stay in power. In the early days of the war he declared Cambodia neutral, but then turned around and severed diplomatic relations with Washington, allowing North Vietnam and the Viet Cong to use Cambodian border areas as a sanctuary and infiltration zone. In 1967, he did another about-turn: facing a rural rebellion against his autocratic rule and convinced that the Communists were out to get him, he began cracking down harshly on leftists. Two years later, the United States launched devastating B-52 bombing raids against guerrilla base camps in eastern Cambodia. When, in March 1970, Sihanouk was mysteriously deposed while on a trip to France by a rival faction led by General Lon Nol, he changed his political colors once again, taking up exile in Communist Beijing at the head of a rebel Cambodian movement that he had dubbed the "Khmer Rouge."

Richard Nixon's invasion of Cambodia in April 1970 triggered savage warfare between the Khmer Rouge and Lon Nol's government forces. It raged for five years, and despite American military and economic assistance, the Lon Nol regime was

no match for the rebels, commanded by a French-educated revolutionary whose name has since become synonymous with genocide, Pol Pot. When Phnom Penh fell to the Khmer Rouge on April 17, 1975 — two weeks before the Communist victory in Vietnam — these fanatical Maoist revolutionaries, characterized by their black peasant uniforms and traditional red-checkered scarves, wreaked a barbarous revenge on their people.

One only has to visit Cambodia today to see the damage and horror that the Red

Khmers inflicted during their demented four-year purge of Cambodian society. Proclaiming "Year Zero" as the start of a complete restructuring of Cambodian society, the revolutionaries virtually closed down Phnom Penh, forcibly evacuating most of its people to the countryside to work as slave labor on farming and rural development projects. Families were broken up, the parents separated and forced into work units that were often many kilometers from each other, the younger children placed in political education camps.

OPPOSITE: A Vietnam War flashback — panic at the United States Embassy in Saigon as Communist troops close in. ABOVE: Government tanks in Da Nang.

Meanwhile, thousands upon thousands of people were consigned to what has now become a morbid catchphrase of Cambodia's darkest hour — the "killing fields." Almost the entire intelligentsia and middle class were wiped out — dancers, writers, teachers, artists, anyone wearing glasses (a sign of education). The victims, some of them mere children, were imprisoned, interrogated and brutally tortured before being taken to rural mass-execution grounds where they were put to death — their skulls smashed with hammers and pickaxes to conserve bullets. There is no need to relate more about this wholesale murder, except to add that between one and three million people are believed to have perished at the hands of the Pol Pot regime. It takes just one visit to the terrible Tuol Sleng Genocide Museum in Phnom Penh — formerly one of the key interrogation centers — and the genocide monument erected over one of the killing fields 15 km (nine miles) from the city, to sense the terrible chilling darkness that swept across the country at that time.

VIETNAM INVADES CAMBODIA

In December 1978, after a series of Khmer Rouge border provocations, Vietnam invaded Cambodia, mercifully putting an end to the pogrom. While it's highly unlikely that humanitarian aims triggered the invasion — the Khmer Rouge had been liquidating thousands of ethnic Vietnamese living in Cambodia — the outcome was another quite shameful show of international cynicism. China and the United States, both alarmed at the prospect of Vietnamese expansion in Indochina, supported the Cambodian rebel factions, including the Khmer Rouge. Thailand, equally nervous about Vietnamese power, became the sanctuary for Red Khmers and other rebel groups forced westward by the occupation.

The Vietnamese behaved relatively well during the 11 years they controlled Cambodia, providing a period of security in which the country could recover from the trauma of the Khmer Rouge "revolution." In 1989, under tremendous pressure to mend its political fences with the rest of the world — particularly the United States — and re-

open its society to foreign aid and investment, Vietnam withdrew its forces from Cambodia. The United States immediately severed its support for the Khmer Rouge and instituted its so-called "road map" of moves — orchestrated in concert with the hunt for American MIAs, or servicemen still missing in Vietnam — to establish diplomatic relations with Hanoi.

THE AFTERMATH

In September 1990, the United Nations Security Council instituted what was hailed as a major step toward eventual peace and stability in this war-weary nation — setting up a Supreme National Council in which a coalition of Vietnam-backed government figures and the major rebel groups, including the Khmer Rouge, would run the country while preparations were made for national democratic elections. The indefatigable Prince Sihanouk returned in triumph from Beijing to head the council, and immediately starting plastering huge portraits of himself all over Phnom Penh. Some 15,000 United Nations troops and rear echelon from nearly 30 countries were deployed in Cambodia to help rebuild the country's infrastructure, disarm the rebel factions, resettle thousands of refugees from Thailand and supervise the May 1993 elections.

The elections in mid-1993 returned Sihanouk to power: he was appointed King and his son prime minister. Predictably, the Khmer Rouge boycotted the elections. Allowed to pour back into Cambodia, they dug in again, controlling virtually all the northern half of the country. Backed by Thai political and business interests deeply involved in lucrative logging and gem mining in their territory, they launched increasingly daring attacks on United Nations positions. More than that, they continued the pogram that they launched in 1975, executing and assassinating whole communities of ethnic Vietnamese in their area.

INDOCHINA TODAY

Indochina may not be without its problems, but the situation today is a world away from the strife-torn days of the Vietnam War. In

Cambodia, the most ravaged of the three countries, a degree of stability has been achieved. The power of the Khmer Rouge waned for much of the late 1990s, and by the time Pol Pot died in 1998, disarray within the ranks meant they were spent as a political force. Bowing to foreign pressure — Cambodia remains heavily reliant on foreign aid — it seems likely now that the government will make an important next step, and try the surviving leaders of the murderous regime in cooperation with the United Nations.

The Khmer Rouge was not the only problem for Cambodia in the 1990s. Deep divisions within mainstream politics threatened the social and economic order. United Nations brokered elections in 1993 saw the emergence of a power-sharing government between Prince Norodom Ranariddh and Vietnam-sponsored Hun Sen (who refused to accept the former's election victory). Four years later, in 1997, as both Ranariddh and Hun Sen courted the splintered Khmer Rouge, Hun Sen launched a coup, deposed Ranariddh (the country's true democratic leader) and set about purging the country of his political enemies. For a time it looked as if Cambodia was once again about to be plunged into violence.

In July 1998, however, elections were held, and despite claims of massive fraud by opposition parties, Hun Sen was only able to establish the two-thirds majority he needed to form a government by again joining forces

The That Luang rites cumulate in a candlelit procession around Vientiane's most sacred stupa.

At the crossroads between Southeast Asia and China, Indochina has a mixed heritage, with numerous minority ethnic groups in addition to the each of the country's main inhabitants. Vietnam alone has within its estimated

with Ranariddh. The result: Cambodia has achieved a degree of stability few would have thought possible just a few years ago.

In Laos, on the other hand, it has very much been business as usual, although through 2000 and early 2001 the country was troubled by a series of small bomb explosions that nobody claimed, and the government itself seemed at a loss to explain. Analysts have pointed to an internal division within the Lao government as the source of the explosions — between those who support increased reliance on China and those who support Vietnam — aggravated by the fact that the pro-China group won the day in the Lao Communist Party Congress in early 2001.

The Vietnamese government, as in Laos, has followed the Chinese model of allowing increased economic freedoms but keeping a tight control on political power. Nevertheless, economic growth has remained sluggish, despite predictions prior to the Asian crash that Vietnam was poised to emerge as the next "Asian tiger." Meanwhile, four years of negotiations resulted in a historic visit by Bill Clinton to Vietnam in late 2000 and the normalization of trade relations; an agreement that was finally ratified by the United States Congress a year later.

population of 78 million, 54 ethnic minority groups, although the Viets comprise something around 85 percent of the population. The ethnic minorities fall into three main groups. The northern minorities, or Montagnards, as they were called by the French, are of the Austro-Asian family who migrated from the tribal lands of southern China and encompass the Hmong, the Zao, the Tai-Kadai, the Tai, the Nung and the Muong. In central Vietnam are the Austronesian groups, which include the Jarai, the Ede, the Ria Gia and the Cham, who live around Phan Thiet and also on the Cambodian border near Chau Doc. Thirdly, smaller communities of Sino-Tibetan heritage, encompassing such obscure groups as the La Hu, the Hoa, the Ha Nhi, the Lo Lo, the Si La and the Phuia, live in the far northwestern tip of the country where it borders Laos and China.

ABOVE and OPPOSITE: Four faces of Vietnam — "beginning to enjoy life again."

Laos, with a population of around 5.5 million, comprises 47 ethnic groups, many living traditional lifestyles high in the mountain areas bordering China and, to the east, bordering Vietnam. In the south a large percentage of the population is made up of the Laos Loum (lowland Laos), Laos's main population group. Existing alongside the different groups are the Chinese, estimated at around five percent, who have come over the centuries for trade and more recently as imported labor from southern China, especially to the northern provinces such as Oudomxai.

Cambodia has a population of around 12.5 million, around 90 percent of which is Khmer. The Khmers are related to the Mons of Myanmar and Thailand, migrating, it is believed, to what is now Cambodia over 4,000 years ago, and intermarrying with the

existing Austronesian population. The remaining ten percent include Chinese Khmers, ethnic Vietnamese (some five percent of the population) who live on Cambodia's two main rivers and the Ton Le Sap Lake, and the approximately 500,000 Chams or Muslim Khmers, descendents of Vietnam's great Champa Kingdom, who live scattered across the southeast. In the northeastern highlands close to the Laos and Vietnamese borders are animist tribal groups known as Khmer

Loeu, who share their ancestors with those across the border.

THE ECONOMY

Ten years ago, Indochina looked to be on the threshold of an economic boom. Rich in agricultural, marine, forestry and mineral resources, and with a huge pool of educated but cheap labor ready, great hope was held out for the region. The results have been disappointing. Vietnam, which was supposed to lead Indochina into a new era of prosperity, has done little to do away with the red tape that makes doing business there fraught with frustration, and the government's much vaunted policy of *doi moi* — liberalization — has turned out to be a mostly disappointing experiment — a government directive in 1996 famously required that all foreign language signs be removed from shop fronts. Meanwhile, as is the case elsewhere in the region, another drawback to Vietnam's development continues to be its decrepit infrastructure — roads, bridges, ports, airports, transportation and communications — a problem that is only now being resolved as one of the results of the lifting of the United States embargo.

Laos and Cambodia have similarly made relatively slow economic progress. Laos began opening its economy in 1986, and averaged healthy growth rates of around seven percent for the following decade. The regional financial crisis of early 1997 changed this, however. The Lao kip was massively devalued, inflation hit 140 percent, and the growth rate slipped to around four percent, where it has remained since. The poorest country in Southeast Asia, Laos is hampered by a rudimentary infrastructure — no railways, a shockingly bad road network, limited communications and an inadequate electricity supply. Official corruption and a government that puts up many informal barriers to foreign investment only add to the country's woes.

Cambodia also suffered as a result of the Asian economic meltdown of 1997, but the situation has been compounded by a lack of political stability. The coup of 1997, in which Hun Sen ousted Prince Ranariddh, led to a mass exodus of the foreign community from Cambodia, though many soon returned. Like Laos, it is hampered by poor infrastructure and corruption.

The Thais are one of the region's most enthusiastic investors, digging in early in both Cambodia and Laos, although one particular industry has embroiled Bangkok in a potentially bitter political and environmental controversy. Logging, much of which is carried out illegally in Cambodia and Laos, costs the governments there millions of dollars in badly needed revenue.

Both Laos and Cambodia are primarily agricultural economies, though they also possess extensive mineral deposits, which require heavy investment to exploit. While the Laos government has instigated some strict and sustainable anti-logging laws, they are not always implemented. Among poor, underpaid officials, a juicy bribe is sometimes difficult to refuse. A former governor of Attapeu Province was sentenced to 15 years in jail for his part in a logging scandal.

The Thais, having already created an environmental crisis with their own wholesale deforestation, have seized this opportunity, and Laos is particularly vulnerable — only 10 percent of its land is arable, the rest is forest. The construction of the Friendship Bridge across the Mekong at Nong Khai, donated by Australia and opened in 1993, is seen by some environmentalists and economists as not just the country's first real physical link with the outside world, but an opportunity for increased Thai exploitation as well. In 2000 a second Japanese bridge linking Pakse in the south with Thailand was completed, far away from the stern eye of the central government — creating, some say, more opportunities for illegal logging.

POLITICS

Despite the talk of a new political openness, Vietnam is still a socialist country, its people still forced to toe the Communist Party line, its economy still centrally controlled. It has opened its doors, but at the higher echelons of government it remains suspicious of foreign activities and motives. Add to this the negatives of greed and corruption and the picture continues to look bleak. But while political change is dragging its feet in the wake of economic liberalization, change is certainly taking place.

The motorbike and bicycle remain Vietnam's main forms of personal transportation as the country tries to modernize.

The *Doi Moi* open-door policy of 1986 came about because a liberal southerner, Nguyen Van Linh, assumed power at the Sixth Congress of the Communist Party. Once the door was opened, once the fundamental decision to bring back free enterprise was made, it would have taken a reactionary crackdown similar to China's Tiananmen Square massacre — especially in the south — to turn the clock of change back.

The switch to a market economy has meant that a whole gamut of laws and regulations have had to be rewritten, and is said to have switched from the unwieldy Communist Party politburo to a smaller and more decisive executive council, with each member responsible for a particular arm of government and administration.

The general trend seems to be for Vietnam to follow the Chinese path, allowing a degree of market liberalization, while at the same time maintaining a firm one-party grip on the reins of power and minimizing the "corrupting" influences that so often come with the market reforms carried out by socialist governments.

new ones made, particularly in that anathema of the Communist state, property ownership. The influx of foreign investment has meant the liberalization of banking laws, allowing private and joint-venture banks to compete with the previous monopoly of official institutions. The search for export markets has meant that Vietnamese are now allowed to travel overseas. Thousands of detainees have been released from re-education camps, and some prominent intellectuals and former capitalists rehabilitated, as the state casts about for people capable of guiding and managing economic reconstruction.

Moreover, the state itself has had to change. Immediate decision-making power

There are two other clear trends that point to comparatively radical political change in the future. The demand for talented, foreign-trained technocrats to run the economic program means that power will ultimately shift from the surviving old guard of wartime revolutionaries. And it remains to be seen how long the Vietnamese will be content with the power to conduct their own business affairs but otherwise not think for themselves.

In Laos, the death of President Kaysone Phomvihane in November 1992 seemed to herald the same passing of the Communist old guard in favor of younger, more liberal

ABOVE: Building fishing trawlers as the economy revives. OPPOSITE: A Cambodian student, Phnom Penh.

blood. However, his successor, General Khamtay Siphandon, who became president in 1998, is a similarly hard-line Communist and ally of Vietnam, underscoring the careful snail's pace of change in Laos and Hanoi's struggle to maintain its political grip on the country in the face of economic incursions by the Thais.

But while Siphandon's accession maintains the supreme power of the Laos People's Revolutionary Party, or Communist Party, governing through its politburo and Central Committee, an undercurrent of economic

reforms similar to those in Vietnam have served notice of the course the country will no doubt take in the future. The first legal code since the revolution was enacted in 1988, establishing a Western-style system of courts and justice, along with liberal investment laws. In 1990, Laos was given its first official constitution since the Pathet Lao victory. It not only ratifies the principle of free enterprise but also removes the term socialism and the hammer and sickle from the nation's political banner.

The Laos government is regarded as one of the most secretive in the world. Access to its 12 ministries is not easy for outsiders, and media publicity is rare. But it is known that Laos shares Vietnam's prime problem

— finding the experience and talent needed to build and manage a modern economy. Otherwise, there's hardly any overt evidence of repression or interference in everyday Lao life; in fact, the society appears to be the most serene and idyllic in Asia. There seems to be complete religious freedom in this devoutly Buddhist domain, and when you witness the passion with which the Laos celebrate their Buddhist festivals, the term "Buddhist socialism" springs to mind. You can't help speculating that this is one popular power that the Laos Communists, at least, prudently came to terms with, instead of trying to conquer.

The same cannot be said of the Khmer Rouge in Cambodia. During their four-year rampage they destroyed Buddhist temples, murdered monks and virtually eliminated all social and political institutions in their crazed vision of a new agrarian society, which, if it had been Europe, would have turned the clock back to the darkest of medieval times. Much of Cambodian society has had to be completely reconstructed — and much is still in waiting. The country as yet has no real legal system, or even workable laws, in place.

Where Vietnam and Laos are resisting democratic reform, rebuilding Cambodia's society was the linchpin of United Nations efforts. Not just the political framework had to be restored — just about everything from public security to social services have required building virtually from the ground up. But it's in the political sphere that the most dramatic reforms have taken place. Since the mid-1998 elections and their crucial significance for Cambodia's redevelopment, more than a dozen political parties representing liberals, conservatives, pressure groups and Buddhists have jostled for a place in the new political order.

Cambodia today is a constitutional monarchy, with the veteran Sihanouk as king. While not without problems, the government, a coalition between Hun Sen's Cambodian People's Party (CPP) and Ranariddh's Funcinpec has brought Cambodia its first spell of stability in decades. In mid-2001, international donors, encouraged by Cambodia's reforms, pledged more than US$500 million in aid to the country.

RELIGION

The rich cultural diversity of Indochina has led to a mosaic of cultural patterns and beliefs in Vietnam, Cambodia and Laos. Basic animistic beliefs, common to each country, formed the basis upon which was overlaid a veneer of first Hindu and then Buddhist beliefs, which in Vietnam have given way to the mass faith of Communism.

When China launched its open door policy after Mao's death, following over 20 years of irresponsible social and economic engineering, it got to work immediately rebuilding and renovating damaged temples, a trend that stemmed not so much from a restoration of religious freedom as from the need to give tourists something to see. Then the monks and worshipers had to be allowed back to give an air of authenticity. Such cynicism does not necessarily apply to all religious restoration, but it is undeniable that tourism development and the demand for exoticism is playing a major role in the revival of traditional culture right through the socialist world.

In Laos and Cambodia, the revival has been more popular, more spirited, reflecting the fact that these communities have been under Communist discipline for a comparatively shorter period. While it's true to say that for every Buddhist or Catholic priest there is a party cadre keeping tabs on the congregation, there's been a wholesale rush back to the images and altars that puts Indochina's socialist experiment into proper perspective — a slight deviation along a well-trodden cultural path that stretches back many centuries.

Hinduism was a major spiritual force in Indochina, with the region's two greatest kingdoms, Champa and Angkor, profoundly affected by the cult of the *devaraja*, or god-king, in which the ruler acquired divine status. The Viets brought Confucianism from China — notwithstanding Confucius's mutterings about them — and this, together with Taoism, percolated down from the north. Confucianism is more a system for the ordering of social responsibilities and relationships than a religion, while Taoism concerns itself with the individual's harmony with nature.

In the second century, a new spiritual influence, Buddhism, began sweeping the region, making its way from India through China to the Red River Delta and then down through the kingdom of the Chams. It eventually became the dominant faith in Indochina, adopted as the state religion by the Ly Dynasty in north Vietnam in the years 1010 to 1225, and spreading from there.

Although Buddhism came under Confucian counter-attack in later years, it prevailed by coming to terms with other faiths around it, most notably, Taoism and Hinduism. One of the region's most precious religious sites, the ruins of Wat Phu near Pakse in southern Laos, is regarded as the first Buddhist temple in Southeast Asia. Yet its architecture is distinctly Khmer Hindu, reflecting the way Buddhism accommodated the faiths it eventually displaced. The great Hindu city and temples of Angkor had likewise been converted to Buddhism by the thirteenth century.

The arrival of the French with their Jesuit missionaries brought Roman Catholicism to the region, and this too eventually flourished, strengthened and promoted by colonial rule, especially among the more cosmopolitan, urban Indochinese. Pockets of Christianity survive to this day, with small congregations gathering in the churches and cathedrals left by the French.

While Catholicism and Buddhism have managed to co-exist for the most part harmoniously, their relationship hasn't been without its trials. When Ho Chi Minh's Communists gained power in North Vietnam in 1954, nearly one million Vietnamese Catholics fled to the south. There they established a Catholic, anti-Communist oligarchy headed by Ngo Dinh Diem and successive presidents, and supported by the Roman Catholic Church in the United States. Their power, not to mention the corruption and favoritism that marked the wartime regimes, provoked and alienated the Buddhist majority in the south, triggered strikes and student unrest and led to the horrifying, internationally publicized self-immolations by Buddhist monks that brought Diem's downfall.

A cyclo driver with a typical load in Da Nang.

Not surprisingly, Catholicism came firmly under the official thumb in Vietnam after 1975. Many churches were closed and congregations intimidated. But a general restoration of religious freedom has taken place since the moves to liberalize the society began.

Throughout Vietnam, old churches and cathedrals are now filled with worshipers each Mass: Saigon's Notre Dame; the striking, almost medieval Saint Joseph Cathedral in Hanoi; the beautiful, domed Notre Dame Cathedral in Hue, just to name a few.

But when you take into account that only about eight percent of Vietnam's population is Christian, the revival of Buddhism and other beliefs is far more dramatic. Prayers, joss and ritual offerings are everyday scenes again at Taoist and Buddhist temples and shrines in all the major Vietnamese cities — places like the Tran Quoc and Quan Thanh temples around Hanoi's West Lake, the revered Thien Mu pagoda and temple overlooking the Perfume River in Hue, and two particularly evocative temples in Saigon; the tiny but elaborate Chinese Thien Hau Pagoda in Cholon, dedicated to the Goddess of the Sea, and the Le Van Duyet Temple, three kilometers (just under two miles) from the downtown area.

But nowhere in Indochina is Buddhism celebrated with such devotion as in Laos, where the faith seems to have stood as a social bulwark against the excesses of Marxism. The great temples of Vientiane and Luang Prabang — and there are literally dozens of them — are flourishing again, apparently undamaged by the Communist reign; and with new supplies of cash flowing in, some are being renovated. In fact, the only damage seems to have been committed in the war years before the revolution, when United States and other foreign correspondents, servicemen and art dealers stole priceless images and relics.

The extent to which Buddhism has triumphed in Laos can be witnessed at two major festivals each year. In November, thousands of monks and novices flock to Vientiane to join the population in a tumultuous three-day celebration centered on the country's most important Buddhist monument, the towering Pha That Luang (Great Sacred Stupa) and monastery on the city's northeastern fringe. In April, elephant processions highlight the three-day lunar new year festival in Luang Prabang.

In Cambodia, Buddhism and other faiths are emerging from the cultural devastation of the Khmer Rouge era. Christian churches were completely destroyed during their rampage, and one of the country's most sacred Buddhist monuments, the hilltop temples and mosque of Odong, only 40 km (25 miles) north of the capital, bears evidence of the suppression — the two main temples are in ruins, and huge reclining and sitting Buddha images were dynamited by the revolutionaries. For all this, much of the country's Buddhist heritage is reasonably intact, most notably the elaborate Royal Palace in Phnom Penh, a complex of halls and temples fashioned in the style of the Grand Palace in Bangkok, which the Khmer Rouge are said to have preserved in an effort to bolster their international image.

Of all the religions of Indochina, one bears special mention for its unique color and ritual — the Cao Dai of southern Vietnam. Based in Tay Ninh, northwest of Saigon

ABOVE and OPPOSITE: Buddhism has survived the Marxist revolution in Laos, proving to be a powerful cohesive force.

on the Cambodian border, Cao Dai has a priesthood modeled on that of the Roman Catholic Church and a doctrine which borrows much from Mahayana Buddhism, but otherwise combines beliefs from the world's major religions. It was founded in 1926 by a Vietnamese civil servant, Ngo Minh Chieu, and most of its early followers were Vietnamese bureaucrats working in the French administration.

The Cao Dai virtually ruled Tay Ninh Province and parts of the Mekong Delta in their early days, and resisted the Communist Viet Cong during the Vietnam War. They came under revolutionary suppression after the war, but are flourishing again today — you have only to visit their ornate Great Temple in Tay Ninh to realize why. With Masses celebrated four times a day, the vast congregations resplendent in white robes and the almost medieval costumes of priests, cardinals and other clergy, the Cao Dai have become one of South Vietnam's biggest tourist drawcards.

GEOGRAPHY

Indochinais a physically beautiful region, and one of many remarkable contrasts. A fleeting overview would compare the dramatic offshore karst, or limestone, formations of Ha Long Bay, north of Hanoi, with the vast, dazzling sweep of flooded riceplains in the Mekong Delta, the crumpled, green-swaddled folds and sharp junglecovered peaks of the mountains of northern Laos with the tranquil surrealism of Cambodia's southern rice lands — flat green pastures broken with the distinctive outlines of tall sugar palms.

Each country has its own contrasts. Vietnam, stretching more than 1,600 km (990 miles) down the eastern seaboard of Indochina, is virtually two huge rice-bowls — the northern Red River and southern Mekong Deltas — connected by a spine of jungled mountains, the Annamite Cordillera, which form the Central Highlands. Within this general physical profile, other distinctions appear: long swathes of sandy, untouched beaches which stretch one after the other from north to south; the pristine coastal bays and flat rice fields of the region between Da

Nang and Hue, set against the rising foothills and high mountain passes of the Central Highlands; the largely arid central region of the country, beyond Quang Tri and what used to be the Demilitarized Zone (DMZ), compared with the lush riverine landscape and rich farming communities that lead into the delta area south of Saigon.

Laos is far more rugged, with nearly three-quarters of its landlocked terrain covered with mountains and plateaus, networked with clear water rivers that rush west to the Mekong. Some of the hills are more than 2,000 m (6,500 ft) high in Xieng Khoang Province, home of the Plain of Jars. In stark contrast, the Mekong River Valley around Vientiane and Savannakhet is a flat, fertile plain and the source of most of the country's food. The mood of the landscape changes dramatically between Vientiane and the upland regions — sultry farmlands, dotted with palms, on the one hand, and a harsh, somewhat bleak red-soiled terrain that's reminiscent of outback Australia minus the eucalyptus in the Xieng Khoang area.

Cambodia is basically a broad and flat central alluvial plain, densely populated and fed by the Mekong River, with hills, mountain ranges and escarpments to its southwest, north and east. The broad expanse of the shallow Ton Le Sap, which spreads below the Angkor region towards Phnom Penh, is a great provider of fish and marine life, reputed to have more fish per cubic meter than almost any other water body in the world. The Mekong Delta begins in this central region, and the river is several kilometers wide in some areas. It splits into two separate courses, the Mekong itself and the Bassac River, at Phnom Penh before sprawling eastward into southern Vietnam. Forests cover the Eastern Highlands and hills in the southwest, close to the Thai border, where the Khmer Rouge have been operating their lucrative lumber trade with the Thais. The southern coast, facing the Gulf of Thailand, is the country's future tourism drawcard, a potential resort playground of sandy palmfringed beaches and islands.

A sacred white elephant is paraded through Vientiane during the That Luang festival.

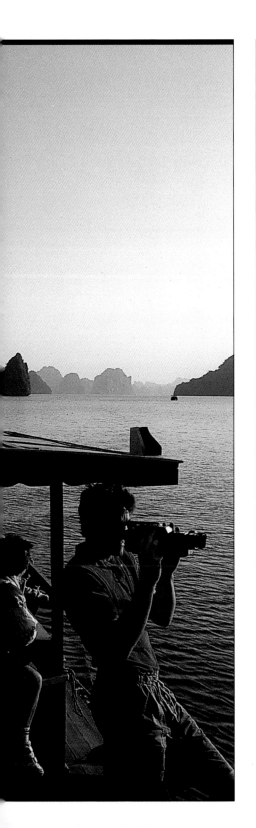

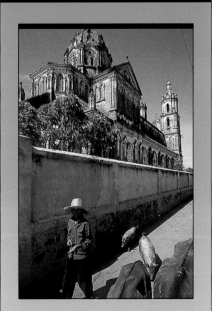

Northern
and
Central
Vietnam

Northern Vietnam holds a special fascination for visitors to Indochina — a mysterious and forbidden citadel throughout the Vietnam War and the years of isolation that followed. For decades it was a society that most people could visit only in the imagination, piecing together sketchy media images and accounts of revolutionary rallies, United States bombing statistics, peasant work units rebuilding bridges and dams, human ants struggling in their thousands along the jungled supply lines of the Ho Chi Minh Trail — and Ho Chi Minh himself, his wispy, bearded features symbolized the stubborn heroism of a society that is only now showing what it actually cost to win the war.

What it cost was progress. Aside from some uninspiring Soviet-era construction — mainly banks and other public buildings — development throughout the north stood still for more than 40 years, leaving the society to muddle through with an antiquated infrastructure left behind by the French. The north is poorer and more rustic than the south, its industrial capacity comparatively ramshackle, its roads in chronic disrepair, its bridges barely able to handle today's traffic, let alone what's likely to come as the region modernizes.

On the one hand, this predominantly agricultural society illustrates the futility of the Vietnam War — how fundamentally reckless it was to wage a high-tech bombing campaign against rural roads, dikes, bridges, grain storage facilities and rail lines that could be bandaged back together as fast as they were damaged. Even today, the railway bridges serve a dual purpose as one-way vehicular bridges between trains. Controlled by traffic lights, they illustrate the brilliant Vietnamese capacity to maximize use of valuable properties.

But perhaps northern Vietnam's most winning feature is its quiet historical charm — an architecture that's languished in a time warp since 1945 and a lingering innocence that's refreshing amid the increasingly hard-nosed growth-driven economies of East Asia.

There's already a well-worn tourist route between Hanoi, Hai Phong and beautiful Ha Long Bay, while access to the rest of northern Vietnam has opened up to reveal destinations of great beauty. It is true that some of the roads need work, but a little discomfort is a small price to pay for the wonders and magnificent scenery revealed in the northern mountain ranges — after all, Indochina is Asia's last great adventure.

HANOI

Stately, sedate and oh so polite, Hanoi makes an interesting introduction to Vietnam. Dun-colored buildings line the streets, the drab shades only relieved by splashes of red from the ever-present flag with its

bright yellow star and the scarlet hatbands of the omnipresent guards. Still, there's a slightly oppressive air in Hanoi, a restrained kind of tension, a "big brother is watching" sensation. Quite often, locals speaking with foreigners tend to look over their shoulder, perhaps a flashback to the old days. It's an atmosphere that is all the more noticeable for those arriving from freewheeling Saigon, so far to the south.

One thing that astonishes any visitor to Hanoi is the extent to which the capital's French colonial heritage survived the Vietnam War and, even more remarkably, survived the onslaught of developers since the

Hanoi's Tran Vo Temple OPPOSITE and a Buddhist temple-keeper ABOVE.

war — so much so that it seems there is hope the historic parts of the city, and especially the 36-Streets district west of Hoan Kiem Lake, may remain. Although much of the architecture is neglected and crumbling, in the summer months particularly, when the city's tree-lined boulevards are in full leaf, Hanoi exudes an exotic, early-European character that is not much in evidence elsewhere in Vietnam.

Many of the old villas are being renovated for use by big business concerns, such as the ANZ Bank near the Hoan Kiem

Lake and up-market residences that have been taken over and renovated for the executive managers of major companies. A series of inner-city lakes and small parks and its location on the Red River add to the rustic beauty.

GENERAL INFORMATION

Unlike most other destinations in Asia, where government information offices can be sources of information, in Hanoi (and elsewhere in Vietnam), hotels and tourist-oriented cafés are far more useful places to get local tips than anything offered by the government, which essentially runs its offices on strictly commercial lines. Should you still be

interested, the **Vietnam National Administration of Tourism** ((04) 942-1061, 80 Quan Su, is the place to go. Private operators, such as the famous **Sinh Café** ((04) 934-4103 E-MAIL sinhcafetour@hn.vnn.n WEB SITE www .vietnamopentour.com, 56 Hang Be Street, tend to be a lot more helpful.

Emergency numbers in Hanoi are as follows: **police** (113, **fire department** (114, and **ambulance** (115, though you will need the help of a Vietnamese speaker.

The **Vietnam International Hospital** ((04) 574-0740, Phuong Mai Road, has a 24-hour

emergency clinic. Another 24-hour medical service is **International SOS** ((04) 934-0555, which has medical teams on call.

Taxi rental can be easily arranged at rates of around US$30 a day at any hotel or travel agency. A reliable agency is **Hanoi Taxi** ((04) 825-4074, 5 Le Thanh Tong Street.

There are numerous foreign banks around town, including the Australian **ANZ** ((04) 825-8190, 14 Le Thai To Street, which has an ATM that takes major credit cards. Other banks include the **Bank of America** ((04) 824-9316, 27 Ly Thuong Kiet.

The following airlines have Hanoi offices: **Air France** ((04) 825-3484, 1 Ba Trieu Street; **Cathay Pacific** ((04) 826-7298, 49 Hai Ba Trung Street; **China Airlines** ((04) 824-

2688, 18 Tran Hung Dao Street; **Lao Aviation** ((04) 822-9951, 41 Quang Trung Street; **Malaysia Airlines** ((04) 826-8820, Hotel Sofitel Metropole, 15 Ngo Quyen Street; **Singapore Airlines** ((04) 826-8888, Unit 2, Ground Floor, International Center, 17 Ngo Quyen Street; **Vietnam Airlines** ((04) 821-6666, 1 Quang Trung Street.

GETTING AROUND

Densely populated Hanoi sprawls for miles in all directions, although most of the sights to visit are located in the relatively small city center. Streets are laid out in a simple grid system created by its French planners. The four principal lakes make convenient reference points for the various districts, and visitors will find most tourist sights within the boundaries set by the lakes.

To the north, Hoan Kiem Lake is the tourist Mecca. Located nearby are most of the newer hotels, galleries, tourist shops and, most important of all, the magical Old Quarter and the main market area around Silk Street and Dong Xuan Market.

Continuing northwest you arrive at West Lake (Ho Tay), the site of the newer big hotel complexes and business developments. En route you pass by the finest surviving examples of the colonial culture — streets full of old French villas, and the imposing and monumental neo-socialist construction and vast square of the Ho Chi Minh Mausoleum.

To the south, Thien Quang and Bay Mau Lakes are the center of the city's "new" business district, where foreign and local companies are clustering their offices in renovated commercial blocks and villas.

From a tourist's point of view, the city's key thoroughfares are Hai Ba Trung Street (close to Hoan Kiem Lake), running east–west, which has become a hot spot for imported consumer electronics; Ngo Quyen Street, running north–south, where you'll find the Sofitel Metropole; and Trang Tien Street, which leads east–west from the Opera and new Hilton Hotel down to numerous restaurants and galleries before veering north (right) into Pho Dinh Tien Hoang, site of the main Post Office, and Lake Hoan Kiem.

To the north and west of Hoan Kiem Lake is the Old Quarter. West Lake is further northwest of the main city center. To the city's northeast, the antique but elegant Long Bien Bridge, built by the French, is one of the city's main cross-river accesses to the international airport and the road to Hai Phong and Ha Long Bay; it's packed most of the day with thousands of rural people flocking in to sell produce and buy supplies in the markets.

Remember that in Hanoi, major streets (as well as smaller ones) change names every

few kilometers or so. This can make getting around extremely disorienting, and it is easy to lose your direction unless you are well armed with a decent map to help to keep your bearings.

All the major hotels have cars, minibuses and limousines at the disposal of their guests, but it is cheaper to jump in a metered taxi, which are abundant. For the authentic local experience, cyclos are good for short hops, but they are something of a tourist trap, and bargained prices have a tendency to get inflated en-route. Nevertheless, the cyclo — something akin to a

OPPOSITE: Hanoi market vendors LEFT and ramshackle public transport RIGHT. ABOVE: Cyclo drivers still provide the city's main transportation.

Northern and Central Vietnam

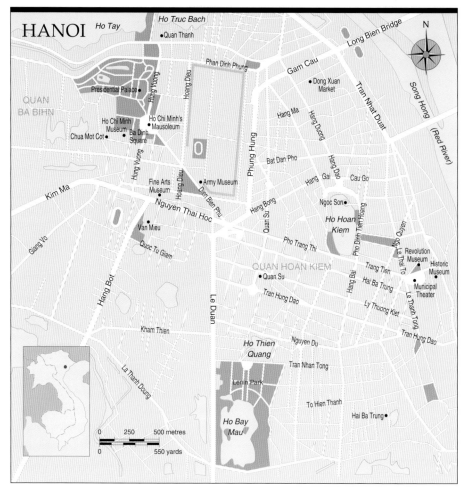

front-end loader powered by a bicycle — are exceedingly comfortable and provide a perfect way to take in the street scenes, the noise, the smells and the passing kaleidoscope of tree-fringed shop-houses, markets and villas. While some cyclo drivers are educated and polite, there are some sharks out there — if you sense a driver is planning to take you for more than the ride you are bargaining for, feel free to walk away and try someone else. Costs run to about US$5 per hour. It's possible to hire a driver on an exclusive stand-by basis at around US$20 a day. Some of the cyclos have seats wide enough to take two people, which makes cyclo-touring in Hanoi especially cozy for couples.

Motos or motorcycle taxis are great for getting around and cost about US$1 for a short trip. Bicycles (US$1 per day) and motorcycles (US$5 per day) are also available for rent, but spend some time strolling around and looking at Hanoi's chaotic traffic conditions before leaping into the fray — for those who have never taken to the roads in a busy Asian city before, this is probably not a sensible option.

WHAT TO SEE AND DO

The logical place to start any tour of Hanoi is in the Hoan Kiem District (Quan Hoan Kiem), where most sights are within easy walking distance or a short cyclo ride away from the lake.

OPPOSITE: Ngoc Son temple bridge on Hanoi's Hoan Kiem Lake TOP and, BOTTOM, the entrance to Quan Thanh Pagoda.

Hoan Kiem District

In Hoan Kiem District, the **Old Quarter**, a teeming rabbit warren of narrow streets and old colonial shop-houses, undeniably ranks as Hanoi's most interesting sight. Lying north of Ho Hoan Kiem lake, it is Hanoi's main market area and most populous district. Also known as the **36 Streets**, the area became the center of 36 guilds — or *dinhs* — centuries ago, when craftsmen came in from the surrounding countryside, each guild forming its own community. The area's origins linger on in the names of the streets — Silk Street, Paper Street, Rice Street, etc. In spite of the profusion of motorcycles, satellite antenna dishes and other signs of burgeoning wealth, something of a traditional atmosphere remains in this area, making it a fascinating area to wander around aimlessly.

Within the 36 Streets is a mix of historic temples, guild and clan houses, colonial villas and the so-called "tube houses," some of which are no wider than two-and-a-half meters (eight feet) across, but tunnel back 100 m (300 ft) or more, with living quarters off the main tunnel or "tube."

Discoveries can be made at every corner — ancient craftsmen making wooden drums the way their forefathers did, bamboo crafts for sale on Bamboo Street (Hang Tre), and shops selling the handmade paper favored by artists and exclusive wrappings for gifts on Paper Street (Hang Ma). Perhaps the only disappointment in this area is Silk Street (Pho Cau Go), which was once home to Hanoi's silk merchants, but in recent years has become a little touristy. Today it is filled with galleries and souvenir shops selling Russian watches, jewelry, new "antiques" and embroidered linen.

The area of 36 Streets is also the home of numerous "mini hotels," many catering to the backpacker market, although they increasingly offer facilities such as air conditioning, color satellite television and international dial-direct telephones. It is also home to backpacker cafés, such as the **Darling Café ℂ** (04) 826-9386, 33 Hang Quat Street, and **Green Bamboo ℂ** (04) 826 8572, 42 Nha Chung Street, which tend to concentrate less on food and more on selling cheaper alternative tours to attractions such as Ha Long Bay and Sa Pa, as well as one-day pagoda tours.

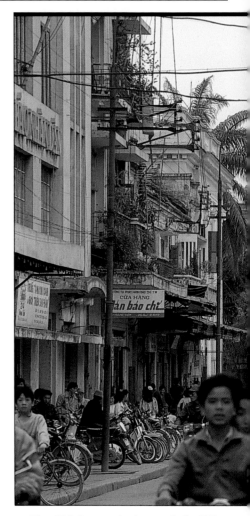

The Old Quarter is the symbol of Vietnamese entrepreneurial spirit at its best. Virtually every inch of the area has a shop or pavement vendor operating on it. Some of the best street food can be found in these tiny pavement eateries, and it is not uncommon to see a big car pull up, it's occupants piling out to sit down at the doll-size chairs and indulge in some delicious specialty before heading off to ritzier entertainment.

It is an easy walk from the 36 Streets to **Hoan Kiem Lake**, which sits at the heart of the tourist hub. A small pagoda in the middle of the lake commemorates an old legend, according to which a golden tortoise snatched the magical sword that the famed fifteenth-century warrior Emperor Le Loi had used to drive the Chinese from northern

Vietnam. The tortoise later returned the weapon to the gods — hence the lake's name, which translates as the Lake of the Restored Sword.

On the lake's northeastern shore, close to the Silk Street market district, is the small and extremely picturesque **Ngoc Son**, or Jade Mountain Temple, which is reached by a traditional Chinese-style hump-backed wooden bridge called **The Huc** (Touched by Morning Sunlight). Ngoc Son is dedicated to General Tran Hung Dao, who drove the Mongols out of Vietnam in the thirteenth century (and who is also commemorated with a towering statue in Saigon's Hero Square), but the temple's main attraction is its bridge and its location — a popular venue for photographers. Every morning,

the lakeshore attracts local enthusiasts for tai chi exercises and badminton.

Of all Hanoi's colonial buildings, the **Municipal Theater** ((04) 933-0131 is the most centrally located and the most splendid. Standing at the eastern end of Trang Tien Street, a short walk from the south of Hoan Kiem, it dominates a huge square formed by six intersecting roads. Built in 1911 as an opera house, it is still more commonly referred to as the **Opera**. The Communist takeover of Hanoi on August 16, 1945, was proclaimed from one of its balconies. In 1992 it provided the opening orchestral setting of the French movie *Dien Bien Phu*. Today, the opera house, with its

Hanoi's colonial-era Opera House still flourishes after two wars and a Marxist revolution.

Northern and Central Vietnam   *109*

elegant 900-seat auditorium, is the cultural center of Hanoi and has both local and international performances most nights of the week. Behind the Municipal Theater, at 1 Pham Ngu Lao, is the **History Museum** (open 8:15 to 11:45 AM, 1:30 to 4:30 PM, closed Thursday), a minor attraction but worth a brief visit if you are in the area — the exhibits feature Vietnamese history from the Neolithic period through to the arrival of the French.

To the north of the 36 Streets, the huge **Dong Xuan Market** has several floors packed with electronic goods, household products, linen and merchandise of every description. An open market for vegetables, fresh fish and produce sprawls around it — crowded beyond imagination every morning with rural vendors in their conical hats, hauling bicycles and bamboo baskets full of produce in from the country. Government concerns about the "messiness" of these street vendors has led to a clean-up, and the area is not as lively as it once was, but it's still worth a visit.

On the northern side of this melee is a small Taoist temple, surrounded by gardens but hidden discreetly behind high walls. Images of Taoist gods, Buddha and various immortals adorn its prayer halls.

Built in 1886, the remarkable square-towered **Saint Joseph's Cathedral** on Pho Nha Tro Street, west of Hoan Kiem Lake, is a well-weathered shell in an unkempt garden, its walls stained and flaked by the elements. But when the light is right, usually in the late afternoon sunshine, it becomes a medieval vision — the effect made all the more profound by weathering and neglect. It's a photographer's dream. Visitors are welcome to take part in Mass, which is held twice a day, from 5 AM to 7 AM and from 5 PM to 7 PM. A side door usually allows visitors to take a look at the interior of the cathedral at other times, though it is on occasion locked.

The mustard-colored **Government Guesthouse** is another photographer's dream, an ornate colonial mansion surrounded by a wrought-iron fence. It was once the residence of the French governor. Located on Ngo Quyen Street opposite the Sofitel Metropole Hotel, it invites closer inspection, but entry is restricted to official state guests,

with little hope of non-VIPs talking their way beyond the locked gates. However, it stands along with the Sofitel Metropole as one of the finest examples of colonial architecture in Hanoi.

At the northeastern end of the Old Quarter, the dramatic 1,682-m (5,518-ft) **Long Bien Bridge**, which was bombed and strafed repeatedly during the Vietnam War, until American prisoners of war were put to work repairing it, provides another key conduit into the district. Every morning the bridge throngs with farmers and workers from the countryside beyond the Song Hong river, many of them struggling across with bicycles and baskets loaded with chickens, ducks, vegetables and fruit as they head to grab a spot in the turmoil

around Dong Xuan Market. The bridge is one of three that span the river.

Ho Tay

Further to the west, on Hanoi's northwestern fringe, West Lake, or Ho Tay, is a tranquil recreational area best viewed at sunset, when the sky and water become a sheet of vivid, changing color. Along the lake's eastern shore, a causeway separates it from a smaller body of water, **Ho Truc Bach** (White Silk Lake), which is also called the "bomb lake." In October 1967, an American pilot landed here after bailing out of his crippled jet, which had been hit by anti-aircraft fire during an attack on an electronics factory. A rather crudely sculptured sandstone plaque at the lakeside commemorates the event.

Both Ho Tay and Ho Truc Bach are now more noted for the new hotels and open-air restaurants that have mushroomed around their shores. On Sundays, particularly, they're packed with wealthier Vietnamese families.

On the eastern shore of Ho Tay, alongside Thanh Nien Street, which runs north between the two lakes, is a fifteenth-century temple that was rebuilt in 1842. **Tran Quoc Pagoda** features a stele, believed to have been erected in 1639, which recounts the temple's history, and a main prayer hall and altar decorated with row upon row of Taoist and Buddhist images.

Hanoi's Central Market lies roughly at the borderline between the city's old and "new" quarters.

At 44 Ngu Xa Street, standing at the southern end of Thanh Nien Street on Truc Bach Lake, the Ly Dynasty (1010–1225) **Quan Thanh Pagoda** has a huge, hand-cast bronze Buddha image almost four meters (13 ft) tall, the biggest bronze statue in the country; it weighs nearly 10 tons. It was made in Ngu Xa village, famous for bronze casting. The Buddha and a bell date back to 1677. Everyday, late in the afternoon, the temple courtyard becomes the setting for children's martial arts practice.

Hanoi's ancient university, the Temple of Literature or **Van Mieu**, is an acclaimed example of early Vietnamese architecture. It is located about two kilometers (slightly over one mile) west of the city center at the intersection of four streets, Nguyen Thai Hoc, Hang Bot, Quoc Tu Giam and Van Mieu. Set in spacious tree-shaded gardens, most of this complex of walled courtyards and pavilions was built in 1070, dedicated to Confucius, and became Vietnam's first university six years later, educating the sons of mandarins. A number of steles, each erected on a stone tortoise, record the names of scholars who were successful in the civil service examinations held there from 1442 to 1778. One structure, the Khue Van Pavilion, was built as late as 1802; the complex underwent repair and renovation in 1920 and 1956.

Housed in the former French Ministry of Information at 66 Nguyen Thai Hoc Street, close to the Temple of Literature, the **Fine Arts Museum** (open 8:30 to 11:30 AM and 1:30 to 4:30 PM, closed Monday) features some good examples of Vietnamese sculpture, painting, embroidery, lacquer ware and other art, but the same people who deified Ho Chi Minh's remains have been at work here, turning traditional crafts into a commentary on the Communist triumph.

Other Areas

The delightful wooden structure of the **One Pillar Pagoda (Chua Mot Cot)**, set in a lily pond, was built by Emperor Ly Thai Tong, whose reign lasted from 1028 to 1054, to celebrate a dream in which he was presented with a son and heir by the Goddess of Mercy, Quan The Am Bo Tat. Shortly after he had the dream, he married a young

peasant girl who bore him his first son. He built the pagoda in 1049, but the French destroyed it in 1954. The revolutionary government rebuilt this newer pagoda. Today, childless Vietnamese couples pay homage at the shrine, praying for a son. It is also a popular spot for young artists, who can be seen amid the trees sketching the pagoda from every conceivable angle.

The pagoda's location, just off Ong Ich Khiem Street at the southern end of Ba Dinh Square, makes it easy to combine with a visit to **Ho Chi Minh's Mausoleum**

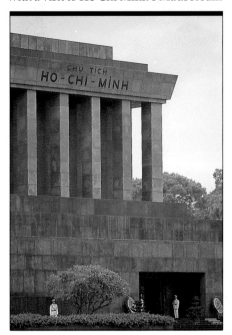

(open 7:30 to 10:30 AM, closed Monday and Friday). This towering, marble-clad, Soviet-style edifice radiates such power and melancholy that it's a wonder "Uncle Ho" isn't turning in the glass sarcophagus that holds his embalmed corpse. It's known that in his will Ho ordered that his remains be cremated. Nonetheless, this is still the most revered monument in Vietnam. **Ba Dinh Square**, which sprawls before it, is the site of annual Kremlin-style victory parades. The whole area is closed to traffic, and on most days the only movement you'll see is a uniformed, armed guard stretching his legs in the trees alongside the mausoleum as an endless stream of cone-hatted, devout peasants await their turn to pay their respects to their revered former leader. A profusion of rules govern visits — absolutely no photography inside the building, no stopping to gaze at the remains, no cameras or bags admitted, no hats, no shorts or tank-tops, no hands in the pockets, no spirited or demonstrative behavior. Each year, Ho's corpse is taken to Moscow for a couple of months — usually September to November — for remedial work to keep it preserved.

Near the mausoleum is **Ho Chi Minh's official residence**, built in 1958, and the 1906

The **Hai Ba Trung Temple**, dedicated to the Trung sisters and their rebellion against the Chinese in AD 40, isn't on Hai Ba Trung Street — it's about two kilometers (a little over a mile) to the south of the city center on Tho Laos Street. It features a statue of the two ill-fated sisters kneeling Joan of Arc-style with raised arms. After proclaiming themselves queens of the Red River Delta region, they committed suicide rather than surrender to a Chinese counter-attack.

The marvelous new **Vietnam Museum of Ethnology** (open 8:30 AM to 12:30 PM

palace of the French governor-general of Indochina, now the **Presidential Palace** and used for official receptions.

Lying to the south of Hoan Kiem, the smaller **Ho Thien Quang** lake is another early morning venue. In fact, it's something of a shock to find such huge crowds in the tree-lined squares and pathways around it — and so early, just after dawn. At the southern end, off Tran Nhan Tong Street, are rows of housewives bending and swaying to the instructions of tai chi instructors. Elsewhere, hundreds of children and adults take part in badminton tournaments, keep-fit classes and all sorts of other sports and pursuits, much the same as in China and Thailand.

and 1:30 to 4:30 PM, closed Monday) is located about 10 km (six miles) out of town, at Dich Vong, Cau Giay District, on the western outskirts of the city. The building houses a comprehensive ethnological collection delineating cultural facets of Vietnam's 54 minority groups, which divide neatly into three broad categories: the Austroasiatic family, the Sino-Tibetan family and related Tai group, and the Austronesian group. The center has received major support from France and Holland and offers excellent introductory insights into the cultural mores of some of Vietnam's ethnic minority groups.

OPPOSITE: Hanoi's Ho Chi Minh Mausoleum. ABOVE: Reminders of the apocalypse in the Hanoi War Museum.

War Museums

An ever-growing number of museums commemorating Vietnam's struggle against French rule and what is referred to by the Vietnamese as the "American War" are burgeoning across the city. A certain jingoistic fervor is to be expected in such venues but, rhetoric and sloganeering aside, most of these museums make for fascinating viewing.

Situated suitably on Dien Bien Phu Street, the **Army Museum** (open 8 to 11 AM and 1:30 to 4:30 PM, closed Monday) features weaponry and scale models depicting Viet-

namese victories from the French collapse at Dien Bien Phu to the 1975 fall of Saigon.

At 25 Tong Dan Street, the **Revolution Museum** (same opening hours as the Army Museum) is no less significant as a national monument, but if you have already visited the Army Museum it can be safely skipped — unless you have a deep interest in the Vietnamese version of their anti-foreign wars — as most of the exhibits comprise documentation and faded photographs.

The **Independence Museum** at 48 Hang Ngang Street is the house where Ho Chi Minh drew up Vietnam's Declaration of Independence, marking the break from French rule in 1945. More interesting to visit, though, is the **"Hanoi Hilton."** This very truncated complex is all that remains of the once sprawling prison known as the **Hoa Lo Prison** (open 8 to 11 AM and 1 to 4 PM, daily). Situated just off Hai Ba Trung Street, the prison was built originally by the French and was later dubbed the Hanoi Hilton by United States prisoners of war — mostly downed pilots — incarcerated there during

the Vietnam War, often after being paraded through the streets. While most of the original site has been used to build the glittering Hanoi Tower, a part of the original complex has been opened to visitors.

SHOPPING

For general souvenir shopping the best area is around Hoan Kiem Lake. North of the lake are countless shops selling everything from clothing to ersatz antiques, while the area in the south of the lake has more a boutique atmosphere, with some good arts and crafts shops to choose from. Naturally, the 36 Streets Old Quarter is another good area for shopping — for silk go to Hang Gai Street.

There are numerous art galleries around town that do a steady business selling the work of local artists, and it is definitely worth taking a look at what is on offer. It is probably not a good idea to make expensive purchases, however, without the advice of someone who knows the local art scene. In the Hoan Kiem District, the **Hanoi Studio** ((04) 934-4433, 13 Trang Tien Street, is a good place to start — the art on sale is generally by Hanoi's better known artists and the gallery provides an overview of what Hanoi artists are up to. Aimed more at the tourist market — though still worth a look — is **Co Xanh** ((04) 826-7116, 56 Hang Gai Street, which is also in the Hoan Kiem District. The gallery also sells some handicrafts.

WHERE TO STAY

Gone are the days when finding a room in Hanoi was a hit and miss affair. Today the city has what almost amounts to a glut of accommodation, and it is possible to choose from five-star luxury to budget backpacker digs, depending on your budget.

Note that many of the hotels below offer substantial discounts if you book online.

Very Expensive

It may be the longest-running hotel, with some stiff competition from new arrivals, but there's still a lot to be said for making the elegant 244-room **Sofitel Metropole** ((04) 826-6919 FAX (04) 826-6920 E-MAIL sofitel

@sofitelhanoi.vnn.vn WEB SITE www.accor-hotel-vietnam.com/sofitel-metropole hanoi/, 15 Ngo Quyen Street, your first choice. This turn-of-the-twentieth-century French building, formerly the Thong Ngat Hotel, was renovated by the French group Accor to capture the fledgling but growing business travel market in Hanoi in the early 1990s. The result is a deluxe property incorporating all its former colonial architecture and fittings, with a top-class bar and main Continental restaurant, business center and swimming pool, and plans for more

nightclub, shopping and sports facilities, it is hardly necessary to leave the place.

Expensive

The new **Hilton Hanoi Opera** ((04) 933-0500 TOLL-FREE IN THE US (800) 774-1500 FAX (04) 933-0530, 9 Le Thanh Tong Street, is, as the name suggests, adjacent to the opera, and it has already won fans by the tasteful way it complements Hanoi's most famous landmark. Inside it is slightly disappointing, however — many of the rooms seem small and, while well appointed, fail

rooms, executive offices, conference facilities and additional restaurants.

The **Hotel Daewoo Hanoi** ((04) 831-5000 FAX (04) 831-5010 E-MAIL info@hanoi-daewoohotel.com WEB SITE www.hanoi-daewoohotel.com/, 360 Kim Ma Street, Ba Dinh District, gives the Sofitel a run for its money, not in atmosphere, but simply by piling on the luxury and amenities in a way that no other Hanoi hotel does. An example is the swimming pool — allegedly one of the biggest in Southeast Asia. Its chief drawback, like many hotels of this sort, is its relatively isolated location, which means getting into town involves taking a taxi. It is, however, a world-class establishment, and with four restaurants, a poolside bar, a lobby lounge,

to live up to the promise of the exterior. That said, it's hard to fault the Hilton in terms of its location — probably the best in town — and the restaurants and other amenities are up to the usual Hilton standards.

A good alternative to the more impersonal style of the big hotel chains can be found at the **De Syloia Hotel** ((04) 824-5346 FAX (04) 824-1083 E-MAIL info@desyloia.com WEB SITE www.desyloia.com, 17A Tran Hung Dao, a small boutique-style hotel in the Hoan Kiem Lake area, with just 27 rooms and six suites. Housed in a nine-story former French villa, it is within easy walk-

OPPOSITE: The Sofitel Metropole remains one of Hanoi's most prestigious hotels. ABOVE: A street barber bears scars of the Vietnam War.

ing distance of most of the downtown tourist attractions. Amenities are limited — there is, for example, just one restaurant — but the high service standards compensate.

Moderate

For those looking for moderate accommodation with good access to Hanoi's sights, the oddly named **Chains First Eden Hotel** ((04) 828-3894 FAX (04) 828-4066 E-MAIL sales @chainsfirstedenhotel.com WEB SITE www .chainsfirstedenhotel.com, 3 Phan Dinh Phung Street, has an excellent location in the

Old Quarter, making it a perfect base for walking tours of the city. The rooms could be a little better maintained, but they still represent good value for money. Basic business services are available, along with tour bookings and baggage storage, but there's little more than this in the way of amenities.

Very close by, and similar in price, is the colonial-era **Galaxy Hotel** ((04) 828-2888 FAX (04) 828-2466 E-MAIL galaxyhtl@netnam .org.vn WEB SITE www.vietnamhotelinfo .com/galaxyhotel, 1 Phan Dinh Phung Street. The building dates back to 1918 and has been tastefully renovated. Rooms vary in size, but the larger ones — particularly the corner rooms — are excellent value. The hotel has a good restaurant (called the

Roadside Café) a bar and a small but efficient business center.

The **Thuy Nga Hotel** ((04) 826-6053 FAX 828-2892, 24C Ta Hien, is a small and slightly cheaper option, with tastefully furnished rooms ranging from around US$15. It has a good location in the Hoan Kiem Lake area, making it popular with backpackers who have a little more money to spend.

Inexpensive

Very popular with the backpacker contingent is the **Queen Café** ((04) 826-0860 FAX (04) 825-0300, 65 Hang Bac, WEB SITE www.queen cafe.com.vn/index1.htm, one of those one-stop travelers' destinations that provide everything from dormitory accommodation and budget tours of the rest of the country to inexpensive Internet access. Dormitory beds here cost as little as US$3, but single and double rooms are also available. Two other branches take the spillover (its popularity means it is often full) — one at 50 Hang Be Street and the other at 3 Tanh Ha Street.

WHERE TO EAT

For many visitors the sheer diversity of dining choices comes as a surprise in Hanoi. The influx of expatriates working in Hanoi has led to an explosion of restaurants offering everything from Thai to Mexican cuisines, with some excellent French and Italian along the way — not to mention the cuisine the locals do best: Vietnamese.

But before starting on the local cuisine, it's worth bearing in mind — this being a former French colony — that in the haute cuisine stakes it's French that dominates. French chefs have descended on Hanoi, and while many complain that local ingredients leave a lot to be desired, there are still enough international-standard French restaurants around to satisfy even the most determinedly fussy Francophile.

Heading the list is Sofitel Metropole's **Le Beaulieu Continental Restaurant** ((04) 826-6919 EXTENSION 8028, which was earning approving reviews of its food as early as 1901. China chronicler Edgar Snow wrote about the dancing parties that were held here into the wee hours of the morning in the 1930s. Today it is still regarded as *the* place in Hanoi to indulge in a classic French meal. And the price? Reckon on around US$30 per head.

Also highly recommended is **Le Splendide** ((04) 826-6087, 44 Ngo Quyen Street, which not only features impeccably manicured decor and a classic range of French dishes, but also offers live jazz on Friday and Saturday nights. Le Splendide is slightly less expensive than the venerable Le Beaulieu, but it is still wise to count on spending at least US$20 per head for an evening meal — lunches are more reasonable at around US$10.

For French (perhaps Mediterranean is a better description) cuisine at more affordable prices, the **Press Club** ((04) 934-0888, 59A Ly Thai To Street, has a delightful deli below and fine dining upstairs. The deli does pizza and sandwiches that the expat community swear by. In warm weather, the terrace area is a delightful place to enjoy lunch or dinner.

A tourist favorite for Vietnamese cuisine is **Indochine** ((04) 824-6097, 16 Ngam Ngu Street, in the Hoan Kiem Lake area. The menu is a list of crowd-pleasers, and in the evenings the restaurant features live classical Vietnamese music. Local residents complain that the service sometimes leaves something to be desired, but the wonderful colonial setting — with both indoor and alfresco seating — and the quality of the food usually compensate. It is a surprising inexpensive place to eat, with main courses ranging from around US$2. A similarly (somewhat touristy) dining experience can be had at **Nam Phuong** ((04) 824-0926, 19 Phan Chu Trinh Street. Like Indochine, it is housed in a converted French villa, features live traditional music and has a menu that provides a good overview of Vietnamese cuisine.

A not-to-be-missed Hanoi institution evocative of the old French-Vietnamese atmosphere is **Cha Ca La Vong** ((04) 825-3929, 14 Cha Ca Street, in the Old Quarter, or its newer incarnation at 107 Rue Nguyen Truong To ((04) 823 9875. The name comes from the house specialty: a grilled fish dish — *cha ca* — cooked at the diners' tables and usually washed down with cold beer. At Cha Ca they have been serving this dish for three generations, and while the restaurant is in danger of becoming something of a tourist trap, it is still well worth a visit. It is open daily from 10 AM to 10 PM, and a meal will cost US$10 or less per head with drinks.

Another Hanoi institution is its cafés, some of which serve not only coffee and croissants, but also superb Vietnamese food. One of the most popular examples is the relatively new **Brother's Café** ((04) 722-3866, 26 Nguyen Thai Hoc, which is housed in a beautifully restored Chinese home more than a century old. The inexpensive buffet lunch is a treat that is not to be missed. In the evenings it is possible to eat from the à la carte menu for US$10 per head or less.

Hanoi has a surprisingly large number of good Italian restaurants **A Little Italian** ((04) 825-8167, 78 Tho Nhuom, is worth including on the agenda, if for no other reason than because it was a ground-breaker. Established by an Australian in 1992, it was the first foreign-run restaurant in Hanoi, and has been a popular meeting spot for locals and expatriates ever since. Main courses start at around US$7. The **Mediterano** ((04) 826-6288, 23 Nha Tho, is especially recommended for its authentic pizzas cooked in a real wood fire oven, and prices are similar to those of A Little Italian. **Il Grillo** ((04) 822-7720, 116 Ba Trieu, has a cozy interior, making it a good place to retreat from the fray and order from an à la carte menu that includes some very good steak dishes. An evening meal costs around US$10 per head, excluding drinks.

Thai food is, not surprisingly, also popular. **Siam Corner** ((04) 829-1200, near Westlake in the Oriental Park, Quang An, Tay Ho District close to the Tay Ho Pagoda, is considered by many to be the best in Hanoi (combining agendas could be a good idea here — a temple visit and lunch). Also very authentic (the chef is Thai) is **Bangkok Hanoi** ((04) 934-5598, 52 Ly Thuong Kiet Street. Prices are very reasonable, with mains running from as little as US$2.

Lastly, a local favorite in the atmosphere stakes is the **Moca Café** ((04) 825-6334, 16 Nha Tho Street, which has a superb location opposite Saint Joseph's cathedral.

A Hanoi street vendor.

The two-story café is — as the name suggests — celebrated for its freshly brewed coffee, but it also serves a good selection of Vietnamese cuisine, making it a great place for a lunch with a view.

NIGHTLIFE

Nobody, it seems, makes a visit to Hanoi without taking in a water puppet show. Unique to Vietnam and having its origins in the villages of the Red River Delta, the next best thing to witnessing an actual village performance is to head down to Hanoi's **Municipal Water Puppet Theater** ((04) 825-5450, 57 Dinh Tien Hoang Street, opposite Hoan Kiem Lake. Performances are held nightly at 8 and 9:15 PM, and tickets can be bought at the door.

The **Central Circus** ((04) 822-9277 performs nightly at 7:45 PM except Monday at the northern gate of Lenin Park. It's a good outing for those who are traveling with children, but is otherwise a modest affair that can safely be missed in favor of other evening entertainment.

The **Hanoi National Opera** ((04) 826-7361, at 15 Nguyen Dinh Chieu, has shows on Mondays, Wednesdays and Fridays at 8 PM.

Hanoi Cai Luong Theatre ((04) 825-7823, 72 Hang Bac Street, has performances every Saturday and Sunday night for US$2. The 70-year-old theatre has achieved recognition as a classical theatre where players dressed in costumes similar to those of Chinese opera re-enact tales that vary from classical to modern themes of love and deception. While performances are in Vietnamese, the color and costumes make a visit worthwhile.

On the drinks and non-traditional nightlife front, Hanoi is no Saigon (or Bangkok for that matter), but it is not without its drinking and dancing venues. The most famous of them is **Apocalypse Now** ((04) 971-2783, 5C Hoa Ma. Not for the fainthearted, particularly late on a busy night, it is nevertheless a fascinating glimpse of a Vietnam that is worlds away from the Party line. Backpackers, tourists, investment bankers, lawyers and ladies of the night swap games of pool, clink drinks and dance the night away in this busy venue — it's said that everybody who visits Vietnam passes

through it doors at some point. If nothing else, it's a good place to meet people who know the city and the latest in-spots in Hanoi's ever-changing nightlife scene.

For those who find Apocalypse Now a little too true to its name, a more sedate evening can be had at the **Jazz Club** ((04) 828-7890, 31 Luong Van Can Street. The owner, Quyen Van Minh, is considered the father of Vietnamese jazz — his first CD was the first ever jazz recording released in Vietnam — and he and his band members can be seen performing nightly. It is a highly recommended evening out.

HOW TO GET THERE

While most travelers arrive in Ho Chi Minh City (Saigon), Hanoi is a good place to start a Vietnam tour. Less frantic than its southern rival, Hanoi is a more subdued introduction to Vietnam. The catch is, it's not as well served by international flights as Saigon. There are no direct flights from the United States, and while most major Asian destinations serve the city, flights from Europe and Australia are limited.

This being the case, most Vietnam travelers arrive in Hanoi from other parts of Vietnam, either by air, bus or train. The public buses, which run to other parts of Vietnam from several bus stations in Hanoi, are sensibly avoided by most travelers as unsafe. An alternative is provided by the Open Tour Bus service, pioneered by the **Sinh Café** ((04) 824-2457, 56 Hang Be Street, and now offered by other grassroots traveler services such as **Queen's Café** (see WHERE TO STAY, above). These services provide comfortable transportation between Hanoi and Saigon, with multiple stopovers at any of the main attractions en-route. The same cafés offer comfortable minibus services out to Ha Long Bay — they leave early every morning from the northern end of Hoan Kiem Lake.

The *Reunification Express* — or *Thong Nhat* — is the 2,010-km (1,249-mile) train service that links Hanoi and Saigon. Sleeping berths are available for those traveling

TOP: The Municipal Theatre in Hai Phong. BOTTOM: Decrepit vehicular ferries provide the only means of crossing Hai Phong's Cam River.

to Hue or Saigon, and are particularly recommended for those doing the long 56-hour haul all the way south. Petty theft is a problem on the train, and it is wise to take precautions — at the very least lock your bags, and best of all secure them to your berth with a chain and padlock.

Two twice-weekly train services go to China — one to Nanning and on to Beijing, the other to Kunming in Yunnan province. The Beijing service takes a staggering 56 hours, but Kunming can be reached in a little over 17 hours. A Chinese visa is required.

car and driver will cost a lot more money, but provide the freedom to stop at will and take photographs, take in the scenery or simply stretch the legs.

Chua Tram Gian, about 25 km (17 miles) along Highway 6 is Hanoi's nearest pagoda. Founded in 1168 and restored in the seventeenth and eighteenth centuries, it looks out from a hill over a landscape of rice fields.

Tay Phuong Pagoda (West Pagoda), about 40 km (27 miles) southwest of Hanoi, is a complex of three small pagodas housing 79 lacquered wooden carvings. Dating

Hanoi's airport is easily accessible from downtown — most cheaply by the minibuses that leave from the Vietnam Airlines office at 1 Quang Trung. A car with driver will cost upwards of US$15. The travelers' cafés in the Hoan Kiem district have shared taxi services that cost around US$5 per person.

AROUND HANOI

The Hanoi environs are dotted with dozens of Buddhist temples and pilgrimage sites, many of which can be visited with a minimum of fuss on day tours from Hanoi — all of which can be organized by Hanoi hotels, or more cheaply by the travelers' cafés in the Hoan Kiem District. Hiring a

from the eighth century, these carvings illustrate stories from Buddhist scriptures.

The nearby eleventh-century **Thay Pagoda** (Master's Pagoda) was built into the side of limestone cliffs rising from the rice fields. It is dedicated to Thich Ca Buddha and 18 *arhats,* or monks who attained Nirvana through a life free of impurity and desire. A statue of the eleventh-century monk, Tu Dao Hanh — the master after whom the pagoda was named — is placed near the central altar. Within this beautiful complex is a small pond and the Dinh Thuy, a small temple dedicated to one of Vietnam's unique performing arts — water puppetry — where performances are staged for pilgrims and visitors at the temple's annual festival from the fifth to seventh day of the third lunar month (March/April). These two pagodas can easily be visited in one day.

Chua Huong Pagoda, usually referred to by the tourist services in Hanoi as the Perfume Pagoda, is one of Hanoi's most popular daytrips, about 60 km (40 miles) southwest of the city in Ha Son Binh Province. Many regard this complex of pagodas and Buddhist shrines built into the limestone cliffs of Huong Tich Mountain as Vietnam's most beautiful spot. A steady stream of small sampans transport visitors for an hour through verdant rice fields, dotted with pagodas and surrounded by towering and often misty limestone karsts, passing several smaller pagodas before reaching the main pagoda. It is especially busy during the pilgrimage season, which runs from February to April.

Hoa Lu, the ancient capital of northern Vietnam, which flourished in the Dinh and early Le Dynasties between 968 and 1009, lies in a region of karst hills. It is often described, for the benefit of tourists, as "an inland Ha Long Bay," and is 95 km (63 miles) south of Hanoi on Route 1, not far from Ninh Binh. Though once rivaling Hue as a royal citadel, and covering an area of three square kilometers (slightly over one square mile), all that's now left of this once grand city is a shrine to Confucius and two sanctuaries, restored in the seventeenth century, commemorating the emperors of that time. One of them features early weaponry, drums and gongs among other relics.

Built by the French in 1907, the hilltop settlement of **Tam Dao** is northern Vietnam's version of the south's Da Lat — a highland retreat where the colonials sought relief during the hottest summer months. Some of their villas are still there, though suffering considerably from years of neglect, but the environment has remained fairly pristine — a series of wooded peaks offer hiking amid giant ferns and wild orchids, and visits to hill tribe communities. Tam Dao is in Vinh Phu Province about 85 km (53 miles) northwest of Hanoi.

The large natural reserve of **Cuc Phuong National Park** was established in 1962 — a hilly rainforest embracing a wide variety of flora, insects, animals and reptiles. The park is home to the **Endangered Primate Rescue Center** WEB SITE www.primatecenter .org/index.htm, which can be visited on organized tours offered by many of the travelers' cafés in Hanoi. The park is a long way from Hanoi — 140 km (87 miles) on a potholed road that is occasionally washed out and impassable — but accommodation is available in a range of options: everything from Muong-minority huts to Swiss chalets. For information on accommodation, call the park ((030) 848006.

The riverside border town of **Lang Son**, 150 km (93 miles) northeast of Hanoi, is the last stop in Vietnam on the road and railway to Nanning, China. It sprang back into prominence in the 1979 border war, when it was almost destroyed by invading Chinese forces. It has little to recommend it as an attraction, though as one of the major conduits of trade — official and unofficial — between the two former enemies it is not without interest. It's possible exchange dollars or dong here for Chinese yuan if you are heading on into China. There are a couple of places to stay here, but nothing that can be recommended — travelers using Lang Son as a jumping off point to China are advised to leave Hanoi early in the morning and continue on to China the same day. The Lang Son area is home to several ethnic minority groups, including the Dao and the Nung.

HAI PHONG

This rather dilapidated coastal city, 103 km (64 miles) east of Hanoi, is Vietnam's third largest city and strategically important as the key port of northern Vietnam. From a visitor's point of view, it is important as the gateway to the fishing port of Hong Gai and the Cat Ba Islands, with ferries leaving from the main city terminal, a short cyclo ride from Hai Phong Railway Station. It also provides the main road access to Ha Long Bay, northern Vietnam's dramatic vacation "resort," and the route north to this beautiful bay is even prettier than the approach from Hanoi — taking two river ferries and

A fishing family in Ha Long Bay — this region spawned much of the refugee migration to Hong Kong.

running through farming communities before melting into a surreal landscape of green fields and towering karst formations.

Although a prime United States bombing target during the Vietnam War, the regular presence of Soviet freighters — and the risk of a much more dangerous conflict — saved it from destruction. Nonetheless, it was mined by the Americans to halt the flow of Soviet military supplies. Military aspects aside, Hai Phong is the proud possessor of some wonderful, although dilapidated, French colonial buildings lining the river — in times past the main harbor.

WHAT TO SEE AND DO

Hai Phong is a bustling commercial city and market place. Much of its character comes from being an international entrepôt. Its shops and open markets offer consumer goods straight off the ships. While Hai Phong is not blessed with many attractions, it's worth spending an hour — perhaps while waiting for the ferry to Hong Gai or to the Cat Be Islands — going by cab to see **Du Hang Pagoda**, south of the city center at 121 Du Hang Street. This tenth-century pagoda, rebuilt in 1672, is the oldest in the city and of some architectural interest.

The **Hang Kenh Tapestry Factory** and the **Hang Kenh Communal House** on Hang Kenh Street, to the southwest of the downtown area, are worth a stop. The communal house features a collection of 500 wooden sculptures, and the 65-year-old Hang Kenh Tapestry Factory produces traditional and modern woolen carpets and tapestries for export. Both are open daily from around 7 AM to 5 PM, with an hour-and-a-half lunch break from 11 AM.

Twenty-one kilometers (14 miles) southeast of Hai Phong is the hilly coastal peninsula and beach of **Do Son**, once a popular seaside resort for the French. Crumbling colonial villas still line the shore. Do Son is now best known for its casino.

WHERE TO STAY

Being an international port, Hai Phong's hotels cater more to business travelers than to tourists. The top hotel in town is the **Tray Hotel** ((031) 828222 FAX (031) 828666 E-MAIL trayhotel@hn.vnn.vn, 50 Lach Tray Road, which has well-appointed rooms from US$50, a central location and good business facilities. Those looking for some ambiance, however, are better off staying at the Hotel du Commerce, which is now called the **Huu Nghi** ((031) 823244 FAX (031) 854673 E-MAIL huunghihotel@vnn.vn, 60 Dien Bien Phu Street. This well-renovated place of faded French elegance, operated by Hai Phong Tourism, offers moderately priced rooms from US$45. Alternatively it's possible to stay on the beach at Do Son's **Hai Au Hotel** ((031) 861 221 FAX (031) 861 176. It's next to the casino and has rooms from around US$12 to US$30.

Hoa Binh Hotel ((031) 859029, 104 Luong Khanh Thien, is popular with backpackers, and has rooms from as little as US$5; better quality and, of course, more expensive rooms are available in a new annex.

WHERE TO EAT

There are a number of small, friendly restaurants and coffee shops around the central market area of Hai Phong, most of them offering very palatable Vietnamese food. For fine dining, the **Shin Shin Restaurant** at the Tray Hotel (see WHERE TO STAY, above) has the best Chinese cuisine in town for about US$5, while the **Rooftop Garden**, on the ninth floor of the same hotel, has surprisingly good Western favorites at similar prices.

The **Bong Sen Restaurant** ((031) 846019, 15 Nguyen Duc Canh Street, serves both Vietnamese and Western cuisine, though it's better to stick to the former. A meal goes for US$3 to US$5.

HOW TO GET THERE

By either road or rail, the journey from Hanoi to Hai Phong passes through some of the prettiest countryside in the Red River Delta. Traditional farming methods are still carried out in this part of the world — fat water buffaloes plow the flooded paddies, women in conical hats sow seed and spread fertilizer by hand, flocks of ducks are shepherded to new feeding grounds, rows of bamboo hats nod amid the green and golden

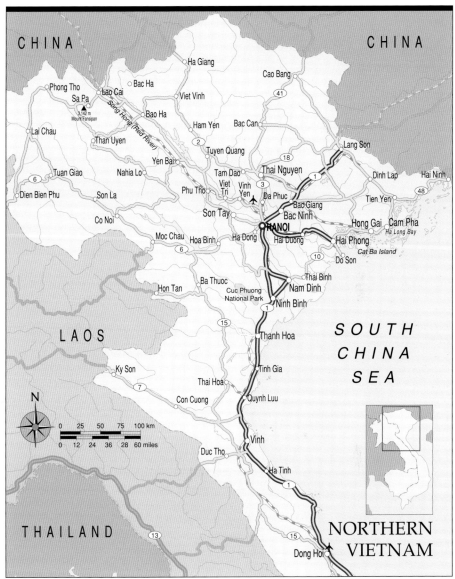

CHINA

CHINA

Ha Giang

Cao Bang

Phong Tho
Bac Ha
41

Lao Cai
Sa Pa
Viet Vinh
3,142 m
Mount Fansipan
Song Hong (Red River)
Bao Ha
Ham Yen
Bac Can

Lai Chau
Than Uyen
2
Tuyen Quang
Lang Son

Yen Bai
18

Tuan Giao
Nahia Lo
Tam Dao
Thai Nguyen
Dinh Lap
Hai Ninh

6
Viet
Vinh
3
1
48

Dien Bien Phu
Son La
Phu Tho
Tri
Yen
Da Phuc
Tien Yen

Co Noi
Son Tay
Bac Giang
Bac Ninh
Hong Gai
Cam Pha

HANOI
Ha Long Bay

Moc Chau
Hoa Binh
Ha Dong
Hai Duong
Hai Phong

6
Do Son
Cat Ba Island
10

Ba Thuoc
Thai Binh

Hon Tan
Cuc Phuong
National Park
Nam Dinh

Ninh Binh
1

15

Thanh Hoa

SOUTH
CHINA
SEA

Ky Son

7
Thai Hoa
Tinh Gia

N
Con Cuong
Quynh Luu

0   25   50   75   100 km
0   12   24   36   28   60 miles

Vinh

Duc Tho

Ha Tinh
1

THAILAND
13
15
NORTHERN

Dong Hoi
VIETNAM

rice as the women harvest it with small curved knives. Because of the speed with which the day heats up, the farmers and their families are usually working in the fields at first light and are on their way home to shelter and rest by mid-morning. In the late afternoon, the road becomes a social spot for families gathering to chat and enjoy the cooling air.

While many travelers opt for a tour from Hanoi, it is well worth making the trip with a car and driver, which allows stops for views of the countryside and even visits to

the small villages set back from the road. If you're with a group, forget it: like much of Asia, the average Vietnamese driver or tour guide has one responsibility in mind — to get you as fast as possible to wherever you're supposed to go.

HA LONG BAY

Ha Long Bay, 60 km (37 miles) north of Hai Phong, invokes the cliché journey back in time. The clear emerald waters are dotted with the tattered bat-wing sails of old sailing junks that have disappeared from China's coastal seas. When you place these beautiful working antiques against the dramatic backdrop of some 1,600 chalk and limestone formations that form a dragon's tail across the bay, it doesn't take much to imagine what this natural wonder was like 100 years ago. That said, Ha Long Bay is shaping up as a major tourist destination, and things are changing fast — chances are it will not remain the quiet retreat it has been for long. Nevertheless, a cruise in its waters — and this is what everybody comes for — remains one of Vietnam's most enjoyable excursions.

Apart from the cruises, the other much-touted Ha Long attraction is the island caves, some of them extending up to two kilometers (one mile) into the rock and featuring magnificent formations of stalactites and stalagmites. Shop around for a good guide, as some of them — enthusiasm and friendliness notwithstanding — carry out their trade with smoky kerosene lamps that don't really throw much light on the caves' natural beauty.

Ferries to Ha Long Bay stop at Hong Gai, the area's key fishing port. Worth a trip on its own, this bustling working village is neglected by many visitors. Most of the fishing junks are based here, and there is a splendid bustling fish and seafood market that starts in the early hours. The food at the market is exceptionally good.

Fast boats and slow ferries run from the harbor to the islands of the Cat Ba Archipelago, 80 km (50 miles) to the east (see THE GREAT OUTDOORS, page 25 in YOUR CHOICE).

WHERE TO STAY AND EAT

The town of Bai Chai, set on a long pebbled beach, is the tourist center of Ha Long Bay, and is where all the hotels can be found. Most of them charge about the same rate for foreigners — US$20 to US$50, depending on the usual variables. Rooms are generally clean, and most have open balconies with a sea view, but the bathrooms are often antique. Most visitors arrive on a tour that includes accommodation.

The **Ha Long Hotel** ((33) 846321 FAX (033) 846318, Vuon Dao, Bai Chai, is a renovated old colonial hotel that has been modernized

and extended to 300 rooms. Rates start at US$40 and rise to US$90 for the suites. The hotel has a good seafood restaurant.

HOW TO GET THERE

Ha Long Bay is accessible both by road from Hai Phong and by ferry to the thriving fishing port of Hong Gai, a short drive away. The bus trip can take more than three hours from Hanoi or two hours from Hai Phong, allowing for photo stops, passing by picturesque inland ports fringed by karst hills amid the rural setting. A far more pleasant route is to take the two-hour train from Hanoi to Hai Phong, then take the two-hour bus to Ha Long Bay (Bai Chai). Or take the three- to four-hour ferry to Cat Ba and use it as your base, taking advantage of one of the numerous tours from Cat Ba to Ha Long Bay run by local fishermen.

Alternatively, take the ferry to Hong Gai (from Hai Phong) and then take a bus, motorcycle or taxi to Ha Long Bay, only an hour including the car ferry ride from Hong Gai. There is also an expensive heli-jet operating directly from Hanoi to Ha Long Bay.

Since access is a little complicated, most visitors take a tour. Numerous tours are available from Hanoi, including many reasonably priced tours from the travelers' cafés, as well as the larger travel agents. A recommended agency is **Green Bamboo** ((04) 828-6504 WEB SITE WWW.greenbamboo travel.com, 2A Duong Tanh Street, Hanoi, though their tours are no longer as cheap as they used to be, charging around US$40 all inclusive for a daytrip to Ha Long Bay. Less expensive two- to three-day tours to Ha Long Bay, including accommodation, can be booked readily in the tourist enclave of Hoan Kiem in Hanoi.

DIEN BIEN PHU

Vietnam's northern mountain ranges are home to numerous ethnic mountain minority people and magnificent panoramas. On the northwestern frontier bordering Laos is the historic market town of Dien Bien Phu, located on Highway 42 — a diversion from the main route, Highway 6. The border crossing from here into Laos is now open, though you need have to have all your paperwork in order if you want to make the crossing — the crossing is called Tay Trang, after the pass on the Lao border.

One of Vietnam's most remote destinations, it is famous as the place where the French were overran by Viet Minh forces after a 54-day siege and forced to abandon their attempts to maintain control over the country. Apart from exploring the surrounding countryside, make a point of visiting some of the sights associated with the campaign. The **History Museum of the Dien Bien Phu Victory** chronicles the entire battle through a diorama and other exhibits. The hills that the French once commanded are still littered with campaign detritus.

It's possible to fly to Dien Ben Phu from Hanoi (flights are once daily), but the best way to visit is in a rental jeep or car — preferably the former, given the state of the roads. Jeep rental in Hanoi can cost as much as US$100 per day, but for anyone who is serious about exploring this rarely visited part of Vietnam, it is worth it.

There are several hotels in town, though none that deserve a special recommendation. The **Dien Bien Phu Hotel** ((023) 824319, Highway 42, has inexpensive and clean rooms and is an acceptable place to stay for a day or so.

LAI CHAU

North of Dien Bien Phu and around 460 km (300 miles) from Hanoi along Highway 6, over the 1,005-m (3,300-ft) Din Bin Pass (heaven and earth), Lai Chau is really out there — somewhere between heaven and earth. Lai Chau is part of the great northwestern road loop that runs from Hanoi west to Lai Chau and Dien Bien Phu before turning east and looping down southwards to Sa Pa and Lao Cai and eventually back to Hanoi, passing through magnificent rural panoramas. Lai Chau Province borders both Laos and China, one of the most remote parts of the country. Almost 25 ethnic groups inhabit these rugged mountains, where small communities nestle surrounded by jungle. While Highway 6 sounds a comforting name, the reality consists of steep climbs, dramatic switchbacks and abundant use of

low gears — to say nothing of spectacular, sweeping panoramas. Only four-wheel drive vehicles or serious motorcycles need try to navigate. From Lai Chau, the highway changes its name, but not its condition, to Highway 12, as it heads north to Phong Tho then east to the relative urbanity of Sa Pa.

SA PA

The hill town of Sa Pa has become one of the most popular destinations in northern Vietnam, particularly with backpackers. Not only

is it approachable by the long mountain route via Dien Bien Phu, but it can also be reached by overnight train from Hanoi to Lao Cai, followed by a connecting 45-minute bus ride through lush mountains. The latter route is the one most visitors take.

Before the Chinese invasion of 1979, this one-time French retreat had over 200 villas. Today most of the remaining 11 villas have been somewhat renovated, but in a rather charmless Vietnamese fashion — no foreigners are allowed to get their hands on them.

Sa Pa is the center of several tribal groups, who converge in town on Saturdays for the morning market. In times past tribal boys

The Sunday market fills with Hmong "Flower" girls at Bac Ha.

woud perform Red Zao, or courtship, here, singing poetic stanzas to girls dressed in all their tribal finery. They have since moved elsewhere — 35 km (22 miles) away from the prying eyes and taunts of local tourists. Now the market in its new concrete building is a lively spot all week, and although much of the charm has gone, it is still a magnificent place to visit.

The 3,142-m (10,309-ft) **Mount Fansipan** (Fang Xi Pan), Sa Pa offers marvelous trekking country in the Hoang Liem Nature Reserve and a cool climate conducive to

good place to gather information on destinations further afield.

Right at the bottom of the main road through town is **Dang Trung Auberge** ((020) 871243 FAX (020) 871282, the most popular budget guesthouse in Sa Pa. The welcoming owner, Mr. Trung, speaks French and takes great pride in showing favored guests his magnificent flower garden. Rooms — some with fireplaces — range from as little as US$5 to US$20. The hotel can organize tours and car rental, and the restaurant is one of the most popular places

physical exercise (see EXPLORE THE TONKINESE ALPS, page 15 in TOP SPOTS).

Among several not-so-appealing larger hotels, the new French **Victoria Hotel** ((020) 871522 FAX (020) 871539 E-MAIL victoria sapa-fo@hn.vnn.vn WEB SITE www.victoria hotels-asia.com/english/h_sapa.htm is the pick of the pack, with well-appointed rooms and a slew of amenities that include a pool and tennis courts. Room prices range from US$60.

The best mid-range choice of accommodation in Sa Pa is the **Green Bamboo** ((020) 871214, which has comfortable rooms with mini-bar and television for around US$25. The hotel also offers a large number of tours to villages in the Sa Pa area, and is a

to eat in town. With rooms from US$5, the **Rose Guesthouse** ((020) 871263, right on Sa Pa's main street, is yet another popular budget choice.

BAC HA

An even newer destination, available through tours from both Hanoi and Sa Pa, is the Sunday market of Bac Ha, a three-hour drive from Sa Pa, or two hours from the railhead at the Chinese border town of Lao Cai. Here the predominant minority group is the variegated Hmong who come from miles around to preen and parade their colorful costumes while shopping for basic necessities and, for the young girls, a husband.

Most travelers visit Bac Ha as a daytrip from Sa Pa. All the hotels and guesthouses offer Sunday market tours to the village. At the budget guesthouses these cost as little as US$7.

While Bac Ha does have accommodation options, none can be recommended.

HEADING SOUTH

Most travelers make the long journey from Hanoi to Hue without any stopovers. Buses make the journey overnight as does the

to 1972; it was rebuilt with East German assistance, a dismal architectural feat of gray, formless concrete drabness. Its one attraction is **Kim Lien Village**, the birthplace of Ho Chi Minh, 12 km (nine miles) west of Vinh. Outside the urban areas, towards the west, the mountains of Nghe Tinh Province are heavily forested, home to numerous minority groups, including Muong, Tai and Khmer. It is said that the mountains are still home to a wildlife population that includes elephants, gibbons, leopards, deer, rhinoceros, squirrels and monkeys.

train, and the few places of interest along the way are barely worth the extra effort involved. The area around **Ninh Binh** with its pagodas and weaving villages can be explored as a daytrip from Hanoi. Further to the south, Thanh Hoa, and the village of **Dong Son**, the reputed site of the Bronze-Age Dong Son culture whose influence spread through Southeast Asia, while of historical note, offers little in the way of things to see or do.

Vinh is similarly of little interest to travelers. One of the poorest and most backward areas of Vietnam, the region is plagued with floods and typhoons as well as poor soil. The city was bombed by the French in the 1950s and later by the Americans from 1964

HUE

Hue stands apart from other Vietnamese cities, having managed to retain much of historical interest, despite the depredations of war. A cultural center of long standing, it still has a tranquil air not much in evidence in Saigon, or even in Hanoi these days. It's worth spending several days exploring the city and its environs.

Built in the late seventeenth century, Hue became the capital of Vietnam in 1802

OPPOSITE: This Bac Ha sugar cane merchant does a roaring trade with minority customers. ABOVE: The Hue Citadel is Vietnam's equivalent of China's Forbidden City. OVERLEAF: Fantastical karst outcrops, island caves and grottoes promise a rich tourism future for northern Vietnam's Ha Long Bay.

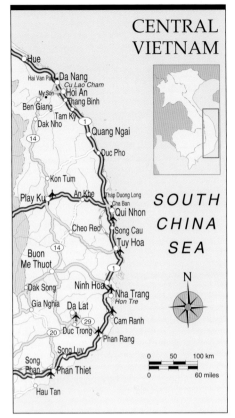

CENTRAL VIETNAM

SOUTH CHINA SEA

N

0   50   100 km

0   60 miles

government troops fought their way through the surrounding hills and down the coast to Da Nang. But bounce back it has, and today it is one of Vietnam's most charming cities.

Hue's attractions are not limited to the ruins of the Citadel alone. It has a number of interesting imperial mausoleums, and a scenic boat ride on the Perfume River to Thien Mu Pagoda is a must-do for anyone who visits the city. A number of sampan communities live along the inner city riverfront and it is not unusual to see the hoop-covered country boats making their way up and down the river. Add to this a lively market and a home lacquerware industry, and it is easy to while away a few days here.

Those with time to spare should consider exploring the lush countryside surrounding Hue. On a motorcycle (the traffic is minimal on the country roads) or a bicycle, it's possible to visit the surrounding villages and come up with some delightful surprises — a farmer and his buffalo at work in the rice fields perhaps, an ancient royal tomb in the background.

GENERAL INFORMATION

Hue City Tourism ((054) 823577 is at 18 Le Loi Street, though you are unlikely to find the staff here to be of much assistance; the travelers' cafés around town do a better job of serving out information.

The Hue **Vietnam Airlines** office ((054) 824709 can be found at 7B Nguyen Tri Phuong Street. The main **post office** is at Hoang Hoa Tham Street. In the event of a medical emergency, the best hospital in town is the **Hue General Hospital** ((054) 822325, 16 Le Loi Street, though if it is something serious you should go to either Hanoi or Saigon, or better yet to Bangkok.

The **Sinh Café** booking desk for its famed Open Tour Bus service, which runs from one end of Vietnam to the other, is at the Mandarin Café, 12 Hung Vuong.

WHAT TO SEE AND DO

Although only a shadow of what it once was, the **Citadel** stands behind high stone ramparts and the huge Ngo Mon (Meridian) Gate, the main access to the imperial

under the Nguyen Dynasty and remained so until 1945. During that time, the Citadel (the court of the Nguyen emperors) was almost comparable in grandeur to the Forbidden City in Beijing. From 1945, the Citadel gradually fell into disrepair, and during the Vietnam War it was the scene of intense fighting between United States Marines and North Vietnamese regulars in the 1968 Tet Offensive — the result was a near demolition job. At that time more than half the population of Hue lived within its outer walls, and in the battle to drive out the Viet Cong, a great deal of this national treasure was destroyed.

Given what Hue went through in the war years, it's something of a miracle that it bounced back at all. During the Tet occupation by Communist troops, some 3,000 pro-government people and Buddhist monks were executed and buried in graves all over the city. In 1975, Hue was one of the first major South Vietnamese cities to fall to the Communists, triggering a violent mass panic in which thousands of civilians and fleeing enclosure. Looking at its sweeping yellow-tiled roofs, red wooden pillars and huge yellow doors, you're reminded of the Meridian Gate of the Forbidden City in Beijing, though it's not quite as majestic. Along the Citadel's outer walls stand other surviving ceremonial gates. Mounted with intricate carvings, colored porcelain and mirrored glass chips and snarling dragon decorations, they give a sense of the imperial city's former scale and authority.

Sadly, all that's really left of the Citadel today is the **Purple Forbidden City**, once

ing costumes, furniture, porcelain, a sedan chair, musical instruments and other relics of the imperial reign.

The evocative ruins of Hue's imperial past are dotted among small farms and rice fields along the Perfume River. The easiest way to see them is to join a tour, but bear in mind it's also possible to rent your own covered sampan. You can do this at the same agencies that offer tours at around US$20 to US$25 for the day.

Four locations inspire real interest. The **Mausoleum of Tu Duc**, who ruled from

the inner, exclusive domain of the emperors, where the Ngo Mon Gate leads to dank lotus pools; the vast, wing-roofed **Thai Hoa (Supreme Harmony) Palace**, which was used for state and ceremonial events; the **Halls of the Mandarins**; the renovated **Imperial Library**, featuring ornate ceramic sculptures of mandarins and other figures on its roof; and the nearby **Royal Theater**, which is now the home of the National Conservatory of Music. It's possible to enter the conservatory grounds and listen to the students practicing — and catch an impromptu chamber recital if you're lucky. The **Imperial Museum**, just beyond the north wall, completes the Citadel tour. It is housed in another impressive hall and features surviv-

1848 to 1883, is among the closest, located in **Duong Xuan Thuong Village** about seven kilometers (slightly over four miles) from town. It's best to visit in the afternoon, when the light is particularly pleasant. Inside an octagonal stone wall, the monarch's sepulcher lies alongside a small lake surrounded by a pavilion, a temple, an honor courtyard lined with stone sculptures of elephants, horses and mandarins, and a stele pavilion sheltering a 20-ton stone tablet recording Tu Duc's virtues and triumphs.

The **Mausoleum of Khai Dinh**, who ruled from 1916 to 1925, reflects how Westernized even the imperial court had become

On Hue's Perfume River, sampans are still a common means of transport.

by then — the architecture and statues have vague European characteristics. The stele pavilion is in the middle of the traditional honor courtyard, with its guardian beasts and mandarins, and an image of Khai Dinh himself sits under a concrete canopy in the complex's ornate main hall, its walls decorated with elaborate frescoes.

The most impressive tomb, the **Mausoleum of Minh Mang** (1820–40), lies 12 km (seven and a half miles) from Hue at **An Bang**, one kilometer (a little over half a mile) from a beautiful section of the Perfume River. Three great ceremonial gates and three granite staircases lead to the stele pavilion. Three terraces then lead to **Sung An Temple**, dedicated to the emperor and his empress. Three bridges cross the tiny **Lake of Impeccable Clarity**, the central one made of marble and reserved for the emperor. Lastly, three more terraces representing Heaven, Earth and Water provide the foundation for another magnificent building, the **Minh Lau Pavilion**. Minh Mang's burial mound lies inside a circular wall representing the sun at the top of a stone staircase flanked by sculptured dragons. To finish off the day, make sure your boat reaches the **Thien Mu Pagoda** in the late afternoon to watch the sun setting across the Perfume River.

There is no other place of worship in Vietnam in such a beautiful location as Thien Mu Pagoda, a seven-story octagonal tower and adjacent prayer hall perched on a promontory right over one of the most dramatic sections of the Perfume River, where the river widens and stretches through green pastures and paddies toward misty blue mountains. The pagoda was founded in 1601, but the present tower was built by Emperor Thieu Tri in 1844. Adjacent to the tower, in a two-story pavilion, is a giant bell that was cast in 1710 and which the monks will sometimes toll for you if you ask them. It is said one can hear it resonate up to 10 km (six miles) away — which must be annoying for the neighbors, if tourists are constantly having the monks toll it. There's also an Austin car that was used to take the bonze Thich Quang to Saigon in 1963, where he was one of the Buddhist martyrs who burned themselves to death in protest against the Diem regime.

Back in Hue central on the right bank of the river, in Nguyen Hue Street, the strange spire of **Notre Dame Cathedral** rises up over the skyline. The cathedral is a grand but somewhat bizarre blend of European and Vietnamese architecture, and the spire is distinctly Asian. Built between 1959 and 1962, it hardly rates as a historical attraction, but it does make a useful point of reference if you get lost.

WHERE TO STAY

Surprisingly for such a popular tourist destination, Hue is disappointing on the hotel front. Budget travelers should have no problems, but those looking for a good tourist hotel will have little satisfaction.

Most tour groups are taken straight to the **Huong Giang Hotel** ((054) 822122 FAX (054) 823102, which is located right on the banks of the Perfume River at 51 Le Loi Street, facing across to Hue's distant central market. It's a somewhat tacky effort, with a lobby full of backbreaking traditional rosewood furniture and lots of lacquer. The panoramic view of the river and bustling sampan communities compensate for a lot, and the ground-floor restaurant terrace is a fine place to sit and watch the river traffic. Rates are from US$70. The hotel operates a villa at 3 Huong Vong called **Indochine** ((054) 826070 FAX (054) 826074. It's an atmospheric place to stay, with an intimacy guaranteed by the fact that it has just 12 rooms. Rates are from US$50.

Next door to the Huong Giang is the monumental **Century Riverside** ((054) 823390 FAX (054) 823394 E-MAIL cenhotvn @dng.vnn.vn WEB SITE www.centuryhotels .com/hotels/vrh_location.htm, 49 Le Loi Street, Rates are reasonable, ranging from US$60, and it has all the amenities — including swimming pool and tennis courts — that you would expect of a big tourist-class hotel. Rooms are a little on the small side, however, and many guests complain of bad service here.

More atmospheric is the newly renovated **Saigon Morin Hotel** ((054) 825870 FAX (054) 825155 E-MAIL sgmorin@dng.vnn.vn WEB SITE www.morinhotel.com.vn/index.htm, 30 Le

The Linh Mu Pagoda in Hue, overlooking the Perfume River.

Loi Street. It was originally built a century ago and is now a very attractive place with a giant garden courtyard and a small pool. Most rooms come with spacious balconies and cost from US$60 for a superior room to US$300 for the executive suites.

The **Thang Long Hotel** ((054) 826462 FAX (054) 826 464 at 16 Hung Vuong Street, may be a gaudy looking building in the Vietnamese style, but it has rooms to suit almost everyone, ranging from US$10 to US$60, making it a popular backpacker accommodation.

WHERE TO EAT

For authentic Hue imperial cuisine, the better hotels around town are the best places to start looking. At the **Huong Giang Hotel** ((054) 822122, 51 Le Loi Street, the Royal Restaurant on the ground floor specializes in imperial Hue cuisine. At the **Century Riverside** ((054) 823390, the Royal Restaurant also offers imperial cuisine, though the atmosphere resembles a Chinese banquet restaurant, and is disappointing on the atmosphere front. The **Saigon Morin Hotel** ((054) 823039 also has a restaurant specializing in Hue cuisine, named appropriately the Royal Cuisine Restaurant. It also has a unique offering in the **1US Restaurant**,

which serves traditional snacks all priced at US$1. The hotel's main drawcard, however, is its Garden Bar, nestling in a tree shaded courtyard, it is one of the best places in Hue for lunch or dinner, or simply some drinks — barbecue dinners are a nightly event.

To try Hue cuisine in a less formal setting, visit the **Ong Tao Café** ((054) 822037, 134 Ngo Duc Ke, which is actually in the grounds of the Citadel. The family of owner Hoang Xuan Minh was in the business of preparing meals for the imperial family for generations, and he has been interviewed by the *New York Times*. Meals come with fresh leaf vegetables for wrapping the delicious morsels.

Dine on the river at the **Song Huong Floating Restaurant** ((054) 826655 on Le Loi Street near the bridge, where seafood and "steamboat" — a variety of meats or seafood and vegetables cooked on the table in a rich meat stock — are specialties. Like the Ong Tao Café, the **Huong Sen Restaurant**, a pavilion-style establishment set over a lotus pond, is in the Citadel itself and makes for a good lunch stop for inexpensive Vietnamese cuisine.

The **Am Phu** ((054) 825259, 35 Nguyen Thai Hoc, serves Hue specialties in a simple setting. For travelers' favorites — stir fries, banana pancakes, etc. — the **Mandarin Café**, 12 Hung Vuong, is one of the most popular hang-outs in town.

HOW TO GET THERE

Vietnam Airlines operates regular services from Saigon, Hanoi and Da Nang to Hue's Phu Bai Airport, which is situated about 17 km (just over 10 miles) south of the city. Airport buses meet incoming flights and cost around US$1 per person. Taxis are also available and cost around US$8.

From the north, the overnight train from Hanoi is a fine way to arrive. Book ahead and reserve a soft sleeper for optimum comfort at around US$50. The journey takes around 14 hours.

OPPOSITE: Minh Manh Tomb in the imperial burial grounds outside Hue. ABOVE: Sampan and harvested bamboo on the Perfume River. OVERLEAF: Sunrise on Hue's busy Perfume River.

If you are coming from Da Nang, 108 km (67 miles) to the south, both the road and train trip are extremely enjoyable. The trip is about three hours — six if you allow for photo-stops and lunch — and it takes you through some of Vietnam's most scenic countryside. The road weaves through three high mountain passes interspersed with coastal farmland, fishing communities and a couple of vast agricultural plains set around wide bays.

Bicycle and motorcycle rental is available in Hue from almost anywhere that deals with

tourists, the former costing as little as US$1 per day, and the latter costing upwards of US$5, depending on the condition and make of the bike. Renting a car with a driver usually costs between US$20 and US$30.

AROUND HUE

Hue has become the center for a busy Vietnam War nostalgia trade, with virtually every hotel and café in town offering tours of the area that saw the heaviest fighting during the war. It is worth taking one of the tours if for no other reason than to actually see some of the places, such as Khe Sanh, that have become part of the popular imagination of the West.

Demilitarized Zone (DMZ)

In 1954 Vietnam was divided in two along the Seventeenth Parallel under the terms of the Geneva Accords. Elections intended to unite the country in 1956 never took place and, as the saying goes, the rest is history. "Demilitarized" shortly became something of a misnomer, as the area became the scene of some of the heaviest fighting of the Vietnam War, the North Vietnamese overrunning the zone in 1972 and pushing it south some 20 km (12 miles).

One of the more interesting stops on the DMZ tours is **Vinh Moc Tunnels**, a fascinating underground village in which hundreds once sheltered from United States bombing. Parts have been restored to allow tourists to play at "tunnel rats." Villagers started carving out the tunnels in 1966, and by the time they reemerged in 1972, the tunnels had everything from family rooms to an underground hospital. The tunnels have been enlarged somewhat for Western tourists, but the 15-minute tour is still not recommended for those who suffer from claustrophobia.

Khe Sanh is the most famous stop on the tours, as the site of a massive North Vietnamese Army (NVA) and United States buildup of forces in 1967. The face-off commanded worldwide media attention, and in early 1968 resulted in a ferocious nine-week battle, only to have the NVA forces melt away, having successfully diverted United States attention from their buildup to the now famous Tet Offensive in the south. The cratered landscape is still today littered with unexploded ordinances, and a guide is essential for exploring the area.

The **Con Thien Firebase** was the largest United States installation on the DMZ, and provides good views over the zone. It is usually followed by a visit to the **Truong Son Martyr Cemetery**, which commemorates the Vietnamese who died on the Truong Song Trail (better known as the Ho Chi Minh Trail) — perhaps as many as 25,000, around 10,000 of whom rest here.

Other popular stops include the ruined shell of a church, pockmarked with bullet holes, and the hill known as the **Rockpile**, which was occupied by a United States

ABOVE: Da Nang's splendid Cham Museum.
OPPOSITE: The Cham ruins in Singhapura.

reconnaissance patrol that had to be rappelled into position from a helicopter.

Day tours of the DMZ can be booked at any agency or hotel in Hue and cost less than US$20.

Hai Van Pass

This 496-m (1,627-ft) spur in the towering barrier of the Truong Son Mountains, 30 km (19 miles) north of Da Nang, is the first and highest pass on the route of National Highway 1 to Hue. It marks the great gulf between north and south, a traditional barrier

that the Chinese invaders never managed to overcome. It is not only the climate that seems to change at this latitude, but the people too become sunnier and more relaxed as the road heads farther south.

Both sides of the pass enjoy spectacular panoramas — to the south, it looks over Da Nang and its coastal headlands and bays while to the north it looks across a valley to the coastal plains on the way to Hue. In the more immediate vicinity, it's interesting to watch the dilapidated long-distance "express" buses that labor to and from Saigon and Hanoi, absolutely packed to the roof with passengers and luggage, hauling themselves at a painful snail's pace up both sides of the mountain. Everyone stops at the

pass. While passengers scramble out of their crowded coaches to stretch their legs and photograph the spectacular view, enthusiastic hawkers descend with brimming baskets and a scrimmage begins, the hawkers usually the victors, but never mind — it provides great amusement for other coachloads who have already survived it.

Hai Van Pass also looks down on two of Da Nang's longest beaches, **Nam O** to the south and **Lang Co** to the north — neat palm-fringed crescents of sand that are still relatively undeveloped.

DA NANG

The approach by air to this key port of central Vietnam reveals a city surrounded by beautiful beaches, bays and hills. It also reveals the pockmarks and the bomb scrapes of Da Nang's suffering during the war, and how the ever-innovative Vietnamese farmers have used them to advantage, converting them to fish ponds in the midst of their rice paddies.

As a major United States Marine base, the conduit to both the central highlands and base camps up toward the DMZ (Demilitarized Zone), the city was the scene of some of the fiercest fighting of the war. When it fell to the advancing Communists in 1975, it became a nightmare of violence as thousands of South Vietnamese soldiers and civilian refugees fought to escape by sea to ports further south. Due no doubt to negative after effects of the war, Da Nang continues to exude an edginess that is less common in other parts of Vietnam — belligerent children and beggars crowd around you the moment you step into the streets, and incidents of theft from hotel rooms are reported from time to time. This is no doubt why many people give Da Nang a miss, except for Vietnam war veterans and those on tour packages. For most travelers it is somewhere to make a one- or two-hour stopover to visit the important Cham Museum before heading on to Hue to the north or to the charming ancient trading port of Hoi An just to the south.

Da Nang is well located for future development. Lying between the Han River and the South China Sea, flanked to the north and south by beautiful white-sand beaches that seem to go on forever. Only the Furama Resort Da Nang (see WHERE TO STAY, overleaf) has capitalized on this beach until now.

To its north and west, the foothills of the central highlands begin their ascent in terraced ranks over sandy bays and rice fields; and a series of coastal mountain passes lead through spectacular highlands and coastal plains toward the ancient capital, Hue. Along the old riverfront tree-lined boulevard of Bach Dang are street-side cafés and

Vishnu alongside carved altars, lingams, garudas and other Hindu symbols. The mood of most of these seventh- to fifteenth-century statues and sculptures is sensual, reflecting the essential role of fertility in this creed. Elsewhere, sculptures of *apsaras* (celestial nymphs), musicians and scenes from the Hindu epic *Ramayana* are reminiscent of the temple carvings of Bali and Java, which share a similar heritage.

At 63 Hai Phong Street, east of the railway station, is **Chua Cao Dai** — the biggest and most important temple of the Cao

marvelous old colonial villas from the time when Da Nang was a busy French trading port known as Tourane.

WHAT TO SEE AND DO

If few travelers actually overnight there, almost everybody makes at least a pit stop in Da Nang, usually en-route between Hue and Hoi An, to visit the **Cham Museum** (open 8 to 11 AM and 1 to 5 PM daily). Located at the intersection of Trung Nu Vuong and Bach Dang, it is a world-famous cultural attraction. This well-planned series of open pavilions houses the world's best and most diverse exhibition of Cham relics, sandstone carvings of Shiva, Brahma and

Dai cult outside Tay Ninh Province in the south. The actual number of followers in Da Nang is disputed, but may be as many as 50,000. The temple was built in 1965 and, like the Great Temple of Tay Ninh, its colorful daily services are worth a visit.

There are three temples in the city area, the **Phap Lam Pagoda**, 373 Ong Ich Khiem Street, and the **Tam Bao** and **Pho Da Pagodas** on Phan Chu Trinh Street. They hold little in the way of historical value — the oldest was built in 1923 — but the Phap Lam Pagoda features a brass statue of Dia Tang, the God of Hell, who most surely played a part in Da Nang's recent history.

OPPOSITE: Worshipers at Marble Mountain, near Da Nang. ABOVE: Fishing boats anchored at day's end.

WHERE TO STAY

Foreign travelers tend to either visit Da Nang from Hoi An or Hue as a daytrip or en route between the two, while the more well-heeled visit from the nearby Furama Resort.

The best of Da Nang's hotels are the **Bamboo Green Harborside** ((0511) 823942 FAX (0511) 824165 E-MAIL bamboogreen @dng.vnn.vn, 177 Tran Phu Street, and the **Bamboo Green Central** ((0511) 822996 FAX (0511) 822998 E-MAIL bamboogreen @dng.vnn.vn. Both cater to the tour-group and business market and have rates from US$45 upwards.

The **Bach Dang Hotel** ((0511) 823649 FAX (0511) 821659, 50 Bach Dang Street, is an older establishment and has air-conditioned double rooms from US$30 to US$80 a night. It serves a buffet breakfast and has a good verandah restaurant.

Budget travelers will find the best inexpensive lodgings at the **Tien Tinh Hotel** ((0511) 834566 FAX (0511) 820748, 448 Hoang Dieu Street, a comfortable but basic mini-hotel that has doubles from US$10.

Out of town at China Beach is the **Furama Resort Da Nang** ((0511) 847333 FAX (0511) 847666 E-MAIL furamadn@hn.vnn.vn WEB SITE www.furamavietnam.com/, 68 Ho Xuan Huong, a US$90-million development that is the only truly international hotel in this part of Vietnam. Rooms range from US$140 to US$400 and the hotel has some excellent restaurants including Café Indochine, which features Asian favorites served in ambient French colonial surroundings, and Ocean Terrace, which offers authentic Italian pizza among other things.

WHERE TO EAT

Café Indochina ((0511) 847333, at the Furama Resort (see above) is the place to go for a splash-out meal, while the resort's **Ocean Terrace** offers a superb Italian lunch if you're visiting China Beach.

To see where the locals dine out, try the **Phi Lu** ((0511) 823772, 249 Nguyen Chi Tanh Street, a Chinese-style eatery that packs in the crowds and serves very tasty meals at

reasonable prices. The **Hana Kim Dinh Restaurant** ((0511) 830024 at No. 7 Bach Dang Street offers inexpensive local cuisine.

HOW TO GET THERE

Vietnam Airlines operates daily flights to Da Nang from Saigon and Hanoi. The airport is around three kilometers (just under two miles) from town, and both airport buses and taxis ferry passengers in. The Open Tour Bus service stops at Da Nang for visits to the Cham Museum en route to Hoi An, and the city is on the main train route.

AROUND DA NANG

Marble Mountains

Eleven kilometers (nearly seven miles) south of Da Nang, the Marble Mountains Buddhist complex is actually five "mountains," all solid lumps of marble, representing the five elements — fire, water, earth, wood and metal. The biggest, generally referred to as Marble Mountain itself, is pitted with grottoes containing stone carvings and more recently erected stone Buddhas. During the Vietnam War, it was from here that Viet Cong soldiers would sit and watch the American GIs frolicking on the beach, a mere bazooka blast away. Getting up and down is something of a workout — it's a tremendous climb — and is not made any easier by the over-enthusiastic child hawkers who relentlessly pester climbers every step of the way with offers of joss sticks and poorly fashioned marble souvenirs. In all honesty, Marble Mountain is somewhat overrated and can be safely dropped from a busy itinerary.

To get there, take a taxi or try to pick up one of the truck taxis that await passengers outside the short-haul pick-up truck station on Hung Vuong Street, a block from Con Market. Buses also leave frequently from Da Nang's inter-city bus station, but they are only recommended for the brave or foolhardy.

My Son

The series of about 20 scarred Cham ruins at My Son, 60 km (37 miles) south of Da Nang along National Highway 1, was the key religious and intellectual center of Champa from the fourth to the thirteenth centuries.

As such, My Son is probably the most important remnant of the Champa Kingdom, and one that survived the centuries only to tragically become a battlefield during the Vietnam War. The Cham kings are thought to have been buried in a complex that was probably as sacred to the Shivaite Chams as Angkor Wat was to the Khmer Hindus and Borobudur to the Javanese Buddhists.

The ruins lie in a valley near a coffee plantation and the towering **Cat's Tooth Mountain**. While nearly 70 structures have been identified from the stone remains (twelfth century) are part of a long-term restoration plan.

The remaining structures include the eleventh-century stone base and lingam of a temple believed to have been first built seven centuries before, the walls of a tenth-century library with bas-relief brickwork of elephants and birds, a reasonably preserved tower, and a meditation hall earmarked for renovation as a new Cham museum. Restoration work is ongoing at these sites, and the plan is to eventually restore other groups that have been re-

around the large site, only 20 have survived in a state that allows visitors to get a sense of what the complex must once have looked like. The main deity is Shiva, whom the Chams believed to be the creator and defender of the Cham Empire. The structures have been categorized alphabetically into 10 groups by the archaeologists, but only Group B (tenth century), Group C (with an eighth-century shrine to Shiva, whose statue has been removed to the Cham Museum in Da Nang) and Group D (tenth century) are intact. An eighth-century site, formerly the best preserved of the ruins, was tragically destroyed by American bombers. Group E (eighth to eleventh century), Group F (eighth century) and Group G

claimed by the surrounding bush or were badly damaged during the war.

My Son is a daytrip by road from Da Nang, or better still, from Hoi An. If driving to My Son, the 35-km (20-mile) dirt road is about seven kilometers (four and a half miles) south of the Hoi An turn off located 27 km (17 miles) south of Da Nang. A reliable driver is essential, otherwise take a day tour. There is no accommodation in My Son.

Tra Kieu Museum

The interesting 100-year-old Catholic church in the small town of Tra Kieu, 20 km (12 miles) beyond My Son, is a museum of Cham relics

One of several idyllic, untouched beaches between Da Nang and Hue.

collected from the local people by the priest. They include ceramic artifacts bearing the features of Kala, the God of Time. Close by, another far more modern church, the Mountain Church, overlooks the stone foundations of what was once Simhapura (or Singapura, the Lion Citadel), the first Cham capital from the fourth to the eighth centuries.

HOI AN (FAI FO)

It is difficult to imagine that anyone could visit Hoi An and fail to be charmed by the became home to both Japanese and Chinese traders, who used the town as a base while waiting for favorable monsoon winds. By the seventeenth century, Hoi An had become a major trade entrepôt. By the time the Japanese had left in 1637, by decree of the Japanese emperor forbidding further contact with the outside world, Dutch, Spanish, Portuguese, English and French merchant ships had started to arrive, drawn by the promise of trade in precious cargoes of silk, paper and textiles, molasses, pepper, porcelain and tea, among other things.

place. Situated 30 km (19 miles) from Da Nang via the Marble Mountains, this historic trading port enjoyed for several centuries a prominence similar to that of Malacca and Macao as one of the great emporiums of the east.

Hoi An's long history would make marvelous background for a novel. From the fourth to the tenth centuries Hoi An was the main trading port for the nearby Champa Kingdom. Early ninth- and tenth-century Arab documents refer to the port, mentioning it as a provisioning stop.

After a long period of unrest between the Chams and ethnic Vietnamese, in the fourteenth century order was restored, and by the fifteenth century Hoi An or Fai Fo

Thai, Indonesian, Filipino, Arab and Indian traders all added both to the cultural mélange and to the stock of items for trade.

While most of the old town was destroyed during the Tay Son Rebellion in the late eighteenth century, it was quickly rebuilt, and trade continued to flourish, right up until the end of the nineteenth century when, with the silting up of the Thu Bon River, business gradually moved to the newer trading port of Da Nang (Tourane). By the early twentieth century, Hoi An's glory days were a thing of the past. For visitors today this is good news. Unlike industrialized Da Nang, Hoi An is a delightfully preserved slice of history. Discovered in the early 1990s by backpackers, today many of the town's more historically interesting homes, shop-houses, warehouses and clan halls have been restored and put to new use as enticing bars, restaurants and galleries for the ever-growing stream of visitors. Newer tourist amenities are, of course, beginning to have an impact on the town, although thankfully still on a small scale. Hopefully this will continue to be the case, a fact that was recognized by UNESCO, which declared the city a World Heritage Site in April 2000.

The main thoroughfare of Tran Phu Street has several historically interesting houses. The most well known is at **No. 77**, a private house nearly three centuries old. At 176 Tran Phu Street the **Quang Dong (Cantonese) Communal House** was founded in 1786, while the slightly older **Chinese All Community House**, founded in 1773, was used by the four Chinese communities who traded in Hoi An — the Cantonese (Guangdong), Hokkienese (Fujian), Hainanese (Hainan) and Teo Chew (Chaozhou) — before they assimilated into the local culture.

WHAT TO SEE AND DO

With over 800 historically significant buildings, Hoi An is an architectural treasure house, making it a perfect place to wander at random. Many of the café and travel agencies around town have giveaway maps that help identify the sights.

Open only to pedestrians, the sixteenth-century **Japanese Covered Bridge** was built in 1593. Before the Japanese left Hoi An in the mid-seventeenth century, it connected their community with a community of Chinese traders. It has been reconstructed several times since then, but always to the same design, and has become emblematic of Hoi An's diverse architectural and cultural heritage.

Also on Tran Phu Street, at No. 46, is the **Phuok Kien (Fujian) Assembly Hall**, whose hall is dedicated to Thien Hau (Tian Hou), the Protector of Sailors and Fishermen. Nearby is the **Quan Cong Temple**, founded in 1653.

A 20-minute bicycle ride past paddy fields and a lagoon brings you to the **Cua Dai Beach**, where deck chairs and vendors await new victims.

Tour agencies around town offer daytrips to **Cham Island**, 21 km (15 miles) away. The boat leaves from the town's main jetty on Bach Dang Street.

OPPOSITE: The Cham ruins in Singhapura. ABOVE: An old wooden bridge crosses the Cai River at historic Hoi An.

Hoi An is also known for its quality tailoring. It is a rare person who leaves without at least one new addition to his or her wardrobe.

WHERE TO STAY

From just one or two tiny guesthouses in the early 1990s, Hoi An's accommodation scene has blossomed to include dozens of guesthouses and hotels that between them offer a good range of accommodation today.

Hoi An's best hotel is the 60-room **Hoi An Riverside Resort** ((0510) 864800 FAX (0510) 864900 E-MAIL hoianriver@dng.vnn.vn WEB SITE www.hoianriverresort.com, Cua Dai Road. Its only drawback is its location, some three kilometers (just under two miles) out

of town and close to Cua Dai Beach. By way of compensation, the grounds are delightful and feature a good-sized swimming pool. Rates range from US$110, but significant discounts are available for those who book on line.

The low-rise **Hoi An Hotel** ((0510) 861362 FAX (0510) 861636 E-MAIL hoianhotel@dng.vnn .vn, 6 Tran Hung Dao, is not quite in the same league as the Riverside Resort, but it wins in terms of location, being a short walk from Hoi An's charming old quarter. The 120-room hotel has a large garden and a swimming pool, and rooms range from US$40 to US$100.

For those looking to savor the atmosphere of old Hoi An, the **Vinh Hung Hotel** ((0510) 861621 FAX (0510) 861893 E-MAIL

The **Pho Hoi 1** ((0510) 861633 FAX (0510) 862626 E-MAIL phohoiht@dng.vnn.vn, 7/2 Tran Phu Street, is close to the market and is a functional and friendly mini-hotel, where rooms — all equipped with IDD phones, satellite television and air conditioning — cost US$25. The **Pho Hoi 2** ((0510) 862628, its sister operation, is located just across the bridge at Cam Nam and can be booked through the original hotel.

The **Cua Dai Hotel** ((0510) 862231, 18A Cua Dai Street, is the budget traveler's favorite and, along with very reasonably priced and well-maintained rooms costing from US$10, offers tours, Internet access and a host of other backpacker services.

WHERE TO EAT

Hoi An has emerged as one of those legendary backpacker destinations, and as is always the way with such places, its popularity has led to an explosion of cafés catering to their budget needs — many of them lining the picturesque Bach Dang riverside. Places come and go, but some have stayed the course, and some are actually very good at what they do. The **Café Des Amis** ((0510) 861616, 52 Bach Dang, is one such. Deservedly popular, is runs on a simple principle — limit the menu to a handful of dishes and offer them at great-value prices. The cuisine is Vietnamese, and the set-menu format forces guests to try dishes they might not otherwise order themselves; few are disappointed. The duck is a special treat reserved for those who make three visits.

The **Champa Bar** ((0510) 862974, 75 Nguyen Thai Hoc Street, has taken Des Amis' winning formula, and even offers very much the same dishes. The added extra is the evening performances of traditional Hoi An music in the upstairs area, which makes for an atmospheric experience.

Also extremely popular, and with good reason, is the **Ly Cafeteria** (no phone), which has an extensive Vietnamese and European menu, is very reasonably priced, and pulls many of its guests back for repeat visits. It's a favorite breakfast destination with budget travelers.

vinhhungha@dng.vnn.vn, 143 Tran Phu Street, is housed in a 125-year-old Chinese merchant's house. One of the rooms on the second floor has a small balcony overlooking historic Tran Phu Street — be sure to book in advance if you want to secure a stay in it. Room rates are US$50. Don't expect creature comforts, as the hotel makes little in the way of compromises for modern conveniences, preferring to retain the atmosphere of the original building. The nearby **Vinh Hung 2** ((0510) 863717 FAX (0510) 864094 E-MAIL vinhhungha@dng.vnn.vn, Nhi Trung Street, is not quite as atmospheric as the original operation but is nevertheless designed in traditional style, although it is more of a modern operation — rooms are slightly cheaper, at US$35.

Morning at the fish market in Quy Nhon.

The **Han Huyen Floating Restaurant** ((0510) 861462, close to the Japanese Covered Bridge on Bach Dang Street, serves Vietnamese and Chinese food in a romantic setting on the river.

How to Get There

Being a backwater off the main highway, Hoi An is a little difficult to access by public transportation, but then hardly any foreign travelers arrive by public transport anyway. Budget travelers mostly stop off here with

the Open Tour service (either from Hue and Da Nang or from Nha Trang in the south), while others come by taxi from Da Nang (US$10) or Hue (US$25). The nearest airport is at Da Nang.

QUI NHON

A busy little timber port, Qui Nhon is not so important in its own right, but it is the nearest coastal access to the Cham ruins of Thap Doi and Bhan It (or Thap Bac), Duong Long, and the former Cham political capital of Cha Ban (Vijaya). It also provides access to the northern central highlands and centers like Play Cu and Kon Tum, home to many minority villages and the site of

fierce battles fought between the Americans and infiltrating NVA units during the war.

What to See and Do

There area's **Cham ruins** are in three different sites. Close to Qui Nhon, on the edge of town, are the two spectacular towers of **Thap Doi**. Rising to heights of over 18 m (60 ft), these newly restored eleventh-century towers symbolize male and female powers. Standing on a hilltop between two branches of the Kon River are the four twelfth-century "silver towers" of **Ban It** or **Thap Bac**, about 12 km (seven and a half miles) north of town. One of Central Vietnam's largest Buddhist monasteries, the **Nguyen Thieu** is also situated in this holy spot.

About 26 km (16 miles) north is the **Canh Tien** (Brass Tower) and the walled ruins of **Cha Ban** — the only remains of the former Cham political capital that existed here from the tenth to fifteenth centuries. Close by is the still operating **Thar Thap Pagoda**, built in the mid-seventeenth century within the ruins of the old capital. Three other elaborately decorated thirteenth-century towers, **Thap Duong Long** (Towers of Ivory) can be seen about eight kilometers (5 miles) beyond Cha Ban. Some of these lintels show certain similarities with the Khmer style of the Bayon temple at Angkor.

About 37 km (23 miles) to the south of Qui Nhon is the somewhat surreal landscape of **Song Cau**, where breezy, stilted restaurants serve excellent fresh seafood, making it a popular lunch stop for tour buses and anyone else in the know. Beyond the restaurants are beaches and the fishing village of Song Cau, which is also a basketware center.

WHERE TO STAY AND EAT

The beachfront **Qui Nhon Tourist Hotel** ((056) 822401, 8-10 Nguyen Hue Street, next to the Tourist Office, is the best hotel in town, with a wide range of rooms from around US$20 to US$60. Budget travelers, though, are better off heading to the nearby **Phuong Mai Hotel** ((056) 822921, 14 Nguyen Hue Street, where simple rooms can be had for US$7 and upwards.

The **Tu Hai Restaurant**, on the third floor of Lon Market on Phan Boi Chau Street, has an English-language menu and serves a variety of Vietnamese and seafood dishes from 6:30 AM to 10 PM. The **Dong Phuong Restaurant** opens from 6 AM until 11 PM at 39-41 Mai Xuan Thuong Street.

HOW TO GET THERE

Lying 238 km (148 miles) north of Nha Trang, Qui Nhon gets little in the way of tourist traffic as it's not the easiest place to get to. For the rare traveler who flies here, the airport is at Phu Cat, another notorious wartime base, 36 km (22 miles) north of the city. The only other real option is to rent a car with a driver.

Both Saigon Tourist and Especen Tourist offer excellent tours of the Cham Ruins. See TAKING A TOUR, page 59 in YOUR CHOICE.

NHA TRANG

Nha Trang is as close as Vietnam gets to Surfer's Paradise or Phuket — a major resort area that is aimed more at vacationers than travelers. Of course, this being Vietnam, it makes little sense to expect the excitement or amenities that are on offer in

Australia or Thailand. It does, however, make for an interesting visit, in as much as it gives an insight into how the Vietnamese are going about catering to the more hedonistic breed of tourist.

Nha Trang started life as a French colonial resort, on account of its genuinely impressive ribbon of beach. It later metamorphosed into to a GI R&R center, only to fade into gloom as a Russian holiday retreat. What a difference a decade can make: today Nha Trang is reinventing itself into a true seaside resort, complete with swanky hotels and seafood restaurants overlooking the sparkling South China Sea.

The six-kilometer (nearly four-mile) Municipal Beach rivals Thailand's Pattaya (as it looked two decades ago), and although the latter's more raucous entertainment options are not present here, for the average visitor this will be more an attraction than otherwise. To the north are even more beautiful beaches just waiting to be explored, while in the vicinity are 71 islands, some with reportedly pristine diving and snorkeling.

Behind the beach is a cultural backdrop that features relics of the ancient Cham kingdom of central Vietnam. The city and its gently curving beach lie 448 km (278 miles) from Saigon on a promontory that runs south of the Cai River estuary. A beachfront road, Tran Phu Boulevard, extends south from the river, becoming Tu Do Street as it approaches the peninsula. The business and administrative district are to the north of the airport, close to the estuary.

WHAT TO SEE AND DO

Five nearby islands provide fodder for daytrips from Nha Trang. **Hon Tre (Bamboo Island)** is the biggest and is reached easily by boat, while the adjacent **Hon Mun (Ebony Island)** is a popular snorkeling spot. **Hon Yen (Swift Island)**, named after the swifts, or *salangane*, that build their edible nests in its caves, is 17 km (10.5 miles) out to sea and is one of several islands famous for their annual harvest of swift's nests — for that Chinese delicacy, bird's-nest soup. **Hon Tam** has a café and deck chairs, while

Fishing nets laid out for repairs at Hai Duong near Nha Trang.

the closest of the islands, **Hon Mieu (Cat Island)**, has a lively fishing village and several pleasant seafood restaurants overlooking the beach. Although no one will tell you this because they would rather sell you a tour, you can get there by public ferry from the ferry point just beyond the Bao Dai Villas (from where all the island tours leave). Locals will try to extort ridiculous prices from foreigners — the price is around US$1. More expensive private boat trips are available to some or all of the islands at travel agents around Nha Trang.

At the northern end of the town, over the Xom Bong Bridge, are the Cham towers of **Po Nagar** (The Lady of the City). Standing like sentinels on a rocky hilltop overlooking the Cai River and northern entrance to Nha Trang are four of the original eight towers, among the finest examples of Cham architecture in central Vietnam. The towers were built between the seventh and twelfth centuries, although originally the site was a Hindu place of worship, dating from the second century. The North Tower is the oldest and also the best preserved, featuring stone wall carvings of Shiva dancing to the accompaniment of musicians, a stone gong and drum and, in the lofty main chamber, a 10-armed stone image of the goddess Uma. There's a small museum (open 8 AM to 5 PM daily) close to this site exhibiting other Cham relics, though nothing of great interest. The three other towers are of less interest, but a recent restoration job has done much to improve things. Two of them have stone lingams in their main chambers and the other, the Northeast Tower, features more bas-relief sculptures. The North Tower was rebuilt in AD 817 after Indonesian raiders destroyed the original temple complex.

West of the city center at 23 Thang 10 Street, the **Long Son Pagoda** is a far more recent relic. Built in the late nineteenth century, the pagoda lies in the shadow of a towering white Buddha seated on a lotus. The temple's most distinctive feature is the mosaic dragons that adorn its entrance and roofs. It is home to a small community of monks. Meanwhile, on Thai Nguyen Street (which is the eastern extension of Thang 10 Street), the Gothic **Nha Trang Cathedral**, with its stained-glass windows and towering spires, looks medieval but is even more recent; it was completed in 1933. Mass is held twice daily at 5 AM and 4:30 PM.

Nha Trang is also the proud home of a Pasteur Institute, one of three in Vietnam (the others are in Saigon and Da Lat), founded by Doctor Alexandre Yersin (1863–1943) in 1895. Born in Europe, Doctor Yersin came to Vietnam in 1889 after isolating the microbes that caused the bubonic plague in Hong Kong in 1894. After spending several years traveling and making observations in Vietnam, he introduced both quinine and rubber trees to the country. While the institute is woefully short of funding, the dedicated workers carry on regardless.

The **Bao Dai Villas**, about six kilometers (four miles) south of town, are also worth a visit, or better yet, a stay. Bao Dai was the last emperor of the Nguyen Dynasty. He attempted to form an anti-Communist state in cooperation with France during the first Indochina War, then abdicated when the Viet Minh achieved victory. His five seaside villas, built in the 1920s, are just north of the Oceanographic Institute and testify to the lifestyle he obviously feared was threatened by the nationalist forces. President Nguyen Van Thieu took advantage of them when he was in power, and after the 1975 victory, they became resort rewards for the Communist hierarchy. They're now tourist guesthouses, renovated and air conditioned, with lush gardens and excellent views of Nha Trang and the nearby islands.

Just below the villas, the **Oceanographic Institute** in Cau Da village was founded in 1923. Within the institute are 23 aquariums swimming with a wide variety of marine life. The institute also has displays of marine life that will not be doing anymore swimming, featuring around 60,000 preserved exhibits.

Recreational pursuits in Nha Trang include **diving** and **snorkeling** on the islands, and while diving is still in its infancy in Vietnam, several companies are operating in Nha Trang. With 71 islands to choose from, this burgeoning industry has great potential (see SPORTING SPREE, page 30 in YOUR CHOICE). Daily boat trips to the islands are also available. Ask at your hotel for the best operator or book a daytrip from the Ana Mandara Resort for a more up-market tour.

The easiest way to get around Nha Trang is on a rented bicycle, which are available from most hotels and cafés and cost as little as US$1 per day. Motorcycles cost around US$5 per day. Cyclos and Honda Oms are thick on the streets. Cars can also be rented (with a driver) at around US$35 a day.

WHERE TO STAY

The **Ana Mandara Resort** ((058) 829829 FAX (058) 829629 E-MAIL resvana@dng.vnn.vn WEB SITE http://six-senses.com/ana-mandara, Beachside, Tran Phu Boulevard, is right on the beach at the southern end of town, and is Nha Trang's flagship luxury hotel. The chalet-style accommodation is furnished with natural materials — timbers and rattans — and is surrounded by expansive gardens: the idea is to create the effect of a traditional Vietnamese village, although no Vietnamese village was ever this comfortable. It has every imaginable amenity and nice touches include the library, which features a wide range of reading material on Vietnam. Room rates range from US$144 to US$300, depending on the season (the first week of January is the most expensive, with rates starting at just under US$200).

Also on the waterfront, though not quite in the same league as the Ana Mandara, is the **Yasaka Saigon Nhatrang Hotel** ((058) 820090 FAX (058) 820000 E-MAIL sg-nhotel@dng .vnn.vn, 18 Tran Phu Boulevard, which seems to suffer somewhat from lackadaisical service standards. This is a pity, as it has the potential to live up to its four-star rating — a great waterfront location, a good range of restaurants and other amenities and luxurious, if a little unimaginative, rooms. Nevertheless, rates are less expensive here — they start at US$60 — than at the Ana Mandara, and its location rivals the former.

The towering **Nha Trang Lodge** ((058) 810900 FAX (058) 828800 E-MAIL nt-lodge @dng.vnn.vn WEB SITE www.nt-lodge.com, 42 Tran Phu Boulevard, overlooks the sea rather than fronts it — guests have to cross the road to get to the beach — but is a good mid-range choice, featuring well-appointed rooms, attentive staff and unexpected treats

such as a tennis court and a good-sized swimming pool. Rooms range from US$50 to US$145.

Bao Dai's Villas ((058) 590147 FAX (058) 590146 E-MAIL baodai@dng.vnn.vn, at Cau Da just to the south of town, is something of an eccentric place to stay, but it will appeal to some — it's a colonial-style complex where you can get a feel for the grander days of Indochina. Huge, air-conditioned double rooms cost US$25 to US$80 a night, but don't expect facilities like a pool. Some of the villas have splendid sea views.

Nha Trang's most popular budget accommodation is the **Dong Phuong Hotel** ((058) 825986 FAX (058) 825986 E-MAIL dong phuongnt@dng.vnn.vn, 103 Nguyen Thien Thuat Street. It has some acceptable lower mid-range rooms priced from IS$18 to US$25, but also has cheaper rooms that are popular with the backpacker set. A friendly, family atmosphere prevails. There is a **Dong Phuong 2** at 1 Tran Phu Boulevard — bookings can be made through the original Dong Phuong Hotel.

WHERE TO EAT

Nha Trang's beachfront is the place for a seafood lunch or dinner. One of the best places for this is the **Sailing Club** ((058) 826528, 72 Tran Phu, an entertainment/water sports/ restaurant complex run by an Australian entrepreneur who saw a niche and jumped in. This up-market venue is actually three restaurants, serving everything from Vietnamese

A vendor prepares a fruit display in Da Lat's central market.

to Italian, with some excellent seafood in between. The expansive bar area is a popular place for evening drinks, and stays open until 4 AM. **Casa Italia**, an Italian restaurant that is part of the complex, is particularly recommended, not only for its authentic pasta and pizza dishes, but also for its "seafood corner," which offers everything from fresh lobster to fish steaks; the happy hour session in the leafy garden area overlooking the sea from 8:30 to 10:30 PM is a great way to end the day.

Also on the beachfront, and popular with budget travelers, is the **Rainbow Bar**, 52 Tran Phu. It is more a party venue than a restaurant, but also serves snacks and fast-food meals. As the evening wears on, the emphasis is far more on lethal cocktails and dancing than it is on eating, however. **Café des Amis (** (058) 813009, 13 Biet Thu Street, is an inexpensive vegetarian restaurant (but despite the billing, they do actually offer some meat dishes) that also doubles as an art gallery. Take a look at their tours too — they are recommended.

Hoan Hai ((058) 823133, 6 Pan Chu Trinh, is a lively, family-run seafood restaurant that is popular with locals and travelers alike. Prices are very reasonable, and the open-front layout makes for good street-scene watching as you wash down your garlic prawns with a beer.

The **Lizard/Zippo Bar**, 2 Hung Vuong, is a long-runner, and was Nha Trang's original late-night drinking venue. It has become a little more up-market these days, offering some excellent Vietnamese and Southeast Asian dishes, but the bar is still open late and is still a favorite gathering spot for all and sundry.

AROUND NHA TRANG

One of Vietnam's more beautiful beaches is **Doc Let Beach**, 40 km (25 miles) north of Nha Trang past Ninh Hoa. This long stretch of white sand flanked by casuarinas is idyllic and untouched most of the year (don't go on a Vietnamese public holiday). Simple accommodation is available along with a restaurant with changing rooms. To get there, rent a motorcycle or car from Nha Trang or take a *moto* from the turnoff at Ninh

Hoa. Other pleasant possibilities are to rent a car or motorcycle and head north to explore other beautiful beaches that line this magnificent coastline, or take a trip out to Monkey Island. The ferry point is about 20 km (13 miles) north of the city.

HOW TO GET THERE

While most visitors regard Nha Trang as a stop off point on the north–south route, it is quite feasible to spend a whole holiday here at the beach. Vietnam Airlines operates regular flights to Nha Trang from Saigon, Da Nang and Hanoi, but beware: they are subject to change without notice if a higher priority request comes through. The *Reunification Express* stops at Nha Trang and it is also a stop off for the north–south Open Tour Bus route.

DA LAT

A French town transplanted into the foothills of Vietnam's Central Highlands, the "City of Eternal Spring" offers faded charm and crumbling French architecture. It was spared bombing during the Vietnam War, and today it is reaping the dividends in the form of a booming tourism business.

Nestling in a valley, 1,475 m (4,800 ft) above sea level in the south-central highlands, Da Lat makes a wonderful retreat from the rigors of Vietnam travel. Developed by the French at the suggestion of Alexandre Yersin as a cool, high-country retreat from the obsessive summer heat of Saigon and the Mekong Delta, the hilly town is filled with elaborate villas, most of which attempt to recapture the familiar architecture of Normandy and Brittany. The French District is almost a replica of a French provincial hometown, and strolling around this part of town on a cool evening, it is possible to forget for a moment that you are actually in Vietnam.

Much of the city surrounds the hugely ugly Central Market, with hotels and the surviving French villas set on ridges and hillocks around it. Da Lat's centerpiece is the picturesque and newly renovated Xuan Huong Lake — a reservoir lake created by the French in 1919. To the north of the lake, a rolling hill leads to Da Lat's Mecca for honeymooning Vietnamese: the Valley of Love. Surrounding Da Lat are acres of market gardens supplying vegetables and flowers to both Da Lat's and Saigon's markets. One of Da Lat's specialty crops is strawberries, which can be bought as delicious jam, dried and, of course, fresh.

Other Da Lat drawcards include one of Vietnam's most glamorous hotels (see the Sofitel Da Lat Palace in WHERE TO STAY, overleaf), a classic 1920s French structure that has been beautifully restored.

Bicycles are the ideal way to get around town, and cost around US$1 per day. They're a less attractive proposition on the hilly outskirts of town, and for farther destinations a Honda Om or a rented motorcycle of your own is a better idea. Most hotels and travelers' cafés rent out cars and minibuses, and this is the comfortable and convenient way to go any distance, especially to the viewpoints, waterfalls and picnic spots in the hills around the city. Don't forget to do some walking: Da Lat is a city made for strolling, and compact enough not to walk you off your feet.

WHAT TO SEE AND DO

It is the dream of many a honeymooning Vietnamese couple to spend those first days of marital bliss in Da Lat. Perhaps it has something to do with the names of the city's sights — the Valley of Love, the City of Eternal Spring, the Lake of Sighs. Less romantic, Da Lat is also the center of a booming sex industry.

Most of the attractions that feature on the honeymoon circuit are of little interest to foreign visitors. The **Valley of Love**, a commercialized souvenir complex, would be more aptly named the "Valley of Shopping." The stalls are packed with stuffed wildlife from the forests around Da Lat — it flies in the face of every effort that Vietnam is now making to preserve the wildlife that survived years of bombing and chemical defoliation during the war. On a more amusing note are the Valley of Love's tourist touts: young men dressed as cowboys who offer kids pony rides around the hills.

On the other hand, the **Da Lat Palace Golf Course** ((063) 823507, Phu Dong Thien Vuong Street, has to be one of Asia's more beautiful courses. Misty mornings render it almost invisible, then the sun melts the clouds away and colonial edifices, such as the cathedral spire, appear across the rolling hills. The walk-in fee for a game at the 18-hole course is US$85, while for guests of the Sofitel Da Lat Palace or the Novotel Hotel, the fee is US$65. It's open 6:30 AM to dusk daily.

Those who have not seen enough temples already will be relieved to know that in addition to the pink **Da Lat Cathedral** on Tran Phu Street, several Chinese and Vietnamese temples can be seen around the city. Particularly worth a visit is the **Thieng Vuong Pagoda**, Khe Sanh Street, about five kilometers (three miles) from the city center.

Da Lat's **Central Market** may be housed in a particularly uninspired concrete block, but inside you will find fresh flowers and vegetables, strawberry items of every description — including the delectable Da Lat jam — clothing and some souvenirs. On the top floor is a food center crammed with stalls selling Vietnamese specialties, juices and some vegetarian food. The tribal artifacts sold by minority women around the market tend to be of poor quality, but it's worth taking a look all the same; be prepared to haggle for a decent price.

Landmarks around town include **Da Lat University**, 1 Phu Dong Thien Vuong Street, and the **Domaine de Marie Convent**, 6 Ngo Quyen Street, which commands a fine view of the city from its hilltop perch. **Bao Dai's Summer Palace**, on the outskirts of town in a grove of pine trees off Le Hong Phong Street, was built in 1933. While not one of his most beautiful hideaways, those who run the gauntlet of souvenir stall touts, Disney characters, "cowboys" on ponies and troops of photographers to enter the 25-room villa will find it interesting if only because it has been left as it was in 1933.

The Gaudiesque Hang Nga Guesthouse and Art Gallery is better known as the **Crazy House**, and for good reason. Designed by Soviet-trained architect Doctor Dang Viet Nga, the building is fashioned of concrete to look like a tree, and the rooms — it was built to be a hotel — are distinguished by unique acid-trip sculptures. Most people take it in as part of Da Lat's sights, but it is also possible to spend a night here — it will undoubtedly be the strangest hotel experience of your life. For more information see WHERE TO STAY, below.

WHERE TO STAY

The **Sofitel Dalat Palace Hotel** ((063) 825444 FAX (063) 825666 E-MAIL salesdalat@accor-hotel-vietnam.com WEB SITE http://accor-hotelvietnam.com/sofitel-dalatpalace, 2 Tran Phu, is not only the best hotel in Da Lat, it is one of the best in Vietnam. Beau-

Another hotel with a long tradition is the 143-room **Novotel Da Lat Hotel** ((063) 825777 FAX (063) 825888 E-MAIL salesdalat@accor-hotel-vietnam.com WEB SITE http://accor-hotel-vietnam.com/novotel-dalat, 7 Tran Phu Street, opposite the Palace. Formerly the Du Parc Hotel (built in 1932) like the Sofitel it has been restored faithfully in keeping with its colonial origins. Both Novotel and the Sofitel are part of the Accor Group — the idea here is to provide four-star standards at the Novotel with full access to the five-star amenities at the adjacent Palace Hotel.

tifully renovated in 1993 by a joint-venture company, and under the management of Sofitel, the 78-year-old property has just 43 rooms and suites, but this is one of the hotel's winning features. Despite the renovations it remains faithful to its original French style, and its restaurants and bars are the best in Da Lat. Guests can play tennis in one of two courts, have access to the golf course and can enjoy a host of travel services in the Da Lat area. Rooms are appointed in fine period style and start at around US$170. In a parallel renovation, the same company has upgraded some 17 French villas in Da Lat as tourist chalets, and has built Vietnam's first international-class 18-hole golf course north of Xuan Huong Lake.

Rooms start at US$119, and discounted golfing packages are available for those who reserve through the hotel's web site.

For mid-range accommodation in decidedly quirky surroundings (see WHAT TO SEE AND DO, above) **Hang Nga's Tree House** ((063) 822070, 3 Huyhn Thuc Khang, is a hotel nobody forgets in a hurry. Every room is unique, some of them looking more like caves than hotel rooms. Rates range from US$25 to US$55.

Minh Tam Hotel ((063) 822447, 20A Khe Sanh Street, about three kilometers (just under two miles) from the city center, is distinctive for its peaceful location amid wooded hills and its history. Built in 1936 and renovated in 1984, rooms cost US$30 to US$40.

Da Lat's most popular backpacker hotel is the **Hoa Binh Hotel** ((063) 822787, 64 Truong Cong Dinh, which not only has rooms from just US$5, but also provides a host of travelers' services out of its friendly café.

WHERE TO EAT

The Sofitel Da Lat Palace offers the most sophisticated dining in town. For French cuisine **Le Rabelais** ((063) 825444 is the place for a splash-out meal, while **Café de la Poste** serves mostly Southeast Asian favorites, with some generic international dishes thrown into the mix.

For a more affordable meal, the **Shanghai Restaurant** ((063) 822509, 8 Khu Hoa Binh Street, close to the Central Market, has good Vietnamese, Chinese and Western food, though service can be a little hit-and-miss. A popular lakeside restaurant is the **Thanh Thanh** ((063) 821836, 4 Tang Bat Ho, for traditional Vietnamese cuisine and Western dishes popular with tour groups. A family restaurant, the **Maison Long Hoa** ((063) 822934, 6 Duong 3 Thang 2, offers a cozy atmosphere and good Vietnamese and Western food.

Lastly, a great place for a coffee or other drinks is **Café Tung**, 6 Khu Hoa Binh, a colonial-period café that takes its guests back in time. It's easy to imagine Vietnamese intellectuals sitting here in times past, plotting the revolution.

AROUND DA LAT

On the outskirts of town, on the Nha Trang road, the so-called **Chicken Village** is one of Vietnam's oddest tourist attractions. Erected at the entrance to an impoverished Koho village, the massive chicken statue is of obscure origins. For most visitors, though, it is little more than a pit stop on a textile-shopping expedition — the villagers here are renowned for their weaving. The village is around 20 km (just over 12 miles) from Da Lat, easily reached by motorcycle or taxi.

While Da Lat is blessed with numerous waterfalls, most have been turned into unappealing tourist attractions, complete with concrete, kiosks and more ponies and Disney

characters; explore at your own risk. An exception is the **Datanla Falls**, about 20 km (13 miles) from town along Highway 20.

Out of town are coffee plantations, highland walks and minority villages to visit. **Lang Bian Mountain**, at 2,162 m (7,095 ft), makes a good day's hike. Leaving from the village of **Lat**, about seven kilometers (four and a half miles) north of Da Lat, the walk takes three to four hours, passing through many villages of four different ethnic groups along the way. Young local boys are often happy to act as guides for a reasonable fee.

HOW TO GET THERE

Daily Vietnam Airlines flights operate to Da Lat from Saigon (the airport is 30 km, or 19 miles, south of the city), but the best way to arrive is by road, either up the incredibly panoramic road from Nha Trang or by the scenic, inland eight-hour drive from Saigon. After the wide agricultural plains the elevation rises, passing through tea and coffee plantations before reaching the densely forested hills that surround Da Lat. Once there, you'll find that the city meets every description that you may have read elsewhere — it certainly enjoys a sense of mountain magic, especially in the chill of the night, when the heavens are brilliant with stars.

OPPOSITE LEFT: Da Lat Cathedral, built in 1931. RIGHT: Morning on Da Lat's central Xuan Huong Lake. ABOVE: "Cowboys" entertain the tourists in Da Lat.

Southern Vietnam

SAIGON
(HO CHI
MINH CITY)

0   250   500 metres
0   550 yards

QUAN 3

QUAN 1

QUAN 5

QUAN 4

N

SAIGON (HO CHI MINH CITY)

While Hanoi is sedate and orderly, Saigon is brash, entrepreneurial and fast — even the pickpockets are talented. While Ho Chi Minh City remains the official name, southerners continue to call the city by the name they have always used: Saigon.

In the war years, fattened with billions of American dollars, the city was regarded as one of the richest, most advanced and certainly one of the most sophisticated in Asia. It came under heavy suppression after the fall of 1975, when many of its intellectuals and entrepreneurs — the ones who didn't make it to freedom in the West, that is — were jailed or put into reeducation camps. Now Saigon's former capitalists are back in favor, and for the most part are run-

ning the city they lost nearly three decades ago in the war against the north.

Saigon is the center where new hotels are at their glitziest and most luxurious, products of numerous joint-venture deals with international hotel groups from around the world. Omni, Hyatt, Ramada, New World, Equatorial, Hilton are all making their mark in competition with the government-run French colonial hotels and well-loved names like the Rex, the Continental, the Majestic and the Caravelle.

Every Saturday and Sunday evening, the broad square between the Hotel Continental and the Municipal Theater becomes the center of an impromptu show as thousands of adults and teenagers ride their motorcycles down Dong Khoi Street to the riverfront. It's quite a spectacle, a continuous stream of headlights and roaring engines that flows until after midnight. According to some reports, this social outing began as a weekly demonstration, a show of force, by the Saigonese to remind the city's Communist authorities and the government in Hanoi that this is a city not to be messed with.

Another pleasant pastime that gives a feeling of old Saigon is to sit back in a comfortable rattan chair and enjoy a late-afternoon beer or *citron pressé* on the roof of the Rex Hotel, one of the must-visits on any Saigon itinerary. It's difficult to resist the

among the craziest in all Asia, and just crossing the road in some parts of town can be a major headache — if in doubt, stick to some locals and learn from their example how to make your way across busy roads. Do not count on traffic lights as the colors are seldom observed.

Unlike her northern sister city, Saigon is an entertainment hub, with bars, discos, clubs, karaoke and other less salubrious establishments operating late into the night. Although the sprawling suburbs are booming with new housing and joint-venture

temptation to stay on for dinner, and you will not regret it if you do. Breakfast of fresh and crisp baguettes, eggs and *café filtre* among the chirping caged birds is an experience that few forget in a hurry.

Saigon runs on foreign investment, its downtown streets and markets packed with imported luxuries and the latest Japanese, Korean and Taiwanese consumer appliances. The traffic is a heady mix of motorcycles and cars, which have now almost completely swept away the bicycles and pedal-powered cyclos of yesterday. As in China, the sudden transition to motorized transportation has not been a smooth one, and it is easy to get the impression that road rules simply do not exist. Saigon drivers are

factories, the inner city is the main tourist area. It sprawls between District 1 — the downtown business area extending southeast from the elegant Notre Dame Cathedral to the Saigon River, centered on Dong Khoi Street (known as Tu Do Street during the war) — and District 5, the teeming Chinatown or Cholon, to the west.

GENERAL INFORMATION

As is the case in Hanoi, there is little point in seeking out Saigon's government-run tourist offices for useful information. **Saigon Tourist (** (08) 829-2291 FAX (08) 824-3239

Saigon's Opera House and the famed Hotel Continental in downtown Saigon.

WEB SITE www.saigon-tourist.com, 23 Le Loi, District 1, is essentially a profit-making organization with far-reaching business concerns that include some 45 hotels and resorts and many restaurants. They will be quite happy to sell a tour to anyone who wanders in, or to make a reservation at one of their hotels, but not much more. Travelers will have more luck getting useful information at one of Saigon's budget travel agencies, such as the long-running **Sinh Café** ((08) 836-7338 or 246-248 FAX (08) 836-9322 WEB SITE www.sinhcafevn.com, De Tamh,

District 1, or **Ben Tanh Tour & Travel** ((08) 829-8463, 4-6 Ho Huan Nghiem, District 1.

In the event of any medical problems, the best place to go is **Cho Ray Hospital** ((08) 855-4137, Benh Vien Cho Ray, which is Saigon's largest, and has a 24-hour emergency service with English-speaking doctors.

For up-to-date information on what's happening around town, look out for *The Guide*, a monthly listings magazine — though strongly commercial — published by the *Vietnam Economic Times* WEB SITE www.vneconomy.com.vn. A more impartial rundown of current events can be found at the WEB SITE www.groovysaigon.com.

Saigon being the main entry point for international travelers, many airlines have offices here. These include: **Air France** ((08) 829-0981, 130 Dong Khoi, District 1; **Asiana Airways** ((08) 822-2663, 34 Le Duan, District 1; **British Airways** ((08) 829-2262, 114A Nguyen Hue, District 1; **Cathay Pacific** ((08) 824-5408, 58 Dong Khoi, District 1; **Emirates** ((08) 825-6576, 114A Nguyen Hue, District 1; **Japan Airlines** ((08) 821-9098, 115 Nguyen Hue, District 1; **Korean Airlines** ((08) 824-2878, 34 Le Duan, District 1; **Lufthansa** ((08) 829-8529, 132-134 Dong Khoi, District 1; **Qantas** ((08) 823-8844, 114A Nguyen Hue, District 1; **Singapore Airlines** ((08) 823-1588, 29 Le Duan, District 1; **Swiss Air** ((08) 824-4000, 65 Le Loi, District 1; **Thai Airways** ((08) 829-2810, 65 Nguyen Du, District 1; and **Vietnam Airlines** ((08) 832-0320, 116 Nguyen Hue, District 1.

GETTING AROUND

Saigon is divided into 21 districts (16 urban and five rural), to be precise, but most visitors spend almost all their time in District 1, the city hub and the area referred to by locals as Saigon. Dong Khoi, Nguyen Hue and Hai Ba Trung Streets are where most of the key commercial centers, travel agencies, airline offices, shops, banks, cultural centers and hotels are located. The Central Market (Ben Thanh) lies west of Dong Khoi on Le Loi Boulevard, and the imposing New World Hotel fronts a wide traffic circus from which the main access streets to the Chinese area of Cholon (District 5) radiate.

Getting around in Saigon is not as confusing as in some Asian cities. Latin script makes it possible to read street signs, but as is the case elsewhere around the region, street numbering can be somewhat erratic — don't expect that No. 17 is necessarily next door to No. 15, though more often than not it will be.

District 1 has retained much of its historical interest despite the spate of development that has enveloped the city. An everyday itinerary takes in Notre Dame Cathedral and the adjacent Post Office, an architectural masterpiece in its own right,

OPPOSITE: Midday traffic rolls by the landmark Notre Dame Cathedral, Saigon. ABOVE: The graceful lines of City Hall and Ho Chi Minh Square in central Saigon.

and extends south down Dong Khoi to the stately Hotel Continental and the renovated Municipal Theater (Opera House), home to the popular Q Bar, west past the Eden Center and public square to the Rex Hotel and Hôtel de Ville (City Hall), then on to the Central Market and south again to the Doc Lap (Caravelle) Hotel on Dong Khoi or to a series of mid-street photo and souvenir kiosks on Nguyen Hue, and finally on to the Saigon River waterfront.

While this is not all there is to the city, it is certainly the hub of most activity, with virtually everything that any visitor would need. Although the hotels and travel agencies in Saigon have limousines, cars and mini-vans available, the cheapest — and most hair-raising — way to get around is by cyclo. The authorities are slowly banning cyclos from many city roads, however, which means that certain parts of the city center are off-limits to them, and more will probably be so as time passes. Most central destinations should cost around US$1, though it is essential to bargain if you wish to avoid paying a lot more. Cyclo drivers usually lurk outside hotels.

Motorcycle taxis, or Honda Oms, are available for quick visits to the bank and other tiresome necessities. Rental car drivers can also usually be found outside hotels, or can be organized through **Saigon Taxi** ((08) 842-4242 and **Vinataxi** ((08) 811-1111. There are many agencies around town offering motorcycle rental, but it is not recommended — take a look at the traffic conditions and you will understand why.

WHAT TO SEE AND DO

Central Saigon
Notre Dame Cathedral makes a useful starting point for a colonial city tour. This elegant blend of red brick and white stone with two soaring, spired towers faces directly down Dong Khoi toward the Saigon River. Built in 1877, Notre Dame and its spires, viewed across a green bank of trees, add a pastoral touch to Saigon's modernizing skyline. The cathedral fronts a sweeping square that features a tall white statue of the Virgin Mary, and a well-kept tree-shaded public park sprawls to its rear.

Closed by the Communists after the 1975 takeover of Saigon, Notre Dame is now flourishing again, with services beginning at dawn each day.

Adjacent to Notre Dame, the **General Post Office (GPO)** is another striking architectural landmark. Built in 1886, it combines an opulence of colonial bas-relief and charming shuttered windows with a vast central hall reminiscent of a canopied Victorian railway station. Today, it's still the main communications center for the Saigonese, but the hotels have now usurped it as a provider of telephone, fax and postal — not to mention Internet — services for visitors. Take care while walking in this area, as the GPO is also home to some of the city's most talented pickpockets — while there are

periodic sweepings by the police, they quickly return.

Close to Dong Khoi Street (in fact, right on the corner of Dong Khoi and Le Loi Boulevard) the **Givral Café and Pâtisserie**, with its big picture window view of the Opera House, is an old Saigon institution and, for nostalgic reasons as much as anything else, still worth a visit for an expresso. Veterans will remember it for its afternoon coffee and ice cream, while newer visitors will enjoy the same service, no doubt from the same old waiters.

The stately old grande dame of Saigon, the **Continental Hotel**, on the opposite corner from the Givral Café, was renowned for evening drinks and the shoeshine boys in its open verandah bar during the war. It featured extensively in Graham Greene's classic *The Quiet American*, and is as much a cultural attraction as a hotel. Somehow, it's managed to tart itself up yet come down a peg or two — the famous verandah bar is now closed and has been reborn as an airline office, and the standard of service has lowered since Saigon Tourist took over day-to-day running of the operation. Still, it's something of a treat to breakfast on hot croissants, baguettes and coffee in the inner garden courtyard, once favored by foreign correspondents. The international hotel chains would no doubt love to get their hands on the place, but for the time being it remains firmly in the hands of the state.

Saigon's Municipal Theatre was the often stormy legislature of South Vietnam during the war.

Opposite the Continental and facing Le Loi Boulevard, the **Saigon Opera House**, as it's commonly known, with its high, arched entrance, was South Vietnam's National Assembly during the war. Now it's the city's main cultural center, staging concerts, recitals, plays and performances by Saigon's new crop of pop artists. During the war the gardened square opposite this building featured a huge, grotesque concrete sculpture depicting a United States soldier and his ARVN (Army of the Republic of Vietnam) comrade charging into battle. But

occupied by JUSPAO (Joint United States Public Affairs Office), was where the famous "Five O'clock Follies" — a daily media briefing on the war — was staged. The establishment's rooftop was a sprawling officers' bar and mess with a stage for regular go-go dance shows, and a viewpoint from which visitors could watch the war at night — the tracers from jet cannon and helicopter machine-guns pouring into the city's outer suburbs.

Today, a rash of high-rise buildings overshadow the Rex rooftop, but it remains

cynicism was so rife among correspondents and United States troops that it was regarded as a United States soldier pushing his Vietnamese counterpart into the fight. Even more cynical was another popular unofficial description — a United States soldier and ARVN comrade attacking the National Assembly.

The charming, renovated **Rex Hotel** on Le Loi Boulevard, facing Ho Chi Minh Square, also deserves special mention for its wartime role. This was the Rex BOQ (Bachelor Officers' Quarters for United States personnel) during the war, heavily sandbagged against Viet Cong attack and one of the focal points of the United States and international media. Its ground floor,

immensely popular. If nothing else, its open bar is still a good position from which to view the city's fast-changing skyline.

Facing Ho Chi Minh Square and a bronze statue of "Uncle Ho" embracing a child, the excellently restored colonial **City Hall** building is one of the city's prettiest. Once the Hôtel de Ville, it is now the headquarters of the People's Committee. Its opulently decorated façade and clock tower provide a backdrop to the square, which is crowded on weekends with Vietnamese sightseers and families taking snapshots. For those who know this location from the old days and are wondering what has happened to the old Rex Cinema, it has been turned into a new lobby for the Rex Hotel.

The huge hangar-like covered market complex of **Central Market (Ben Thanh)**, west on Le Loi Boulevard from the Rex Hotel, and close to the New World Hotel, is a place that the words "crowded" and "bustling" just do not do justice to. Shoppers come here in hordes to pick and jostle their way through stalls piled high with consumer and household goods, shoes, cheap clothing, poultry, fish and just about every other product and provision you can name. The market has entrances on all four sides, making getting in relatively easy.

open market is also full of imported watches, video games and other electronic products. The main tourist run of **Dong Khoi Street** is another must. Along this tree-shaded thoroughfare are dozens of hotels, gift shops, pickpockets and art galleries, as well as bars and restaurants.

Dong Du Street, which runs west from Dong Khoi from just outside the Bong Sen Hotel, is notable for three attractions — the **Saigon Business Center**, set up to provide modern office facilities and communications for incoming joint-venture companies; the

Getting out again is another thing altogether, such is the general crush of shoppers, wandering hawkers, beggars, monks and novices cadging alms, and the ever-persistent kids selling lottery tickets, maps, postcards and books. Another teeming open market fills the streets around Ben Thanh, and surrounding it are shops and boutiques selling home electronics, watches, jewelry, luggage and fashion clothing.

Ham Nghi Market has become one of Saigon's main venues for consumer electronics, its shops and sidewalks piled with Japanese and Taiwanese televisions, video cassette recorders, hi-fi systems and computer equipment. In the streets between Ham Nghi and Nguyen Hue, a sprawling

Central Saigon Mosque, its white minarets making a welcome change from the drab architecture surrounding it; and a number of new tourist bars that have sprouted up around the long-running **Apocalypse Now**. The name may trade on war nostalgia, but it is essentially a place to unwind, and later in the evening let loose — see NIGHTLIFE, page 175.

All main streets in this central downtown area eventually converge on the vast piazza of **Me Linh (Hero) Square** on the Saigon River. The square is dominated by a towering statue of the hero himself, Tran Hung Dao, who led the resistance against the invading Mongols in 1287. On the river itself

ABOVE and OPPOSITE: Saigon street life — as in most cities in Indochina, two wheels get the job done.

are tourist cruise boats, and bordering the river is the elegant **Majestic Hotel**.

From Hero Square you can rent a launch to tour the **Port of Saigon**, cruising among the container ships and something that's quite unique to southern Vietnam — high-prowed lighters and cargo junks with big eyes painted on their bows.

Museums

Nobody, it seems, leaves Saigon without visiting the **War Remnants Museum** (open 7:30 to 11:45 AM and 1:30 to 5 PM daily). This

ing to view the news pictures of the political giants of the Vietnam War — Lyndon B. Johnson, Dean Rusk, Robert McNamara, Ambassador Elsworth Bunker, General William Westmoreland, Presidents Nguyen Cao Ky and Nguyen Van Thieu — and to contemplate how ignominiously they've passed into history since.

Located in what was once Gia Long Palace, the **Museum of Ho Chi Minh City** (open 8:30 to 11:45 AM and 1:30 to 4:30 PM, closed Mondays), on Nguyen Binh Khiem Street, built in 1886, is a shrine to the Com-

complex of old buildings at the intersection of Le Qui Don and Vo Van Tan Streets is an emotionally debilitating exhibition of American and allied atrocities committed during the Vietnam War. The My Lai massacre, the Phoenix Program torture sessions, the Viet Cong suspects being hurled from helicopters — it's all there, presented in room after room of photographic displays. It says nothing, obviously, about Communist atrocities, and it seems a shame that this litany of crime and suffering could not have embraced the mutual savagery and collapse of human values that make all war such a tragedy. But even so, it does present the war from a perspective that few Western viewers will have seen before, and it is interest-

munist triumph, and is an interesting place to visit. Many of the exhibits reek of propaganda, but others hold much interest — look for the models of homes of revolutionary leaders on the second floor or the diorama of the famous Cu Chi Tunnels, also on the second floor.

Also located on Nguyen Binh Khiem Street, at the zoo entrance, the **History Museum** (open 8:30 to 11:45 AM and 1:30 to 4:30 PM daily) makes a welcome change from modern war history, tracing Vietnam's journey from the Bronze Age to the post-1975 era, and includes a research library. Prior to the fall of Saigon it was the National Museum of South Vietnam, built in 1929 by the Société des Études Indochinoises.

The **Reunification Palace** (open 7:30 to 11 AM and 1 to 4:30 PM daily), erected in 1966 with a blend of Western and Asian design influences, lies in sweeping grounds surrounded by a decorative steel fence beyond the public park to the west of Notre Dame Cathedral. It's a significant landmark — it was the Presidential Palace and home of Nguyen Van Thieu from the height of the Vietnam War until Thieu was finally forced from office shortly before the fall of 1975. It's also significant as a symbol of the Communist triumph — television news footage

The **Fine Arts Museum** (open 7:30 to 11:15 AM and 1:30 to 4:30 PM, closed Sunday) somehow amounts to more than the sum of its parts — much of which is fairly dull revolutionary art. The third floor, which features art from the Funan period, is probably of the most interest, but even the ground-floor revolutionary efforts make for interesting viewing, not least insofar as its Vietnamese characteristics differentiate it from the Soviet art most viewers will be more familiar with. To the rear of the building are some commercial galleries

of a tank crashing through the palace's main gates, a Viet Cong soldier rushing to fly the revolutionary flag from its balcony, has now entered history as one of the most remembered scenes of the war. Today the Palace is a tourist attraction and a trade exhibition center. It's a fascinating place to visit, tastefully appointed, littered with the finest in Vietnamese art, and the sense that once history was made here is particularly strong. As for its former residents, Ex-President Nguyen Cao Ky, once famous for his dashing flight-suits, pearl-handled revolvers and equally flamboyant First Lady, ended up running a store in Los Angeles. And Thieu, he died a virtually forgotten recluse in England.

Southern Vietnam

featuring the art of contemporary Vietnamese artists, and in some cases the prices are very reasonable.

Not exactly a museum, but worth a visit all the same, is the **Orchid Farm**, which even has specimens named after Richard Nixon and Joseph Stalin. It is 15 km (nine miles) from downtown Saigon along the highway to the former United States military base at Bien Hoa. Visits can be arranged through your hotel desk or a travel agency, and the best time to go is in January or February, when the plants are in full bloom.

OPPOSITE: A downed United States jet in the Revolutionary Museum, Saigon. ABOVE: Saigon's Ho Chi Minh Memorial lies alongside the Saigon River port.

Temples

A great many Buddhist and Taoist temples can be seen in Saigon and Cholon, some of them neglected and dilapidated, others gleaming with garish renovations. The oldest is the **Giac Lam Pagoda**, northwest of Cholon at 118 Lac Long Quan Street, which was built in 1744 but completely restored in 1900. This temple and the nearby **Giac Vien Pagoda** at 247 Lac Long Quan Street, dating back to the late eighteenth century, both feature a great many relics and images including white statues of the Goddess of Mercy.

Xa Loi Pagoda, at 89 Ba Huyen Thanh Quan Street, north of Ben Thanh Market, is historically interesting because it was here that dissident monks immolated themselves in protest against the Diem regime in the early 1960s. The ritual suicides followed a raid by government forces in 1963 in which the temple's 400 monks and nuns were arrested. Another historical temple is **Tran Hung Dao Temple** at 36 Vo Thi Sau Street, dedicated to the hero of Vietnam's battle to defeat the invading Mongols of China's Yuan Dynasty.

Two much newer temples are the **Dai Giac Pagoda** at 112 Nguyen Van Troi Street on the way to the airport, and the **Vinh Nghiem Pagoda**, built in 1971 with the support of the

Japan-Vietnam Friendship Society, whose eight-story pagoda towers over the suburban sprawl of Nam Ky Khoi Nghia Street.

Among the Chinese temples of Saigon and Cholon, the **Emperor of Jade Pagoda** at 73 Mai Thi Luu Street is the biggest and most opulent. Both Buddhist and Taoist, it was built in 1909 by Saigon's Cantonese community, and its courtyards and three main prayer halls are crowded with images of the divinities, including the Goddess of Mercy, the Sakyamuni Buddha and the Jade Emperor.

The city's Fujianese immigrants built their main shrine, **Phung Son Tu Pagoda**, at 338 Nguyen Cong Tru Street, and it is dedicated not only to the Goddess of Mercy but the Guardian Spirit of Happiness and Virtue as well.

In Cholon, the renowned **Quan Am** at 12 Laos Tu Street is generally recognized as the district's most important shrine, but you'll find a far more picturesque temple, **Thien Hau Pagoda**, dedicated to the Goddess of the Sea, in crowded Nguyen Trai Street. Above the entrance to this small but colorfully restored temple is an elaborate ceramic frieze featuring mandarins, immortals and scenes from the Taoist legends. The main hall is reminiscent of the famous Man Mo Temple in Hong Kong — huge coils of smoking incense hanging from its rafters. Not far from this temple on Nguyen Trai Street, another Chinese place of worship, the **Nghia An Hoi Quan Pagoda** or **Ba Pagoda** features gilded bas-relief wood carvings and images of Ba Thien Hau and the Guardian Spirit of Happiness and Virtue. It was founded in 1760 by Chinese immigrants in thanks for guiding them to Vietnam.

Cholon District

During the Communist Tet Offensive of 1968, the Viet Cong infiltrated Saigon through the urban beehive of Cholon, populated by ethnic Chinese, to the west of the downtown area. When you see its densely crowded streets you'll appreciate why. Cholon isn't just a hum of activity, it's more like a full-scale orchestra, and you may find yourself exhausted after a couple of hours battling

ABOVE: The entrance to Thien Hau Temple in Cholon. OPPOSITE: Street vendors outside Saigon's Mariammam Hindu Temple.

its traffic and pedestrians. Chinese immigrants began setting up shop here in 1778. As with most expatriate Chinese communities in Southeast Asia, they have suffered their share of discrimination in times of nationalist fervor. During the Vietnam War many were regarded as profiteers, and they came under a certain amount of repression after 1975. Many fled Vietnam, making up a large percentage of the boat people who made it to Hong Kong. However, their value to Vietnam's economic revival has put them back in favor today: it's estimated that

since a Hong Kong investor revived the weekly races in 1991. But don't expect anything as grand as Kentucky or Ascot: the horses look underfed, the jockeys are preteen boys and the race goers are usually the city's poorer people — laborers and cyclo drivers. However, it's a quirky otherworldly sort of entertainment and certainly offers a different day, and if you decide on a flutter of your own, the bets are generally just a few hundred *dong*. Races are held every Saturday afternoon. The track is located north of Cholon near Ho Ky Hoa Park.

for every dollar in foreign investment that comes into Vietnam, two dollars is brought in unofficially by the people of Cholon through family contacts in Hong Kong, Taiwan and other Asian countries.

Hung Vuong and **Chau Van Liem Boulevards** are the central thoroughfares of Cholon, and the district's most crowded spots are the renovated and colorful **Binh Tay Market** and the nearby long-distance bus station. The district has a great many Chinese restaurants, some of which are worth visiting. The tumult of Cholon makes a great daytrip by cyclo, taxi or, if you are fearless, by motorcycle taxi. The old racetrack and the bare, concrete, time-worn grandstand of **Saigon Racecourse** have sprung back to life

WHERE TO STAY

Saigon has Vietnam's widest range of accommodation, but it is luxury travelers who are best served. Bear in mind that the frantic hotel boom of the early 1990s created a glut of rooms in Saigon, meaning that substantial discounts are often available for those who ask, and in the case of the better hotels, for those who book online or through an agency.

Expensive

Several top-line hotel chains that were slated to open hotels in Saigon have yet to open their doors, among them Hyatt WEB SITE www.hyatt.com and Ramada WEB SITE www

.ramadahotels.com. Check with the respective web sites for the latest information.

Recommending the best of Saigon's hotels is a tough proposition, as none completely fit the bill. For many travelers, however, despite the fact it is not perfect, the **Hotel Continental** ((08) 829-4456 FAX (08) 824-1772 E-MAIL continental@hcm.vnn.vn WEB SITE http://continental-saigon.com, 132 Dong Khoi Street, District 1, is the first choice, if only for nostalgic reasons. The location in the center of town is a definite plus, and while the latest restoration job, carried out on the colonial-era building in 1989 by Saigon Tourist, could have been done in grander style, the hotel still has a lot going for it. Standard rooms start at a very reasonable US$60, but it's worth booking a suite, which cost from US$120. The hotel has just 84 rooms, so advance bookings are essential.

In a similar category is the **Rex Hotel** ((08) 829 2185 FAX (08) 829-6536 E-MAIL rex hotel@hcm.vnn.vn WEB SITE www.rexhotel vietnam.com, 141 Nguyen Hue Street. Renovations have failed to drag this old hotel into the twenty-first century, but then this is part of its charm. If it is international standards you are looking for, however, this is probably not the best bet. The less expensive "superior rooms," which start at US$55, are a little tacky. On the plus side, the hotel has a definite Vietnamese ambiance, helpful staff and excellent food in its restaurants.

The 280-room **Hotel Sofitel Plaza Saigon** ((08) 824-1555 FAX (08) 824-1666 E-MAIL sales saigon@accor-hotel-vietnam.com WEB SITE http://accor-hotel-vietnam.com/sofitel-plazasaigon, 17 Le Duan, District 1, is a reliable top-end choice, even if the hotel is somewhat lacking in a distinctive style. It has a good central location and all the amenities you would expect, and room rates range from US$160 to US$350.

Saigon's biggest, if not best, hotel is the **New World Hotel** ((08) 822-8888 FAX (08) 823-0710 E-MAIL nwhs@hcm.vn.vn WEB SITE www.newworldvietnam.com, 76 Le Loi. Its executive floors are very highly rated, coming with a host of personalized services, and are reasonably priced, starting at just under US$100.

The latest arrival on the top-end hotel scene is the **Renaissance Riverside Hotel**

((08) 822-0033 FAX (08) 823-5666 WEB SITE www .renaissancehotels.com, 8-15 Ton Duc Thang Street, District 1, a deluxe 21-story structure that, as the name suggests, enjoys views of the river. With tastefully appointed colonial-era rooms and one of the largest swimming pools in town, it looks set to become one of Saigon's most popular luxury hotels. Rates range from around US$110.

Moderate

Some of the expensive hotels listed above — notably the Continental and the Rex —

have moderately priced rooms that allow travelers to enjoy near international standard amenities at affordable rates.

The popular **Palace Hotel** ((08) 829-2860 FAX (08) 824-4230 E-MAIL palace@hcm.vnn.vn, 56-66 Nguyen Hue Street, charges from US$60 to US$140, but substantial discounts are available if you book through an agency or an Internet site such as WEB SITE www .asia-hotels.com. The hotel has a somewhat dated air, but there is little to complain about in terms of its location or its rooms — the restaurants lack atmosphere and are better avoided for other eateries around town.

Seldom used by Western visitors to Saigon, the **Pastel Inn** ((08) 822-8222 FAX (08) 822-8242 E-MAIL pastel@hcm.vnn.vn WEB SITE www1.sphere.ne.jp/yamachi/ pastelinneng.htm, 99 Pasteur Street, District 1, can be recommended as a stylish mini-hotel with exceptionally good value rooms from US$30. It's mostly used by Japanese

OPPOSITE: Worshipers at the main altar of the Jade Pagoda. ABOVE: The Continental Hotel offers a breath of nostalgia along with comfortably chic rooms.

visitors, which explains the ground-floor karaoke parlor, but don't let this put you off — the Pastel is one of Saigon's best moderately priced hotels.

The **Bong Seng Hotel** ((08) 829-1516 FAX (08) 829-8076, 119-123 Dong Khoi Street, is hard to beat in terms of location, and it also delivers in its service and facilities. Many repeat visitors to Saigon swear by the place. Complete with a business center, sauna and fitness center, rooms range from US$60, but can be booked with discounts of 40 percent or more through Internet booking sites such as WEB SITE www.asia-hotels.com.

Inexpensive

The Pham Ngu Lao area is the place for budget accommodation. One of the best around is the **Lan Anh Hotel** ((08) 836-5197 FAX (08) 836-7394 E-MAIL lan-anh-hotel@hcm .vnn.vn WEB SITE http://1saigon.net/lananh/, 252 De Tham Street, District 1, a delightful family-run establishment with impeccably maintained rooms with a fan from US$8 and air-conditioned rooms from US$15.

More expensive but excellent value all the same is **Hoang Ha Hotel** ((08) 844-3781 FAX (08) 844-3645 WEB SITE www.1saigon.net/ hoanghahotel, 51 Truong Quoc Dung Street, a charming mini-hotel in which all rooms are equipped with mini-bars, IDD phones, satellite television and air conditioning. Rooms cost US$20 to US$44, and they even have a small but efficient business center.

Lastly, **Guesthouse 127** ((08) 836-8761 FAX (08) 836-0658 E-MAIL guesthouse127 @bdvn.vnd.net WEB SITE www.1saigon.net/ guesthouse127, 127 Cong Quynh Street, District 1, has made itself very popular with the backpacker set on account of its friendly service, well-kept rooms and reasonable prices. A lot of the rooms are a little dark, and furnishings are basic, but for US$15 a night for a basic double they are good value.

WHERE TO EAT

Food is where Saigon comes into its own. The city has an abundance of good restaurants, and not just those in the five-star hotels listed above — though any of them is a good place to start looking if you want a splash out meal of international standards.

Some places are worth visiting simply for their historical associations. Probably top of the list on this front — although the food is nothing to get particularly excited about — is the **Givral Café and Pâtisserie** ((08) 829-4727, 169 Dong Khoi Street. It faces the Opera and is run by charming old Frenchified Vietnamese retainers who look to have been there since the 1960s at least. Apart from its cakes, pastries and coffee (excellent), a diverse selection of Western, Chinese and Vietnamese dishes is available — they're more suitable for a light lunch than dinner.

In a similar vein is **La Bibliothèque** ((08) 823 1438, 84A Nguyen Du Street, which is another Saigon institution. An elegant French/Vietnamese restaurant, it is run by Madame Nguyen Phuoc Dai, a former lawyer and member of the Wartime National Assembly, in her villa close to Notre Dame Cathedral. The dining room itself is set in what was once her library — guests eat surrounded by shelves packed with old law books. A meal here shouldn't come to more than around US$8 per head.

The ornate, neon-lit **Maxim's Dinner Theater** ((08) 829-6676, 15 Dong Khoi Street, almost next door to the Majestic Hotel, is another must-visit oddity with an overwhelmingly extensive Continental and Chinese menu, live pop music, singing divas and traditional musicians. Prices are very reasonable, averaging at US$5–6 per head.

A number of new arrivals are challenging the oldies, and one such is **Club-Restaurant Camargue** ((08) 824-3148, 16 Cao Ba Quat, District 1, in which French nouvelle cuisine is served in a wonderful alfresco French villa setting right in the heart of town. Reckon on around US$20 per head, perhaps more if you dip into the restaurant's very good wine list.

Augustin ((08) 829-2941, 10 Nguyen Thiep, is not quite in the same league, but is nevertheless an excellent place for a French meal. Next door at 6 Nguyen Hue Street is **Globo Café** ((08) 822-8855, a hip eatery with an Italian chef and fine woodfired pizzas.

OPPOSITE TOP: The Rex Hotel roof garden, formerly a United States officer's mess. BOTTOM: The Rex Hotel reception area.

For Vietnamese cuisine, **Nam Giao** ((08) 825-0261, 136/15 Le Thanh Ton, District 1, is a wonderful, inexpensive Hue-style restaurant. The specialty of the house is the *banh beo*, a rice-powder and shrimp dish. It's possible to eat a superb meal here for just a few dollars per head. Slightly more up-market and popular with tour groups is **Ancient Town**, or **Pho Xua** ((08) 829-9625, 211 Dien Bien Phu, District 3, which often features live jazz in its alfresco courtyard, and serves delicious regional Vietnamese cuisine. The restaurant is housed in a charmingly converted

when Bill Clinton popped in for a bowl of noodles during his November 2000 Vietnam visit. There is a branch at 1–3 Phan Chu Trinh, next to Ben Tanh Market, along with several others in District 1.

Saigon dining is not limited to Vietnamese and French cuisines. **Ashoka** ((08) 823-1372, 17/10 Le Thanh Ton, District 1, is a long-running (by Saigon standards) Indian restaurant that specializes in northern cuisine and has a traditional tandoori clay oven. The lunch buffet, at around US$8 per head, is recommended.

villa; prices average around US$10 per head. Similarly up-market Vietnamese cuisine can be sampled at **Lemongrass** ((08) 822-0496, 4 Nguyen Thiep, District 1, a classy three-story building with traditional live music nightly and chic decor. An evening meal here will cost around US$10 to US$15.

For Vietnamese cuisine on the trot, keep your eyes peeled for branches of **Pho 2000** around town. Alain Tran, a local restaurateur, opened the chain to celebrate Vietnam's national noodle soup dish, and many who have dined at a branch, say it serves the best *pho* they ate on their Vietnam trip. The media have dubbed the chain, "Vietnam's answer to McDonald's," and the inexpensive diners got a further publicity boost

The Pham Ngu Lao area is the place to look for inexpensive cafés. The prices are right, they're good places to get travel information and meet other travelers, and often the food is not too bad either. A long-runner, with an interesting mix of vegetarian, Vietnamese and international favorites on its menu is the **Kim Café** ((08) 835-9859, 270 De Tham. If you want to see where it all started, take a stroll over to the **Sinh Café** ((08) 836-7338, 248 De Tham, where the Vietnam travelers' café scene kicked off. It still does a steady business, though the food is not wildly exciting. For breakfast, everybody seems to head to the **Saigon Café**, 195 Pham Ngu Lao, which is popular for its croissants, eggs and coffee.

NIGHTLIFE

Saigon is where Vietnam gets hip. Hanoi might frown on decadent nocturnal activities, but in Saigon the bad old days have returned. **Apocalypse Now** ((08) 824-1463, 2C Thi Sach, District 1, is perhaps definitive of Saigon's more liberal approach to nightlife — it has none of the chic of some of the newer watering holes around town, and can be very quiet in the early hours of the evening, but after midnight becomes

HOW TO GET THERE

Saigon is Vietnam's main entry point for foreign visitors, and those who arrive by air will find the city's Tan Son Nhat Airport surprisingly convenient by Asian standards. Just seven kilometers (four miles) from the city center, the drive into town shouldn't cost much more than US$5 with a metered taxi. The Skybus service goes to the Vietnam Airlines office on Nguyen Hue Street and costs US$2, which means if there's more

a heaving party nightly, with ex-pats, backpackers, tourists and ladies of the night rubbing shoulders and clinking drinks, among other things.

Less raucous, and very much more upmarket, is **Saigon Saigon** ((08) 823-4999, on the tenth floor of the Caravelle Hotel, 19 Lam Son Square, District 1. It is an elegant place for an evening drink, and rightly celebrated for its splendid views of the Saigon neon. Another good place for an early evening drink, **Underground** ((08) 829-9079, 69 Dong Khoi Street, District 1, in the basement of Lucky Plaza, is a hip bar with one of the most impressive cocktail menus in town and not a bad selection of bar food either — the pizzas are recommended.

than one of you it's almost as cheap to grab a cab and go straight to your destination. Getting out to the airport is slightly cheaper by taxi — make sure the meter is working or haggle for a decent price.

A reasonably popular way of approaching and leaving Saigon, though mostly with budget travelers, is the land crossing to Cambodia at Moc Bai. The best way to do it is with a rental taxi — easily organized at any of the travelers' cafés (see WHERE TO EAT, above) — which should cost around US$20. You will need to rent another taxi on the

Contrast of color and commerce — OPPOSITE LEFT: Vung Tau's Seabreeze Hotel and RIGHT Saigon's Hotel Continental. ABOVE LEFT AND RIGHT: The Cao Dai Holy See in Long Hoa, north of Saigon.

other side of the border. It's something of a rough trip — the roads are bad — but it's possible to make the entire journey from Saigon to Phnom Penh in around five to six hours if there are no hold-ups (as in customs problems) at the border. Buses run the entire route, but they are only recommended for the truly destitute.

The travelers' cafés in the Pham Ngu Lao area all seem to advertise the "open tickets" that have become extremely popular, not just with budget travelers but also with better-off solo travelers. The Open Tour Bus service essentially allows you to travel all the way to Hanoi in a luxury bus with unlimited stopovers for as long as you like at any of the designated stops along the way — for first-time visitors to Vietnam this provides a trouble-free and inexpensive way to see the best the country has to offer, and is highly recommended. Vietnam's regular buses are overcrowded and dangerous.

Saigon's train station is at 1 Nguyen Thong, District 3, but there is no need to go there to book tickets. Most travel agencies around town can book this for you. Be aware, however, that at short-notice demand usually exceeds supply, and it is essential you book in advance. The fastest way to travel by train to Hanoi is on the *Reunification Express*, which leaves Saigon seven times daily.

AROUND SAIGON

PHAN THIET

Two hundred kilometers (124 miles) east of Saigon, Phan Thiet has been rapidly gaining in popularity the last few years, and for good reason — it is a more attractive alternative to Vung Tau in the south. For the traveler, it makes a fine stop-off for an overnight stay, half way between Saigon and Nha Trang along the coast road. Apart from a beach, there is also a fishing port nearby, so good seafood is assured, as are plentiful supplies of pungent *nuoc mam* fish sauce from the nearby factories. Four kilometers (two and a half miles) to the northeast of town, near the beach at Pho Hai, is an eighth-century Cham tower, marking the southernmost extent of the Champa Kingdom. The triple tower shows a strong Khmer influence.

Several good beaches are in the vicinity, and the Victoria Hotel Group has an up-market chalet-style hotel here: the **Victoria Phan Thiet Resort** ((062) 847170 FAX (062) 847174 E-MAIL victoriapt@hcm.vnn.vn WEB SITE http://victoriahotels-asia.com/english/pthiet.htm, km9 Phu Hai, Phan Thiet. The thatched-roof bungalows — beautifully appointed — start at US$115, but substantial discounts are available for those who book online.

The **Novotel Phan Thiet** ((062) 822393 FAX (062) 825682 E-MAIL salesphanthiet@accor-hotel-vietnam.com WEB SITE http://accor-hotel-vietnam.com/novotel-oceandunes, 1 Ton Duc Thang Street, Phan Thiet, is adjacent to the **Ocean Dunes Golf Club** ((08) 8243749. Golf packages are available at discounted rates from the hotel's web site. Rates range from US$120 to US$180.

The original resort operation in the area stretches along nearby Mui Ne Beach, a stunning 20-km (12.4-mile) strip of sand. The **Coco Beach-Hai Duong Resort** ((062) 847111 FAX (062) 847115 E-MAIL paradise@cocobeach.net WEB SITE www.cocobeach.net, km12.5 Ham Tien, Village 3, Phan Thiet, is a beautiful set-up that somehow manages to avoid the worst excesses of resort developments. The bungalows all face the sea and come equipped with mini-bars and IDD phones. Bungalow rates are US$65 low season, US$85 high season (mid-November to the end of April).

VUNG TAU

Once known as Cap Saint Jacques, Vung Tau's erstwhile colonial charm has been compromised in recent years by its status as a special economic zone and a center of southern Vietnam's oil exploration industry. In fact, it's shaping up to be to Saigon what Pattaya is to Bangkok — a getaway beach resort where life is a party. But, as is the case at Pattaya, the beaches are not that good. Vung Tau makes up for this with a thriving fishing port, a couple of good Buddhist temples and some fine seafood restaurants. It also makes for a relaxing daytrip out of Saigon — a 128-km (79-mile) drive

Flamboyant midday mass at the bizarre Cao Dai Temple in Tay Ninh.

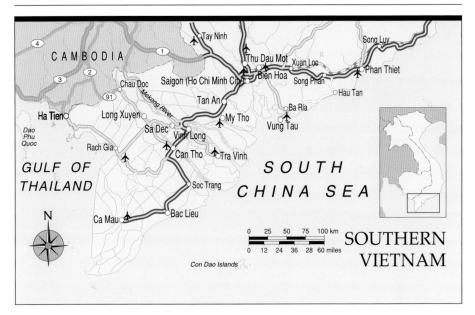

through lush farmland and bustling rural villages, or a one-and-a-half-hour air-conditioned hydrofoil trip. The hydrofoils leave from Vina Express ((08) 829-7892, 6-8A Nguyen Tat Thanh Street, District 4, in Saigon four times daily.

A stroll around the Vung Tau peninsula, from **Front Beach** (Bai Truoc) to **Back Beach** (Bai Sau), takes in just about everything of any note, including the old Russian compound where Soviet oil workers were housed until most of their Vietsovpetro leases were transferred to Western companies after the collapse of the Cold War. The fishing fleet moors at Front Beach, which is fringed with tall coconut palms — a marvelously picturesque spot. A huge **statue of Jesus Christ**, erected in 1974 at the southern tip of the peninsula, is a must see — after you fight your way though the beggars along the steps, the view from the top is unbeatable.

Vung Tau's prime attraction is the **Niet Ban Tinh Xa temple**, on the waterfront between Front Beach and the statue, which features a fairly spectacular reclining Buddha and a huge bronze bell on its roof. In short, Vung Tau is a welcome break from Saigon, a place for relaxation and people-watching but nothing much to write home about. Those who want to relax at a beach resort are better off heading north to Phan Thiet or to Nha Trang.

Where to Stay and Eat

The renovated villa housing the **Petro House Hotel** ((064) 852 014 FAX (064) 852015 E-MAIL petro.htl@hcm.vnn.vn WEB SITE www.vnhotels .net/petrohouse_hotel/petrohouse_ hotel.html, 63 Tran Hung Dao, may not be the top star-rated place in Vung Tau, but it's a charming place that deserves a special mention. It calls itself a "boutique hotel," and in all honesty there's something to be said for the description. The swimming pool in the inner courtyard is a lovely touch, and the well-appointed rooms are great value at between US$30 and US$70.

The 53-room **Royal Hotel** ((064) 859852 FAX (064) 859851 E-MAIL rht@hcm.vnn.vn, 36 Quang Trung, is more representative of Vung Tau's "better" establishments. While it has a good location on the beachfront, the rooms are somewhat uninspired and difficult to justify paying rates of US$100 and upwards for.

Set in expansive parklands, the **Anoasis Long Hai Resort** ((064) 868227 FAX (064) 868229 E-MAIL anoasisresort@hcm.vnn.vn WEB SITE www.anoasisresort.com.vn, Long Hai Ba Ria, Vung Tau, has quite charming "cottage bungalows" from around US$100 midweek, and US$120 on weekends.

A good value option is the **Southeast Asia Hotel** ((064) 859412 FAX (064) 853630, 249 Le Hong Phong, an older but well-maintained operation that has rooms ranging from US$11 to US$20.

The Front Beach has a number of cafés and restaurants, many of them specializing in seafood, and at Nos. 11 and 31 Thuy Van Street at Back Beach are two more seafood restaurants.

TAY NINH

Notwithstanding the beauty of the delta region, it's to the north of Saigon that you will find one of southern Vietnam's most fascinating cultural oddities. Tay Ninh, located three hours by road to the northwest, right on the Cambodian border, is the center for a unique cultural spectacle, the **Cao Dai**. This religious sect, founded in 1926, embraces various religions — mixing Christianity, Buddhism, Islam, Confucianism and even Taoism into its creed and featuring a priesthood and structure based on the Roman Catholic Church. Its most revered symbol is the "divine eye," which may or may not have been borrowed from Tibetan Buddhism, but is found on all Cao Dai temples in Tay Ninh province and the Mekong Delta. The eye is the focal point of the sect's spectacular **Great Temple** at Long Hoa, four kilometers (two-and-a-half miles) from Tay Ninh city, where extravagantly costumed services are held four times each day, beginning at 6 AM. But, whether it's becoming a tourist attraction or not, a Cao Dai service remains something to behold — massed ranks of cardinals, priests and white-robed male and female clergy parade into the vast, pillared and opulently decorated hall of the Great Temple to pray before the altar and divine eye to the chant of choirs and the rattle and chop of wooden instruments.

The Cao Dai lay-women are friendly and only too willing to explain the principles and rituals of Cao Daism to you before the services begin. Tay Ninh itself enjoys an interesting location and contemporary history. With Cambodian territory bordering it on three sides, and the southern end of the Ho Chi Minh Trail nearby, the tunnels of Cu Chi and beyond were part of the whole Viet Cong network. A key United States Special Forces base was established here to monitor the end of the Ho Chi Minh Trail during the war. It also came under the pressure of Khmer Rouge border attacks before Vietnam invaded its neighbor in 1979.

Tay Ninh is another daytrip from Saigon, very easy to reach along a highway, which passes through delightful rural scenery — it can easily be combined with the Cu Chi Tunnels, and for those who take a tour out of Saigon it almost certainly will be.

CU CHI TUNNELS

The famous tunnels of Cu Chi, the vast underground network from which the Viet Cong fought in the Vietnam War, have now taken their place among the great wonders of military lore. They're also one of the prime tourist attractions of the Saigon environs. Although only a small section of what was once a 200-km (124-mile) labyrinth of tunnels, staging camps, hospitals and operations bunkers is actually open to the public today, this is still quite enough to get a sense of how the Vietnamese retreated beneath ground to evade American bombing, defoliation and search-and-destroy missions.

The tunnels have been widened slightly to accommodate bulky Westerners, and if you venture down you will no doubt be glad for it. The guides are mostly Vietnamese soldiers, and along with the tunnels themselves they provide a fascinating glimpse of a war most of us have only read about or seen in Hollywood productions.

The Tunnels of Cu Chi by Tom Mangold and John Penycate (Random House, New York, 1985) offers a good insight into life as it was lived beneath the earth's surface, and details many of the ingenious devices employed, not only to stay alive, but also to win battles.

THE MEKONG DELTA

For some, the Mekong Delta is the heart of Vietnam, a major rice bowl and source of magnificent rural scenery. The Vietnamese call the Mekong River *Song Cuu Long* — River of the Nine Dragons — and its vast delta, culminating a 4,500-km (2,800-mile) journey from the Tibetan plateau, is the nation's richest agricultural area. After flowing down through Laos and Cambodia, the river divides into two main arms at Phnom Penh. As they reach the delta, the upper arm flows into the South China Sea at Vinh Long and the lower at Can Tho. In the rainy season from May to October, the entire delta region is virtually a lake, the river's various arms and tributaries flooding the rice fields as far as the eye can see. In the dry season it's a dazzling sheet of green or gold, depending on the progress of the crop, punctuated by tiny communities hidden in copses of tall palms.

The towns along its banks, and their busy markets, bring this vast waterway alive — and nowhere is this more evident than in the Mekong Delta. There are a great many interesting delta towns: how many you visit all depends on time.

MY THO

My Tho is the closest delta town to Saigon — just 70 km (43 miles) away — and for those who travel by road, the trip itself is perhaps more interesting than the destination. From the moment Saigon's suburbs recede, the road passes through rural areas so pretty it is like driving through a well-kept garden — the ricefields dotted with communities and white ancestral stone tombs. Alternatively, an air-conditioned hydrofoil ferry leaves Saigon at 7:30 AM every day and takes two hours to reach My Tho before continuing on to Can Tho.

Once there, there's not much to see except the exceptionally large and lively **Central Market**, the 100-year-old **Catholic Church** and the **Mekong riverfront**, which is home to a small Chinese community. My Tho's main attraction is **Vinh Trang Pagoda**, which is a short way east of town. It's a picturesque place inhabited by monks, built in an eclectic East-meets-West style in the early nineteenth century.

Many visitors, however, elect to take a Mekong boat trip out of My Tho rather than explore the town itself. Boats can be rented for an idle afternoon of aimless exploration, or it's possible to take chartered boats or public ferries to delta islands.

Probably the most interesting of the islands is **Phung Island**, home to an obscure cult founded by the so-called "Coconut Monk." **Than Long** and **Thoi Son Islands** are scenic enough, but offer nothing in the way of cultural attractions.

For most travelers, My Tho is a daytrip out of Saigon or a stopover on a longer tour of the delta. Accommodation is basic, to say the least, and the only place really worth considering for an overnight stay is the **Chuong Duong Hotel (** (073) 870875 FAX (073) 870876, on 30/4 Street at No. 10, My Tho, which has well maintained mid-range rooms from US$20 to US$30.

CAN THO

The administrative capital of the delta, the bustling and energetic town of Can Tho is surprisingly cosmopolitan — the city was home to thousands of American GIs during the war years. It is located 104 km (65 miles) south of My Tho and is well worth a few days' visit, making a good base to explore the surrounding area.

It's a rough five-hour trip by road from Saigon to Can Tho, with two ferry crossings. Small surprise then that most people elect to take the air-conditioned hydrofoil, which also stops at My Tho en-route. Try to avoid the tours that travel here with everyone cramped into the back of a minibus. It is far better to arrive by hydrofoil and to arrange boat trips on arrival. Enterprising women accost visitors with pictures and glowing recommendations of their tours as they disembark the hydrofoil, and renting a boat is easily done. Short tours can be booked from the **Can Tho Tourist Company (** (071) 821854 FAX (071) 822719, 20 Hai Ba Trung.

The **Ho Chi Minh Museum** on Hoa Binh has pretty eccentric opening hours (essentially, it is closed on Mondays and Wednesdays, and weekend afternoons, and at lunchtimes) and is probably not really of great interest to anyone who has

---

TOP: A woman rows her sampan to market near Can Tho in the Mekong Delta. BOTTOM: Fishing boats and boatyards on the river at Rach Gia in the Mekong Delta. OVERLEAF: The magnificent Munirangsyaram Pagoda at My Tho.

already done tours of war-related museums elsewhere in Vietnam. It is historically very significant for the Vietnamese, as Can Tho was the last southern city to fall to North Vietnamese troops and has thus become synonymous with reunification.

Things to see include the distinctive Khmer Buddhist temple, the **Munirang-syaram Pagoda**, on Huo Binh Boulevard, which is home to a small community of monks. The sprawling **Central Market** in the center of town is another key attraction.

The best hotel by far in Can Tho is the new **Victoria Can Tho Hotel** ((071) 810111 FAX (071) 829259 E-MAIL victoriact@hcm.vnn.vn WEB SITE http://victoriahotels-asia.com/ english/h_cantho.htm, Cai Khe Ward, Can Tho, an impressive resort-style hotel with a fabulous swimming pool and a modern colonial ambiance to its rooms. Rates range from around US$100 to US$175, but discounts are available if you book online.

The 40-room **International Hotel** ((071) 822079, 10-12 Hai Ba Trung, overlooking the river, is a poor second choice, and given its rates of around US$70 and upwards, not a great deal cheaper.

The **Ninh Kieu Hotel** ((071) 824583, 2 Hai Ba Trung, is a popular place to stay with budget and mid-range travelers. It overlooks the river, close to the jetty, and has comfortable rooms from US$20.

LONG XUYEN

Located upriver to the north of Can Tho, the provincial capital and transport hub of Long Xuyen is more interesting historically than as a tourist destination. Up until the stirrings of the Vietnam War, it was the center of an armed religious sect called the Hoa Hao, which rejected churches or temples and the priesthood, which probably accounts for Long Xuyen's singular lack of cultural attractions today. The city's main showpiece was built in 1973, a huge **Catholic Church** that can accommodate 1,000 worshipers. In event of an overnight stay, the **Long Xuyen Hotel** ((076) 841927 FAX (076) 842483, 17 Nguyen Van Cung, is the city's best, with air-conditioned rooms for US$25 a night. Cheaper non-air-conditioned rooms are also available.

CHAU DOC

Lying not far from the Cambodian border, at the confluence of three rivers, the small town of Chau Doc is known as a trading and pilgrimage center. Long under Khmer control, there is still a sizeable Khmer community here, and it was Khmer Rouge intrusions into the area that led to the Vietnamese invasion of Cambodia.

Just under five kilometers (three miles) southwest of town is **Sam Mountain**, a famous Buddhist center with many temples and grottoes around its slopes. **Tay An Pagoda**, at the foot of the mountain, is the most famous and as a result is something of a tourist trap — it's unlikely you will be left alone for a moment if you visit. Halfway up the mountain, on a track, **Cavern Pagoda** is worth a look.

Chau Doc is also notable as the main access point to **Tan Chau**, a famous silk weaving district.

The best hotel in town is the **Victoria Chau Doc Hotel** ((076) 865010 FAX (076) 865020 E-MAIL victoriachaudoc@hcm.vnn.vn WEB SITE www.victoriahotels-asia.com/ english/h_chdoc.htm, 32 Le Loi Street, Chau Doc Town. This hotel is linked with the Victoria Hotel in Can Tho by the so-called Victoria Sprite, a cruise motorboat that travels as far as Saigon, should guests be willing to pay for the service. Like its sister operation in Can Tho, this outfit is superbly done and features all modern amenities, a swimming pool, and well-appointed, atmospheric rooms; rates start at US$85 and range up to US$155. Discounts are available for online bookings.

The very pleasant **Hang Chau Hotel** ((076) 866 196 FAX (076) 867773, 32 Le Loi Street, has rooms with balconies that overlook the river confluence, and makes a less expensive alternative to the Victoria, with rooms from US$15.

Chau Doc is now easily reached from Saigon by a five-hour hydrofoil trip. The hydrofoils are operated by **Proshipper** ((08) 826 3201, at the river end of Nguyen Hue in Saigon. The service leaves three

Young worshipers in the Tay An Pagoda at Chau Doc.

times a week, on Tuesdays, Thursdays and Saturdays, and returns to Saigon on the following days.

THE ISLANDS

Phu Quoc

Beyond the delta towns, the island of Phu Quoc beckons. See it before it gets too popular — already a small but steady crowd trickles down there, and some stay for weeks. Phu Quoc has great potential — a mountainous, forested island in the Gulf of Thailand, 15 km (nine miles) south of the Cambodian border, with long unspoiled beaches and coral diving spots.

At one time the island held 30,000 to 40,000 prisoners, but its days as a penitentiary are done, and now it is setting its sights on the tourist market. There is still a heavy military presence here, however. The island is served by Vietnam Airlines, with nine flights a week from Saigon landing at the main airport in the center of the island near the town of Duang Dong.

Whether you book or not, there will be hotel representatives at the airport to meet the plane and organize transport. A daily ferry runs from Rach Gia to the south of the island and the fishing town of Cay Dua, a very pleasant six-hour voyage. From Cay Dua it costs around US$5 for a motorcycle to take you to one of the resorts or to Duong Dong. If taking the boat, don't forget to bring along snacks, a good book and, if possible, a hammock.

Representative of how things are likely to shape up on Phu Quoc is the new **Saigon-Phu Quoc Resort** ((077) 846999 FAX (077) 847163 E-MAIL sgphuquocresort@hcm.vnn.vn WEB SITE www.saigon-tourist.com/saigon-phuquoc, Duong Dong Town, Phu Quoc. Complete with a large swimming pool, expansive, leafy grounds, restaurants, bars and a wide range of villas to suit almost all budgets, it's as close as Vietnam comes to southern Thailand; rates range from US$22 to US$130.

The **Tropicana Resort** ((077) 847127 FAX (077) 847128, Duong To, Duong Dong, is a much smaller operation, but for some this will be an advantage; advance book-

ings are essential. The nine bungalows here start at US$35, though there are also some cheaper rooms available.

The concrete, government-run **Huong Bien Hotel** ((077) 846050, on the outskirts of Duong Dong town, overlooks the sea, and has rooms from US$20, but is best skipped in favor of one of the resorts.

Con Dau Islands

With its fine white sand beaches, turquoise waters, coral reefs and forests, this group of 14 islands located 180 km (112 miles) southeast of Vung Tau in the South China Sea, is just beginning to attract tourists after years of notoriety as a very tough penal colony. The main island, **Con Son**, was used as a prison

for political dissidents by the French, and then by the United States-backed Saigon government during the war. The inhumane conditions of incarceration are illustrated in its Revolutionary Museum. You can also visit the former prison buildings.

Home to dozens of varieties of endangered species of birds and sea turtles, the island has recently been conferred national park status. It is linked with Saigon by a Russian helicopter service operated by Vietnam Airlines (the round trip costs US$150). The alternative is a 12-hour boat ride from Vung Tau.

The best place to stay is on Con Son is the **Saigon-Con Dao Resort** ((064) 830336 FAX (064) 830335 E-MAIL sgtcd@hcm.vnn.vn WEB SITE www.saigon-tourist.com/hotels/

condao/condao_info.htm, 18 Ton Duc Thang Street, Con Dao. Despite modern amenities like IDD phones, and recreational facilities such as a swimming pool and tennis courts, there's an Old World feel to this resort, and it caters more to Vietnamese holiday-goers than to foreigners. The 27 rooms are housed in five villas, and rates start at US$35.

Ho Chi Minh City Heliport ((08) 884-8814, 286 Hoang Hoa Tham, sells helicopter tickets to Con Dao. **Fiditourist** ((064) 8296264, 73-79 Dong Khoi, also sells tickets, but for US$5 extra.

The fishing boat dock on Phu Quoc harbor is awash with color and activity .

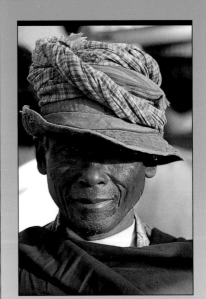

Cambodia

A few years ago, Cambodia looked like a country under a bad spell, the wild card of travel and tourism in Indochina. Despite the demise of Pol Pot and his Khmer Rouge, Cambodia seemed to be slipping further into anarchy. Today, the tides of chaos have mostly receded — it would be foolish to pretend that the country is now an oasis of calm — and Cambodia looks set to put itself on the tourism map. Increasing numbers of visitors are discovering the hospitality of the Khmer people and their fascinating historical legacy, which has granted them Southeast Asia's premier cultural tourist attraction in the Angkor Wat complex near Siem Reap.

That said, it would still be wise to check the situation in Cambodia before visiting. Chances are, however, given the developments of the last couple of years, the news will be good.

In the pioneering days of Cambodia travel, the loop was essentially Phnom Penh followed by Siem Reap, where visitors would spend several days to a week exploring Angkor Wat. Little has changed, except that now, with direct international air links to Siem Reap finally becoming a reality, more and more people are making the famous temple complex their only Cambodian destination. This is something of a pity, as Cambodia has a lot to offer. Even much maligned Phnom Penh easily has enough attractions, restaurants and nightlife to fill a busy three or four days.

PHNOM PENH

Phnom Penh has received more bad press than any other city in Indochina, perhaps all of Asia, but the reality is that it is not without charm. Like Hanoi, much of the old French colonial architecture lingers — moldering perhaps, but in style — and there is a bustle to the city today that wins many skeptical visitors over. A civic beautification project is slowly bringing some grandeur to the city's riverfront, which has vast potential. Around town, colonial villas are being refurbished and put to commercial uses, much as they have in Hanoi and Saigon.

Phnom Penh also has some of Indochina's best hotels — the Hotel Le Royal has been renovated to five-star standards by Singapore's Raffles Group, the Intercontinental has a new property, the Sofitel Cambodiana is a major presence, and other hotels like the Royal Phnom Penh are very attractive.

Nevertheless, Phnom Penh is still something of a rough-and-tumble cowboy town. Anyone who chooses to explore the city's nightlife, or the seedier parts of town, will no doubt find much to lament. But there is also much to celebrate. Given the country's recent history, Phnom Penh has bounced back and is looking ahead.

GENERAL INFORMATION

Despite the fact that tourism is playing an increasingly large role in Cambodia's economic recovery, government tourist offices are thin on the ground and provide only limited information to visitors. Most travelers rely on their guesthouses or hotels for information. The information desk at Phnom Penh's Pochentong Airport is open for most incoming flights (it seems to have variable opening hours) and can direct new arrivals

OPPOSITE: The Cambodian national flag flies from the Foreign Affairs Ministry in Phnom Penh. ABOVE: Traditional music and dance are staged for visitors at the School of Fine Arts near the National Museum.

to the taxi ramp and recommend a limited number of hotels around town, but it is otherwise of little use. The same goes for both **Phnom Penh Tourism**, 313 Sisowath Quay, and the **Ministry of Tourism** ((023) 723949, 3 Monivong Boulevard, at the corner of Street 232.

For up-to-date information on what to do around town, pick up a copy of the bi-weekly *Phnom Penh Post*, which has a pull-out map of the city, or the *Cambodia Daily*.

Phnom Penh, like the rest of Cambodia, works on a dual currency — the riel may be official tender but the United States dollar reigns supreme. Most travelers carry around dollars in small denominations, and accumulate crumpled piles of riels in small change. The city, and indeed the entire country, has just one ATM, which is operated by **Canadia Bank**, 265 Street 110, but with one catch: it is not connected to the international banking network, so unless you have a Canadia Bank account it is useless. It's possible to arrange credit card advances at the **Cambodian Commercial Bank**, 26 Monivong Boulevard, and at the **Foreign Trade Bank of Cambodia**, 26 Norodom Boulevard.

In the event of any medical problems, the two best places in town are the **Tropical & Traveler's Medical Clinic** ((023) 366802, 88 Street 108, and the **SOS International Clinic** ((023) 216911, 161 Street 51. The SOS clinic also operates a 24-hour emergency service ((015) 912765. If you have serious medical problems you are advised to head to Bangkok.

Internet access is widely available in Phnom Penh, particularly on Sisowath Quay in the area of the Cambodian Foreign Correspondent's Club, where you will find many restaurants and travelers' services.

The following airlines have offices in Phnom Penh: **Air France** ((023) 426426, 389 Sisowath Quay; **Bangkok Airways** ((023) 426624, 61 Street 214; **Lao Aviation** ((023) 216563, 18B Sihanouk Boulevard; **Phnom Penh Airways** ((023) 217419, 209 Street 19; **Royal Air Cambodge** ((023) 428891, 206 Norodom Boulevard; **Silk Air** ((023) 364545, 219B Monivong Boulevard; **Thai Airways** ((026) 722335, 19 Street 106; **Vietnam Airlines** ((023) 363396, 41 Street 214.

GETTING AROUND

Greater Phnom Penh is quite small and a fairly easy place to get around, as it is laid out in a basic grid pattern. If you rent a motorcycle at US$10 a day (24 hours), you can head where you please.

The city lies north–south along the left bank of the Tonle Sap River, at the confluence of the Mekong and the Bassac Rivers — beyond which, all three start their long sprawl southwards to finally emerge as the Mekong Delta of southern Vietnam. The most important boulevards, Monivong Boulevard and Sisowath Quay, run north–south, and while the main thoroughfares have names, all other streets are numbered in, it would seem, no particular order. Wat

Phnom to the north is a major point of reference, as is the Central Market in the heart of town, and the Independence or Victory Monument to the south.

The main north–south street is Monivong and as it runs south it passes Phnom Penh's derelict railway station, the flamboyantly ugly Central Market and some of the leading hotels — the magnificent Hotel Le Royal, the Pailin, Singapore, Paradise and the Dusit, before turning towards the river at Sihanouk towards the Cambodiana Hotel, the Naga Casino and the Royal Palace.

In the center of town it is quite feasible to do some exploration on foot, though you should keep an eye out for potholes. Otherwise, particularly on a hot day — and Cambodia has a lot of these — most people

get around on motorcycle taxis — or *motos*, as they're known in Cambodia. A short hop should cost around 1,000 riels, a longer journey 2,000 riels to US$1. You won't have any luck hailing taxis on street corners, but they are readily organized at hotels or cafés, and they also tend to congregate in the Central Market area.

WHAT TO SEE AND DO

Now that the king is often in residence, the opulently decorated **Royal Palace** on Sothearos Boulevard between Street 184 and Street 240 is unfortunately not open to visitors except on special occasions, such as the

Archar Mean Boulevard, Phnom Penh's chaotic main street.

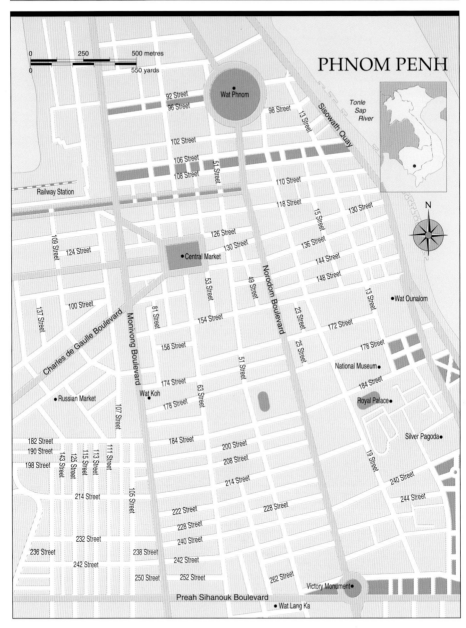

PHNOM PENH

Tonle
Sap
River

N

Wat Phnom
92 Street
96 Street
98 Street
13 Street
Sisowath Quay
102 Street
106 Street
51 Street
108 Street
110 Street
Railway Station
118 Street
15 Street
130 Street
126 Street
109 Street
124 Street
130 Street
136 Street
Central Market
144 Street
53 Street
49 Street
148 Street
Norodom Boulevard
13 Street
Wat Ounalom
100 Street
137 Street
81 Street
154 Street
23 Street
172 Street
Charles de Gaulle Boulevard
158 Street
Monivong Boulevard
25 Street
178 Street
National Museum
174 Street
51 Street
184 Street
Russian Market
Wat Koh
63 Street
178 Street
Royal Palace
107 Street
Silver Pagoda
182 Street
184 Street
190 Street
200 Street
198 Street
143 Street
125 Street
115 Street
111 Street
113 Street
208 Street
19 Street
240 Street
214 Street
105 Street
244 Street
214 Street
222 Street
228 Street
228 Street
232 Street
240 Street
236 Street
238 Street
242 Street
262 Street
242 Street
Victory Monument
250 Street
252 Street
Preah Sihanouk Boulevard
Wat Lang Ka

0   250   500 metres
0   550 yards

king's birthday. Facing a large open park and
the river, this inviting edifice, built in 1866
by King Norodom, with its high walls and
intriguing glimpses of glittering temple
spires and sweeping tiled roofs, is somewhat reminiscent of the Grand Palace in
Bangkok, on which it was modeled.

While the Palace may be off limits, it is
possible to visit the adjacent **Silver Pagoda**,
whose compound is open every morning

from 7:30 until 11 AM and from 2:30 until
5 PM. Spared by the Khmer Rouge during
the years of madness, the entrance houses
an open-air theater for classical dance performances and an open-air entertainment
pavilion for the use of the king. The Royal
Throne Room stands by the Throne Hall,
crowned with a 59-m-high (194-ft) stupa in
a style faintly reminiscent of the towers of
the Bayon Temple in Angkor, recalling some-

thing of the wealth and splendor of the Khmer civilization. Amid wall and ceiling murals illustrating tales from the *Ramayana* are several thrones, including a gilded contraption in which the king was carried at royal processions. In the nearby King's Pavilion, watched over by four garudas, there are two more modest sedan chairs, which the monarch and his queen presumably used for less-official public appearances, rather like using the Toyota to go shopping instead of the Rolls.

One of the more incongruous sights that can be glimpsed from the adjacent grounds of the Silver Pagoda is a complete Normandy-style villa, the **Napoleon III Pavilion**, shipped from France and reassembled in the grounds — a gift from the French Empress Eugenie early in the twentieth century. Outside the main complex is the compound of the white elephant, used for royal occasions, births, deaths, marriages and coronations.

The Silver Pagoda itself, which sits at the heart of the compound, gets its name from the more than 5,000 silver tiles that cover its floor, but it is also known as **Wat Preah Keo (Emerald Buddha Pagoda)**, after the Emerald Buddha displayed inside. The Buddha sits on a dais surrounded by several gold Buddha images, one encrusted with 9,584 diamonds and weighing 94 kg (207 lbs). A huge running frieze illustrating tales from the Khmer version of the *Ramayana*, or *Reamker*, decorates a three-meter (10-ft) wall containing the temple complex. Around the pagoda are statues of Cambodia's most recent monarchs, a ceremonial bell tower, various monuments donated by such historical figures as Napoleon III, and the small Wat Phnom Mondap, displaying a bronze footprint of the Buddha from Sri Lanka.

Adjacent to palace's northern wall, the **National Museum** (open 8 to 11:30 AM and 2 to 5:30 PM, closed Mondays) is housed in a burnt sienna-colored classical building constructed in 1917. It houses more than 5,000 Khmer paintings and sculptures dating back to the sixth century — to the pre-Angkor states of Funan and Chenla. The museum also has some magnificent classical Khmer statues up to the thirteenth century. In particular, look for the twelfth-century statue of Jayavarman VII, a meditative sculpture that sums up the genius of late Khmer art. Later treasures include nineteenth-century dance costumes and royal paraphernalia.

One excursion that can only fill a visitor with hope for the future is a visit to the **Fine Arts School** on Rue des Petites Fleurs (Street 70) for the morning dance class, which starts at 7 AM (see WITNESS A CULTURAL REVIVAL, page 17 in TOP SPOTS). Here in a crumbling colonial-style complex of the university is a huge barn-like room where

hundreds of talented youngsters are being schooled in Khmer classical dance. If you go, please be discreet. These are real classes in progress, not a tourist event.

As with other Buddhist cities, Phnom Penh is busy with wats and pagodas, and although many were decimated by the Khmer Rouge, some have since been renovated. **Wat Phnom** is Phnom Penh's symbol — a distinctly historical place. Located on an artificial hillock north of the city center, it was built in 1434 to commemorate a woman named Penh who reputedly discovered four sacred Buddha images washed there by the river. Hence Phnom Penh — the "Hill of Penh." This crumbling old stupa and surrounding shrines and pavilions were damaged by the Khmer Rouge and later restored; unfortunately a recent major restoration clothed the crumbling stupas and statues in cement and brightly colored hues of paint. It's something of a tourist trap nowadays, with hawker stalls and children

A garish new Central Market building marks the downtown hub of Phnom Penh.

scampering after visitors with birdcages — pay to set one free and improve your merit, though the bird will fly back to its owner. Somehow, this simply adds to the fun, however, and the wat is definitely worth a visit.

Wat Ounalom, on Sisowath Quay, across from Phnom Penh Tourism, was literally torn apart during Year Zero and has since been restored. It features a stupa that is said to contain a hair from an eyebrow of Buddha and a marble Buddha image that was smashed to pieces by the Khmer Rouge. Despite the carnage, the temple has been restored and

has resumed its place as the headquarters of the Cambodian Buddhist patriarch.

Wat Lang Ka, near the Victory Monument (built in 1958 to celebrated Cambodian independence), is another temple that was ravaged by the Khmer Rouge. It is now restored and has a small community of monks back in residence.

Wat Koh, off Monivong Boulevard at Street 178, and **Wat Moha Montrei**, which you'll find near the National Sports Stadium, are also worth a visit.

Marking one of the city's major intersections, the distinctively Khmer **Victory Monument** — sometimes referred to as the Independence Monument — at the junction of Norodom and Preah Sihanouk Boulevards was erected to celebrate the end of French rule in 1953. Although designed in a modern style, it features repetitive *naga* or snake motifs, a motif that permeates Khmer art and culture, both historical and modern. The Victory Monument is now a memorial to servicemen who lost their lives in the Vietnamese-led liberation of Cambodia

in 1979, and wreaths are laid at its base on national holidays.

Nobody should visit Phnom Penh without taking a look at one of its markets, the most imposing of which is **Central Market** (Psar Thmei), also known as New Market, close to the Wat Phnom. This domed, mustard yellow structure may not be architecturally inspired, but it is certainly an unmissable landmark, and downtown Phnom Penh would not be the same without it. Within the cavernous main hall are brightly lit displays of glittering jewelry,

gems (including fakes from Thailand) and watches, among a host of other items, ranging from Khmer textiles to foodstuffs. Surrounding the main building is a warren of lanes filled with open stalls selling everything from vegetables to piles of dazzling handloomed silks. It is the place to pick up some handloomed *krama*, the ubiquitous Khmer scarves that double as sarong, sunshade or towel. They come in silk and cotton — watch out for the polyester — and make great souvenirs and gifts for just a few dollars. It is also the place to find the ubiquitous

ABOVE: A cyclo driver LEFT on Phnom Penh's Lenin Boulevard. Elaborate bas-relief RIGHT at Wat Phnom in Phnom Penh. OPPOSITE: The main gate at the Royal Palace, official residence of King Norodom Sihanouk.

T-shirts and pirated CD-roms and music cassettes. It's the center of town and makes a good reference point for urban navigation. Beyond the market are textile stores, restaurants (including La Paillote) and "black market" currency exchange dealers.

Also worth a visit is **Psar Tuol Tom Pong**, or the **Russian Market**, an enticing, dimly lit bazaar of open stalls selling vegetables, food and clothes (with great deals in very wearable handloomed silk tops or shirts that cost a fraction of the price tagged in the hotel gift shops). Antiques scoured

from the countryside, handloomed silks, tools, ceramics — the market is filled to overflowing with exciting buys. Dedicated browsers might spend hours here, though as in any crowded Asian market it is wise to keep your valuables secure as a precaution against pickpockets.

The city's most dramatic monument is connected with the darkness and brutality of Pol Pot's reign of terror. **Tuol Sleng Museum** (open 7:30 to 11:30 AM and 2 to 5:30 PM, daily) was formerly Tuol Svay Prey High School, which the Khmer Rouge converted into Security Prison 21 — their main detention, interrogation and torture center for class enemies. Within the bleak brick walls on Street 113 is a collection of old

school buildings surrounded by barbed wire, which even now exude an atmosphere of fear. Although a lot of its most hideous features — the various instruments of torture — have been removed, it still chills the heart to think of the thousands of people who passed through this charnel house. Most shocking of all is the vast gallery of small passport-sized before- and after-interrogation photos of the detainees condemned to death and torture — with their ages — exhibited on wall after wall within the main buildings. Most were hardly older than teenagers, stunned and completely helpless in the grip of a regime that was all the more insane for the grim efficiency with which it recorded its purge.

WHERE TO STAY

Phnom Penh has a wealth of accommodation options, ranging from budget guesthouses to some of the best hotels in the region.

Very Expensive

If it's the best hotel in town you want, look no further than the Raffles-operated **Hotel Le Royal** ((023) 981888 FAX (023) 981168 E-MAIL raffles.hir.ghda@bigpond.com.k WEB SITE www.raffles.com/le.htm, 92 Rukhak Vithei Duan Penh, which looks as impressive on the inside as it does from without. Its imposing, ornate French façade, and the role it played during the Khmer Rouge takeover, when the last remaining Western journalists stayed here (part of the movie, *The Killing Fields*, was set here), gives it a certain mystique. The beautifully appointed rooms and public areas are just as grand as the day it opened in the 1930s. Architecturally, as the hotel itself is quick to point out, the building is an interesting fusion of art deco, French colonial and Khmer influences. The facilities are world class, and it is difficult to imagine anyone coming away from a stay here disappointed. Rates start at around US$180 and range up to more than US$2,000.

The **Sofitel Cambodiana Hotel** ((023) 426288 FAX (023) 426392 WEB SITE www.hotel

---

ABOVE: Mixay Monument forms a major orientation point in Phnom Penh.
OPPOSITE: The spires of Wat Botum.

cambodiana.com, 313 Sisowath Quay, has a main wing of 360 rooms surrounded by restaurants, bars, shops, garden bistros and an excellent gift shop, all set on the bank of the Brassac River. It's a grand palace of a hotel, which took from 1967 to 1987 to build, its construction halted for years by warfare and the Khmer Rouge purges. When the first tourists began to trickle into Phnom Penh it was the best place to stay by far; now it is rivaled by newer arrivals and by refurbished colonial-era hotels like Le Royal.

luxury that will not break the budget. The 75 guestrooms have a genuinely homey ambiance, and most overlook the garden, which fronts the Brassac River. The hotel has a pool and a driving range. From US$90.

Less satisfying on the atmosphere front, but maintaining good luxury standards at reasonable prices, is the **Juliana Hotel** ((023) 366070 FAX (023) 880530 E-MAIL juliana @camnet.com.kh, Street 152. It has an excellent swimming pool, and all the rooms come with IDD phones, mini-bars, 24-hour service and Internet access. Prices range from US$80.

If it's a straight international-class hotel you are looking for the **Hotel Intercontinental Phnom Penh** ((023) 424888 FAX (023) 424885 E-MAIL phnompenh@interconti.com WEB SITE www.interconti.com/cambodia/phnom_penh/hotel_phnic.html, 296 Mao Tse Tung Boulevard, is arguably the best in town. Rooms cost US$180 upwards, but substantial discounts are available through agencies and online booking sites such as WEB SITE www.asiatravel.com

Expensive

The **Royal Phnom Penh** ((023) 360026 FAX (023) 360036 E-MAIL sales@cambodia-travel .com, Samdech Sothearoh Boulevard, is a superb choice for travelers looking for some

Moderate

The **Renakse Hotel** ((023) 722457 FAX (023) 428785 E-MAIL renakse-htl@camnet.com.kh, 40 Sothearos Boulevard, opposite the southern end of the Royal Palace complex and just a few blocks away from the Cambodiana, is something of a treat — a rambling old colonial edifice that has not been renovated out of recognition. This former Buddhist institute has comfortable rooms with satellite television, hot water and air conditioning, and charges US$35 to US$40 a night. The charming open, tiled verandah and lobby look out onto gardens of frangipani trees and, on the right night, the moon rising over the temple spires of the Royal Palace. The food is fairly basic — a Continental breakfast is included in the rate and other meals can be taken elsewhere. The coffee is good, and staff friendly and accommodating.

For an accommodation experience few could expect of Phnom Penh, **L'Imprévu** ((023) 360405 FAX (023) 310335 E-MAIL imprevu @khmer.net WEB SITE www.cambodia-web .net.htm, Road No 1 (seven kilometers or just over four miles after Monivong Bridge), is a beautiful set of bungalows in a glade-like setting of coconut palms. With tennis courts and a swimming pool, it is the perfect retreat from downtown Phnom Penh — indeed many

about@bigpond.com.kh WEB SITE http:// travel.to/walkabout, at the corner of streets 174 and 51, is the kind of place that advertises the fact that it sells the local brew — Angkor beer — at less than US$1 per bottle. This makes it popular with the backpacker set, and with good reason: the restaurant downstairs is good and provides a host of travel services, and the rooms range from as little as US$5.

The long-running **Narin's Guesthouse** ((023) 213657, 50 Street 125, is the most sought-after accommodation among back-

expatriates book in here for a weekend out of town. Air-conditioned bungalows with mini-bar cost US$30 per night or US$150 per week.

Inexpensive

The **Golden Gate Hotel** ((023) 721161 FAX (023) 427618, 6 Street 278, is a long-runner that has maintained its popularity, particularly with people who are spending some time in Phnom Penh. It has a friendly, family-run atmosphere, and rooms are immaculately maintained — all come with air conditioning, satellite television and even mini-bars, and some have balconies. Rates are US$30. Book ahead.

For true budget accommodation, the **Walkabout Hotel** ((023) 211715 E-MAIL walk

packers. It has a winning family-run atmosphere and simple but clean rooms ranging from US$4. As it is often full, ring ahead to make a booking.

WHERE TO EAT

If, like many visitors, you go to Phnom Penh with little in the way of expectations on the dining front, prepare to be surprised. The city's huge NGO population has led to a thriving restaurant scene — if you've ever wondered

OPPOSITE: The No Problem pub and Mousson restaurant in Phnom Penh. ABOVE: Handwoven silks and other traditional textiles can be found in shops ringing the Central Market. OVERLEAF: Girls in traditional dress in Siam Reap.

where all that aid money winds up, after a couple of nights dining out in Phnom Penh you will not be wondering anymore.

Worthy of a special mention on this front is the **Foreign Correspondent's Club of Cambodia** (FCCC) ((023) 210142, 363 Sisowath Quay. A pioneer of international cuisine in Phnom Penh, it remains probably the most popular place in town, not only to eat out, but also to enjoy evening drinks. With lazy overhead fans, views of the Tonle Sap River on one side and the National Museum on the other, it easily rates as one of the best bar-restaurants in Asia. Meals average around US$8 per head, though most visitors end up staying on for drinks and spending more.

The section of Sisowath Quay that the FCCC is located on is an excellent place to seek out other places to eat, even if the FCCC is difficult to compete with. Many of the restaurants in this part of town are rough-and-ready places, popular with budget travelers who sit out on the street eating everything from stir-fries to french fries, downing beers, and fending off the never-ending procession of beggars and *moto* drivers. An exception is **Rendez Vous Restaurant** ((015) 831303, 239 Sisowath Quay. Prices are very reasonable in this unassuming little restaurant, which serves French standards along with some unusual specialties of the house. Meals average around US$6 per head.

Also close by is **Ponlok** ((023) 212898, 319 Sisowath Quay, a long-runner that serves some of the best Khmer cuisine available in Cambodia. It is usually packed with well-to-do locals. Like the FCCC, it has great riverfront views, and the English menu is as good a place as any to begin a crash course in a cuisine the world knows too little about. It's possible to eat very well here for around US$5, which is a bargain given the views and the quality of the food.

Two other restaurants in this area deserve mention. **Eid** ((023) 367614, 327 Sisowath Quay, was one of the pioneers of Thai cuisine in Phnom Penh, though in the early days it was down by the Victory Monument. The food is superb and costs next to nothing. It's possible to eat very well here for a few dollars. Close by is **Happy Herb Pizza**

((023) 362349, 327 Sisowath Quay, which has been serving excellent pizzas to the Phnom Penh expat community for some 10 years. Herb's is an institution. If you are confused at all by the menu's references to ordering pizzas "happy" it would pay to ask — the friendly serving staff will fill you in.

For more excellent Khmer cuisines (and some Thai favorites thrown for good measure), the **Khmer-Thai Restaurant** ((012) 881964, 15 Street 94, near Wat Phnom is an excellent choice. A classy establishment, it features a good English menu and — something of a rarity in Phnom Penh — waiters who speak English well enough to guide new arrivals through the more obscure sections of the menu. A meal here is around US$7 per head.

The **Sorya Restaurant** ((023) 210638, Street 142, serves Khmer and Chinese cuisine, in a setting that is more Chinese than Khmer. It's popular with Phnom Penh's large Chinese community but, with more than 300 seats, getting a table is never a problem. Costs are around US$10 per head.

To meet other travelers and swap travel gossip over drinks and overland staples like banana pancakes, head over to the **Walkabout Hotel & Restaurant** ((023) 211715, at the corner of Streets 174 and 51. The **Capital Guesthouse** ((023) 364104, Street 182, is the other popular rendezvous spot among travelers. It's a seedy place and the food is not particularly good — it is, however, a good spot to nurse a beer and meet other people.

NIGHTLIFE

At the time of writing, Hun Sen was imposing a law-and-order campaign on Phnom Penh that was extreme even by, say, Singaporean standards. All drinking establishments were ordered to close, and nobody was saying if and when they would reopen. It is difficult to imagine that Phnom Penh, which until not long ago had a very freewheeling nightlife scene, will turn overnight into an early-to-bed, early-to-rise city, but it does make recommending drinking establishments fraught with danger. The following are several long-running nightspots that will no doubt resurface if the ban is lifted.

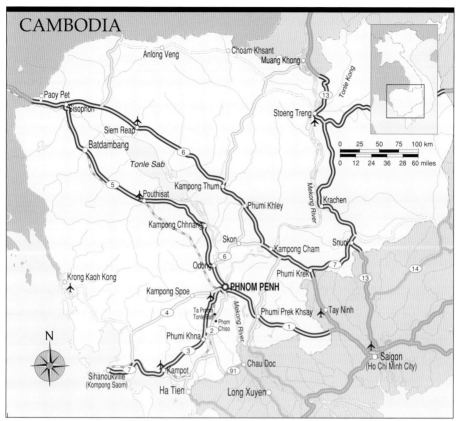

CAMBODIA

The **FCCC** (see WHERE TO EAT, above) is one of the most popular spots in town to start an evening, though most budget travelers shun it due to its relatively expensive drink prices — very reasonable by international standards. The budget travelers tend to do their early evening drinking at the **Walkabout** (see WHERE TO EAT, above), and many of them are still there in the early hours of the morning.

Those who are still up for more drinks from around 11 PM onwards should head down to the **Heart of Darkness**, 26 Street 51. On a busy night it can be a bizarre gathering of NGOs, journalists, backpackers and locals, all jostling together in the darkness, the occasional pin-prick of light highlighting the Khmer statuary littered around the bar.

For late-night dancing, **Manhattan (** (023) 427402, 402 Mao Tse Toung Boulevard, is a long-running disco that still packs in the crowds. It's as close to an international club as Phnom Penh gets.

HOW TO GET THERE

Phnom Penh's Pochentong airport is conveniently located just seven kilometers (just over four miles) out of town. Official airport taxis cost US$7 and are recommended if this is your first time in Cambodia. *Moto* drivers also lurk outside the Arrivals terminal and will ferry brave visitors into town for US$1.

Royal Air Cambodge (see GENERAL INFORMATION, above) has flights to most major destinations around Cambodia (and for the average visitor that means Siem Reap, gateway to Angkor), but with the exception of Siem Reap flights, which are usually available at short notice, advance bookings are essential.

The southwest corner of the Central Market is the place to get buses. Surprisingly, there are now some relatively luxurious services, though they run almost exclusively to the beach resort of Sihanoukville, a four-hour trip. The bus service from Phnom Penh to Saigon is best avoided, but the Capital Guesthouse (see WHERE TO EAT, above) has pioneered an inexpensive minibus service that saves the trouble of having to negotiate fares for two taxis on either side of the border — it is much cheaper too.

Most guesthouses (and luxury hotels, though at considerably higher prices) can sell boat tickets to Siem Reap. The journey takes around four or five hours, and their only drawback is the overcrowding that the operators allow.

AROUND PHNOM PENH

THE KILLING FIELDS

From Tuol Sleng, a visit leads inevitably to the Killing Fields themselves — or rather, to one of the many mass-execution spots that operated throughout Cambodia during the Khmer Rouge reign. You get to the former extermination camp of **Choeung Ek** past tranquil paddy fields and small farming communities. This trip is a perverse contrast of rural industry (with happy children who shout "Hello-goodbye!" as you ride past haughty russet-colored Brahmin cattle hauling traditional rice carts) and the horror that awaits at Choeung Ek. There, about 15 km (nine miles) from the city, a tall glass-faced monument contains nearly 9,000 skulls, the remains of victims dug from mass graves nearby. The grim relics are arranged tier-upon-tier up the tower according to sex and age. No amount of description can really prepare anyone for this monument, and it leaves all a little

humbled by the contrasting good fortune of our own lives.

ODONG

One of the journeys to make beyond Phnom Penh is to a hilltop complex of temples and stupas at Odong, about 45 km (28 miles) north of the city on Road No. 5. This rambling set of ruins was the capital of Cambodia from 1618 to 1866. Tour agencies can provide a car, or it is also possible to get there by motorcycle, but either way, it's a long, hard drive. While little remains of King Ang Duong's masterpiece — the main temple of Vihear Preah Chaul Nipean, nearly 100 pagodas and its main relic, a huge sitting Buddha, were blown to pieces by the Khmer Rouge — three huge stupas nearby were mercifully spared. Decorated with garudas, elephants and ceramic motifs, they stand untouched, even though they commemorate three of the country's kings. From these stupas the view across a vast rice plain again allows one to contemplate the chilling juxtaposition of darkness and light in Cambodia. Below the hill there's a memorial to victims recovered from more than 100 mass graves found in the region. Odong is a popular pilgrimage site where Khmers go to pay homage to former kings.

TA PROMH TONLE BATI

About 35 km (23 miles) south of Phnom Penh on Road No. 2 is a twelfth-century temple dedicated to both Buddhism and Brahmanism. Built by the Khmer King Jayavarman V11 Tonle Bati temple can be combined in a day visit with Phnom Chiso.

PHNOM CHISO (SURYA PARVATA)

Also south on Road No. 2, the eleventh-century Angkor mountain temple of Phnom Chiso stands atop a 100-m (328-ft) hilltop with extensive views over the surrounding countryside. Built by King Suryavarman I, this laterite, brick and sandstone monument has a central sanctuary housing the "Black Lady" or Neang Khmao, a venerated Buddha about 300 years old.

KOH DACH

Reachable by Road No. 6A about 15 km (10 miles) northeast of Phnom Penh, or by boat along the Mekong, past fishing villages and idyllic rural scenes, Koh Dach is a Mekong island of about 30 sq km (12 sq miles), a historical center well known among the Khmers for its quality handloom silk weaving. It is also a center for pottery production, woodcarving, painting and gem cutting, making an interesting day's outing from Phnom Penh.

SIHANOUKVILLE (KOMPONG SAOM)

Beachside resort town of Sihanoukville, on the south coast, bordering the Gulf of Siam, is about 230 km (160 miles) from Phnom Penh — four hours by car or bus. Cambodia's main port and a major fishing town, Sihanoukville is increasingly looking to tourism to revive its fortunes. Unfortunately, a long-anticipated tourism boom has never materialized. This is partly because the beaches here do not quite rival the best beaches elsewhere in the region, but it is also because for years the road to Sihanoukville was considered too dangerous to travel on, and in late 1998 the resort came to further prominence in a toxic-waste scandal.

Sihanoukville today is a sleepy place, and less a compelling attraction than a getaway from the heat of Phnom Penh and Siem Reap for travelers who are spending two weeks or more in Cambodia. It's a surprisingly sprawling place, so if you want to explore it properly you will need to rent a motorcycle, or rent a *moto* for the duration of your stay. Pick up a copy of the *Sihanoukville Visitors Guide*, a free, annually updated publication, with listings of places to stay and eat and things to do in the area.

The most popular beach — though midweek it can be near deserted — is **Sokha Beach**, around a kilometer to the west of town. Further west is **Independence Beach**, which is home to the Independence Hotel, allegedly, according to locals, haunted. North of here is **Victory Beach**, the southern strip of which locals have hopefully named "Hawaii Beach." This is where most of the budget guesthouses have set up shop, and is the center of Sihanoukville's backpacking culture. On the edge of town itself is **Ochheuteal Beach**, which is a fine stretch of sand and home to some of the more upmarket hotels and restaurants.

Several operators offer diving in Sihanoukville, and given they are professional outfits and the islands offshore here do indeed provide some splendid diving opportunities, the idea is not as crazy as it might first sound. The best established of them is **Chez Claude** ((015) 340120 at Ochheuteal Beach.

Sihanoukville has far more accommodation than it actually needs, given the volume of tourist traffic it receives. Most of it, however, is of a fairly poor standard. This will all change when a projected US$30-million joint-venture hotel comes into existence at Sokha Beach, but for the time being the **Seaside Hotel** ((034) 933641 FAX (034) 933640 E-MAIL seaside@khmer.net, Fourth Quarter, Mittapheap Section, Ochheuteal, is probably the best choice. It sits directly on the waterfront, and the rooms are well appointed, with air conditioning, mini-bars and satellite television. Rates range from US$25 to

OPPOSITE: Skulls pack the macabre shrine to Pol Pot's victims at Choeung Ek. ABOVE: The sun sets over the Mekong River in Phnom Penh.

US$50. The nearby **Crystal Hotel** ((034) 933880, Ochheuteal Beach, can also be recommended; it has comfortable, air-conditioned rooms from US$20.

Budget travelers all head to Victory Beach, where a large number of guesthouses can be found. One of the longest running and most popular is **Mealy Chanda Guesthouse** ((034) 933472, which offers basic double rooms for as little as US$3, and has great views over the beach from its restaurant. The **Melting Pot** ((034) 933391 E-MAIL meltingpotkh@yahoo.com is

a British-run operation that has rooms at US$5 and offers a host of travelers services such as Internet access, tours, and even a tattooing service.

On the food front, the **Melting Pot** has become one of the most popular places to eat and have a few beers. The **Mealy Chanda Guesthouse** also has a popular restaurant. For something special, French-Vietnamese Claude has shifted his restaurant **Chez Claude** ((012) 824870 up onto the hill between Sokha and Independence Beaches, away from his original location on Ochheuteal Beach. Specializing in seafood, it's a superb place for an evening meal — there are also pleasant bungalows for rent here from US$20.

Sihanoukville can be easily reached by luxury bus from Phnom Penh nowadays. The journey takes around four hours and costs US$5.

SIEM REAP

Siem Reap is a compact boom town that owes its recent prosperity — compared to much of the rest of Cambodia — to the fact that it sits next to a tourist goldmine: Angkor Wat, which is probably Asia's grandest historical attraction. And given

that tourist arrivals are still relatively low, Cambodia having received so much bad press, the boom is just beginning.

Siem Reap may be developing faster than anywhere else in the country, but for the time being the town still retains a certain charm. Accommodation is plentiful, however, with a broad range of options from the inexpensive to the luxury of the Grand Hotel d'Angkor; restaurants are thick on the ground and there are even a few decent bars in which to while away the balmy evenings.

OPPOSITE: The South Gate at Angkor Wat. ABOVE: Many artistic treasures, such as these incredible bas-reliefs, have survived Cambodia's years of conflict. OVERLEAF: A stone causeway leads to the main entrance and architectural wonders of Angkor Wat.

GENERAL INFORMATION

You will find **Siem Reap Angkor Tourism** ((063) 964347 opposite the Grand Hotel d'Angkor. The only useful service it provides is a representative office for the Khmer Angkor Tour Guide Association. A much better source of local information is the excellent *Siem Reap Angkor Visitors Guide*, a giveaway listings magazine that comes out annually and provides comprehensive information on accommodation, restaurants, tour agencies and transportation. Travelers' cafés, guesthouses and hotels are the best sources of on-the-spot, up-to-date information.

Bangkok Airways (which flies to Bangkok) can be reached in Siem Reap ((063) 380191, as can **Royal Air Cambodge** ((063) 963322.

Several banks around town can change money. They include the **Cambodia Commercial Bank** ((063) 380154, 130 Sivatha Road; the **Canadia Bank** ((063) 964808, Old Market; and the **First Overseas Bank** ((063) 963508, Old Market.

Understandably with such a large number of locals now dependent on tourism for the incomes, whether you arrive by boat or by air, you will be besieged by guides touting their services. Do not rush into anything. The difference between a good guide and a useless one will have a huge bearing on your enjoyment of the Angkor complex. It's better to shop around at leisure in Siem Reap. Most hotels can recommend a guide, as can the very efficient **Khmer Angkor Tour Guide Association**, which is located in the tourism office (see above). Alternatively try one of the many agencies around town. **Angkor Tourism** ((063) 380027 FAX (063) 380027 WEB SITE www.angkor-tourism.com, Street 6, Phum Sala Kanseng, Siem Reap, is particularly recommended.

WHAT TO SEE AND DO

In one word: Angkor. Siem Reap is a pleasant town to spend a day or so in, but it is unlikely that anyone would come here if weren't for the nearby ruins of a great civilization, forgotten for centuries and left to the jungle.

The vast, world-famous complex of Hindu-Khmer temples, the legacy of the Khmer Empire, has been stirring the imagination of visitors for more than a century. Created over the ninth through the fifteenth centuries, Angkor has been compared to Egypt's pyramids, a tribute that is by no means unjustified — and without the crowds too. Angkor is Cambodia's crowning glory as a tourist destination, and it is easily Southeast Asia's foremost historical attraction. To visit Indochina without touring Angkor is almost unthinkable.

A dedicated visitor could easily spend a week or even two exploring the ruins, but most travelers will find two or three days is sufficient to get a feel of this marvelous place.

For many years now teams of foreign and local archeologists have been laboring to restore the complex, and the condition of the ruins continues to improve. Teams of Japanese archeological experts have been working on a restoration project of the Bayon. Meanwhile, a short 300-m (200-yard) walk away, the French-restored Elephant Terrace and Terrace of the Leper King has a replica statue of the Leper King who stands guard over what was possibly the royal crematorium. Nearby, in a tree-shaded grove, a long, stone causeway leads to the mountain temple of Baphuon, where ancient masonry is being rebuilt by a French team and is to be completed by the year 2003. Within the complex, the late tenth-century Phimeanakas has also been restored recently.

The beautiful Banteay Srei Complex and Banteay Samre have been opened to visitors, with the Khmer Rouge threat now a thing of the past, and the roads to these monuments are being upgraded. A much larger part of Angkor is now open to exploration although its three most famous attractions continue to be Angkor Wat, the Bayon Temple with the Baphuon and Ta Prohm.

The Temple Tour

What is left of Angkor today represents only a fraction of its ancient splendor, a small part of what was once a powerful empire whose

---

OPPOSITE: Angkor's main surviving ruins are still in the crossfire of government and Khmer Rouge troops.

influence and architecture spread across Cambodia into southern Laos and Vietnam and towards Yunnan in southern China. Even so, **Angkor Wat** itself, the first stop on the temple tour, continues to awe visitors with the monumental vision and artistry employed in its construction. You approach the outer temple walls along a wide, romantically dilapidated stone causeway that runs across what was once a protective moat. The main gate and its walls are spectacular enough, crowded with sculptures of *apsaras* (celestial nymphs) and Hindu carvings, but

them now headless, victims of vandalism and the lucrative (and illegal) international trade in East Asian antiquities. To the left, demons and, to the right, gods, hold seven-headed snakes or *nagas*, a much-used Khmer symbol. Once the epicenter of the city of **Angkor Thom**, the Bayon stands at the symbolic center of heaven and earth, and five entrance gates are placed at strategic points around the complex.

While Angkor Wat, basking in a golden glow, is an unforgettable sight in the late afternoon sunlight, the Bayon is best visited

this in turn opens on to a vast courtyard that leads to the main temple itself. This gigantic three-story structure, rising 55 m (180 ft) from the ground, was built by King Suryavarman II (1113–50) and dedicated to Vishnu. Of all the monuments of Angkor, it is this great structure, quite apart from the wealth of bas-relief carvings of Hindu epics and Khmer battles adorning the walls and cloisters surrounding it, which testifies to the power and glory of the Khmer civilization.

The second stop on a tour of Angkor's monuments is the **Bayon**. Built in the reign of Jayavarman VII (1181–1201), it lies in a forest clearing. Coming from Angkor Wat, entry is by way of the southern gate, along a causeway lined with 54 statues, many of

in the morning when the rays of sun slanting through the trees dapple it with light. Granite gray, the stone of its walls, towers and stairways crumbled and pitted by time; its artistry arouses a sense of majesty and mystery — its upper level mounted by no fewer than 49 towers bearing some 200 serenely smiling faces of the Bodhisattva Avalokitesvara — the Buddha of compassion — though it is thought they are carved in the likeness of Jayavarman VII. It's an eerie feeling in the first light of dawn to be standing among these serried faces, whose eyes seem to follow you wherever you go. Elsewhere in the galleries and cloisters of this momentous relic, some 11,000 other carvings depict Hindu legends and Khmer life at that time.

　　　　　　　　　　　　　　　　　　　　　　　　Cambodia

Restoration work is being carried out on the Bayon, the Japanese Government Team for Safeguarding Angkor (JSA) discovered that it was in a critical state. Restoration work on the northern library was completed in 1999. A second phase of restoration work has been started on other sections of the temple. Nevertheless, for the time being it remains an awesome chunk of masonry rising through the jungle, like a scene from an Indiana Jones movie.

Adjacent to the Bayon to the east, is the 3350-m (1,150-ft) **Terrace of the Elephants**, which was used as a dais from where Khmer rulers reviewed their armies. From one end to the other it is sculpted with bas-relief cavalry and war elephants. This terrace leads to the **Terrace of the Leper King**, at present under renovation. A replica sandstone statue of the Leper King can be seen within this complex.

Restoration work on all these monuments has been ongoing since the beginning of the 1990s by international teams. By contrast, **Ta Phrom** has been left in the clutches of the jungle, as the entirety of the complex was when it was first discovered. It's a crowd pleaser with tourists, but it has not been uncontroversial, with critics pointing out that tourist nostalgia to experience the temples as they were first discovered should not stand in the way of restoration work. Still, be that as it may, it is difficult not to be taken with a sense of intrepid discovery when you first enter its grounds, as if you are the first to arrive at an undiscovered site.

Built as a Buddhist temple in the late twelfth century by Jayavarman VII (1181–1201), it has since been virtually reclaimed by the jungle, its stonework mingled with the spreading roots of banyan trees, broken and heaved about as though an earthquake had struck it, its passageways and cloisters piled with fallen masonry.

Elsewhere, the impressive **Ta Keo**, built by Jayavarman V (968–1001) in honor of Shiva, rises up out of the jungle in a series of lofty towers with huge stone steps that are exhilarating to climb.

In the forest around the Bayon, huge ceremonial gates, all that remain of the precincts of Angkor Thom, have approaches lined with rows of sculptured guards —

most of them now headless after centuries of looting. In attempt to halt the destruction and pillage at Angkor, the Angkor Conservation Agency has managed to save about 5,000 statues and other relics, storing them in sheds at its compound between Siem Reap and Angkor Wat.

Banteay Srei and Banteay Samre
Farther out, about 32 km (20 miles) from Angkor, Banteay Srei, or the Citadel of Women — long off limits due to Khmer Rouge activity — is one of the oldest Angkor monuments and one of the finest in execution. Built by King Jayavarman V in the second half of the tenth century and dedicated in AD 987 to Shiva, the pink sandstone temple is small and delicate, filled with the finest flutings and carvings of *apsaras* and divinities. At one time the entrance path was lined with lingams, although many have since collapsed or fallen into disrepair. The distance from Angkor deters many visitors, which makes it mercifully quieter than the main complexes. It is best visited in the cool of the early morning or late afternoon.

Also recently opened to tourism, about 18 km (11 miles) from Angkor located at a turnoff before Banteay Srei, Banteay Samre is a twelfth-century complex of some interest and in quite reasonable condition. Its central temple is flanked by two libraries and crumbling wings surrounded by what was no doubt a moat. There are two main entrances in the high, slightly forbidding walls that surround the complex.

WHERE TO STAY

Siem Reap has accommodation to suit all budgets, and the situation continues to improve.

Very Expensive
One of Indochina's most famous hotels, the **Grand Hotel d'Angkor** ((063) 963888 FAX (063) 963168 E-MAIL ghda@worldmail .com.kh WEB SITE www.raffles.com/dang .htm, 1 Vithei Charles de Gaulle, has been renovated and restored to its former glory by Singapore's Raffles Group. As recently

---

Angkor Thom is at its most atmospheric in the early morning.

as the mid-1990s the Grand was a crumbling pile, with a swimming pool that might have served as the setting for a remake of *Creature from the Black Lagoon*. Today the 75-year-old hotel is one of the best in the region, and the 35-m (115-ft) pool is once again fit for a dip. Delightful touches include the library and map room, which brings together a host of Angkor-related literary and cartographic material, the Apsara Terrace, where cultural events are held, and the Performance House in the Riverside Garden, where guests can dine to performances of

Khmer dance and music. Rates range from US$310 to US$1,900.

Not quite in the same league for atmosphere, but a sound luxury choice all the same, and with the closest location to the Angkor complex of any hotel in Siem Reap, is the **Hotel Sofitel Royal Angkor (** (063) 964600 FAX (063) 964611 E-MAIL sofitel@sofitel-royal-angkor.com WEB SITEwww.accorhotels .com, Vithei Charles de Gaulle. The resort-style hotel comes with every five-star comfort and amenity it is possible to imagine. Rooms range from US$280.

Expensive

In Siem Reap, travelers are best off either splashing out in a big way and staying in

luxury at the Grand, or going downmarket somewhat and taking advantage of some of the excellent deals available in the town's more moderately priced hotels. The **City Angkor Hotel (** (063) 380200 FAX (063) 380022 E-MAIL ctangkor@camintel.com, Route 6, is a 204-room monster with all modern amenities, but it is somewhat lacking in character and is mostly used by tour groups.

Moderate

For those with time to book ahead, **Angkor Village (** (063) 963561 FAX (063) 380104 E-MAIL info@angkorvillage.com WEB SITE www.angkorvillage.com, Wat Bo Road, inspired by a traditional Khmer monastic village and designed by the French architect who owns it, is easily the most delightful mid-range hotel (it bills itself as a "village resort") in town. The gorgeously appointed standard rooms are US$55 and there are also duplex suites for US$110. The village has a swimming pool and an excellent restaurant that serves French-Khmer cuisine — it's the perfect place to retreat to after a long day of sweaty sightseeing out at Angkor.

A good alternative to Angkor Village is the charming **La Noria Guesthouse (** (063) 964242 FAX (063) 964243 E-MAIL lanoria@bigpond .com.kh, which is close to the river, not far north of Route 6. It has a family atmosphere, a good French-Khmer restaurant, and evening puppet shows. Rooms start at US$25.

Inexpensive

Backpackers were among the first foreigners to begin trickling into Siem Reap for a glimpse of Angkor when the place first opened up again in the early 1990s, and the budget travel scene is well established. A long-runner and still popular is **Mom's Guesthouse (** (063) 964037 FAX (063) 380025, Wat Bo Street, which is one of those travelers' institutions that serves as one-stop-shop for all travel needs. The rooms are clean, if basic, and range from US$6 to US$15. Mom is more than happy to help guests find a guide to explore Angkor with.

Another popular place to stay is the **Ivy Guesthouse (** (012) 800860, Old Market, which has budget rooms at US$6 and a popular bar and restaurant downstairs; it's a good place to meet other travelers.

WHERE TO EAT

Not so long ago Siem Reap had only a handful of places to eat. The tourist boom of the last few of years has changed that, and the town is now home to a host of restaurants serving excellent Khmer and international fare. Those wishing to simply follow their noses and find a meal are advised to head to the riverside section of the Old Market, which has developed into something of a "scene" in recent years, with restaurants, bars and stalls.

Old Market is **Chao Say** ((063) 964387, an inexpensive Khmer restaurant at which it's possible to enjoy a hearty meal for as little as US$3 — an English menu and English-speaking staff take the trouble out of ordering.

Another very popular place in the Old Market area is **Lotus Restaurant and Bar** ((063) 964381, which serves European favorites at moderate prices with very generous servings. Later in the evening the restaurant converts into one of the most popular bars in town.

Repeat visitors who remember the old days of just half a decade ago will no doubt have fond memories of the **Arun Restaurant** ((015) 638469, just north of Route 6 next to the river, which was celebrated for its "chicken curry in coconut." It has expanded its premises and looks a lot smarter than it used to, but the food is as homey, delicious and inexpensive as it ever was. It's a perfect place for an evening meal. Per head costs are unlikely to exceed US$5.

In a different league altogether is **Only One** ((063) 965318, opposite the Old Market, Siem Reap's pioneering French restaurant (hence the name). It's still a fabulous place for a classic French meal. Reckon on around US$8 per head. Also opposite the

One of the trendiest places in town, and definitely worth a visit, is **Liquid** ((063) 964405, 293–4 Pokambor Avenue, which has a great riverside location and serves Malaysian cuisine with a nouvelle twist.

Restaurant Samapheap ((015) 635619 has been around for years, and has endured despite newly arrived competition due to its incredibly extensive selection of Khmer and Chinese dishes and its delightful Thai-style pavilion setting surrounded by gardens. It's just across the river from the Grand Hotel d'Angkor. Within the Grand Hotel, visitors

OPPOSITE: Siem Reap's Grand Hotel, gateway to Angkor Wat. ABOVE LEFT: Newlyweds in Phnom Penh pose for the camera. RIGHT: A girl in traditional dress at Siem Reap.

can treat themselves to the best in quality and service at the **Café d'Angkor**, which serves a mixture of Khmer and Continental favorites.

Lastly, don't forget to call into **Angkor What?** ((012) 957620, a friendly little bar that deserves a visit for its name alone. It features a pool table and is a good place to meet other travelers; it is open late.

HOW TO GET THERE

In the past, everybody approached Siem Reap via Phnom Penh. But that has changed

with the arrival of an international airport in Siem Reap and the opening up of a land crossing from Thailand.

At present both Bangkok Airways and Royal Air Cambodge fly direct between Bangkok and Siem Reap; Bangkok Airways four times daily, and Royal Air Cambodge once daily. Other international options include Singapore with Silk Air, Saigon with Royal Phnom Penh Airlines and Vietnam Airlines, and Phuket with Bangkok Airways.

For budget travelers the overland route from Bangkok to Siem Reap is becoming very popular. Buses do the journey, via the Paoy Pet border crossing, in around 10 to 12 hours. Travel on the Thai side of the border is painless enough, but once the bus hits

Cambodian roads it turns into a bone-jarring journey of unpredictable duration. But at around US$15, the money saved on flying is hard to resist for many budget travelers. Bus tickets are sold at travel agents on Bangkok's Khao San Road, and at most travel agents in Siem Reap for the return journey.

Siem Reap can be reached from Phnom Penh by twice-daily flights on Royal Air Cambodge, three-times-daily flights by President Airlines, once-daily flights with Siem Reap Airways and twice- to three-times-daily flights with Royal Phnom Penh Airlines.

An interesting alternative is the fast, crowded and not very comfortable express boats that travel between Phnom Penh and Siem Reap daily and take around four hours. It's best to sit on the roof of the boat, as it gets very crowded in the cabin — bring sun cream and a hat for protection. Tickets cost US$25 and can be bought at travel agents and hotels.

A huge Buddha face OPPOSITE at the awesome Bayon Temple alongside the bas-reliefs ABOVE that adorn the walls and niches.

Laos

Sleepy, mountainous Laos is the jewel of Indochina, a golden land where the people remain charming, where saffron-clad monks chant prayers on their morning alms round, where religion and graciousness are more important than money. How long can it last? Probably not long, but while it does, it is something to treasure, and now is the best time to visit this gorgeous country.

Laos is not so much a land of breathtaking sights and historical monuments as a place whose atmosphere seduces and bewitches. Perhaps it helps that travel in Laos still provides a sense of adventure, of striking new paths rather than following the tried and tested routes of thousands before you. In this, travelers today are in debt to laws that, until Visit Laos Year in 1999, kept much of the country off-limits to travelers. Such restrictions are a thing of the past now, though registration processes have to be followed in more remote areas.

The truth is, Laos lingers in something of a time warp. Where Vietnam has its eyes fixed firmly on the future — even if the way forward is faltering — and Cambodia sets about recreating itself from the ashes of the Khmer Rouge holocaust, the Laos government — probably for purely political reasons — has taken a slowly-slowly approach to development. Whether this is a good thing is probably for the Laos themselves to decide; in the meantime it makes Laos a fascinating place to visit for those of us who got to Asia "20 years too late."

It's unlikely this situation will change anytime soon. The Lao government is being very cautious about allowing any rapid change that could lead to political instability and challenge its hold on power. As a result, much of the country remains undeveloped and comparatively undiscovered. Travelers here can expect to be treated graciously, and to encounter little of the price gouging that is so common in, say, Vietnam.

Much of its French colonial character lingers on in the architecture of its cities and towns; its spiritual traditions are still alive and well, its Buddhist temples flourishing, its festivals celebrated as colorfully and joyfully as they ever were. Even the Australian-funded Friendship Bridge over the Mekong River, which links the country directly with Thailand, is little more than a symbolic step into modern Asia, and although there are more of the ubiquitous Thai *tuk tuks* and *samlor* motor transports on the roads, there is no obvious negative impact from this convenient new access.

That's not to say that Laos won't change. The country remains threatened by the struggle between Thailand and Vietnam for economic and political dominance. Its relative poverty — it is the poorest country per capita in Southeast Asia — means that an industrial base of some sort must be developed soon if it is to compete with the rest of the region; but the Laos are taking their time. For now, to travel in Laos is to travel back in time, and to experience first hand the gracious Buddhist traditions that have been corrupted by rapid economic growth and too much tourism in neighboring Thailand.

As elsewhere in this region, Laos has two seasons, governed by the monsoons that bring rain and high humidity during the summer months from May to October, and almost perfect conditions — warm and dry in the daytime, cool and dry at night — from November to April. However, temperatures get more frigid, especially at night, in the northern mountains during the dry season.

VIENTIANE

Sitting on the northern banks of the Mekong, just over the border from Thailand, Vientiane is a small capital city of just under half a million people. Those coming over from Thailand — a good way to approach Laos — will notice the difference immediately. It's not just the city's charming French architecture, it's as if the pace of life has been ratcheted down a few notches, and there is an Old World quality about this city of dusty boulevards and crumbling buildings.

A sedate city, it is immediately apparent that the Vientiane of Paul Theroux's *The Great Railway Bazaar* (1975), which he dismisses so disparagingly as a city where "the brothels are cleaner than the hotels, marijuana is cheaper than pipe tobacco and opium easier to find than a glass of cold beer," has, for better or worse, disappeared.

The courtyard of Vientiane's Pha That Luang (Great Sacred Stupa).

Today the city has the character and feel of a large Southeast Asian market town over-laid with a familiar veneer of French architectural icing, an undercurrent of Buddhist sanctity and a bustle of largely ethnic Chinese and Thai trade and enterprise.

GENERAL INFORMATION

Inter Lao Tourism ((021) 214832 FAX (021) 216306 on Setthathirat Road near Nam Phu Square provides very good maps of Vientiane and the whole country, while the **National**

Geographic Department, adjacent to Le Parasol Blanc just past the Pratuxai Monument, sells marvelously detailed, large-scale maps for a very reasonable price.

In the event of a medical problems, there are several centers in Vientiane that can provide professional help: the **International Clinic** ((021) 214022, Quay Fa Gnum, is open from 6 AM to 7 AM, midday to 2 PM, and 5 PM to 9 PM, and 24-hour emergency treatment is on call: English and French are spoken. The **Australian Embassy Clinic**, on Nehru Road, also has a 24-hour emergency hotline ((020) 509462.

ABOVE and OPPOSITE: Two views of Wat Si Muang, one of Vientiane's many well-preserved temples. OVERLEAF: Sunset on the Mekong River in Vientiane.

The following airlines are represented in Vientiane: **Lao Aviation** ((021) 2120572, Pangham Road; **Thai Airways** ((021) 251168, Pangham Road; **Vietnam Airlines** ((012) 217562, Lao Hotel Plaza, 63 Samsenthai Road.

GETTING AROUND

The city snuggles along a broad curve of the Mekong, hugging the western bank. Most of its main streets, such as Samsenthai Road, run parallel to the river. Others radiate to the north, such as Lane Xang Road, which is a wide triumphal boulevard leading to the city's most notable landmark, the towering Pratuxai Monument, which looks as though it were uprooted from somewhere in the vicinity of India's Taj Mahal (word has it that it was built with United States funds donated to extend the airport some years ago). The city's tourist and business district begins in downtown Samsenthai Road, around the intersection with Lane Xang Road and extends southwest to the river, taking in the very 1960s-style Nam Phou Fountain that dominates a circle lined with restaurants, the Laos Tourism Office, the Diethelm Travel Company and the rear entrance to Lane Xang Hotel.

Vientiane is an easy city to get around — compact, flat, and with most major hotels, restaurants, agencies and attractions within walking distance, or at least in directions you can easily decipher. Only when you head north to locations beyond Pratuxai Monument do you need transportation, which the passing *tuk tuks* handle admirably. If you prefer, a bicycle or motorcycle can easily be rented in Vientiane for a day or week at ridiculously reasonable prices.

WHAT TO SEE AND DO

One of Vientiane's chief pleasures is simply strolling around and soaking up its ambiance. While Hanoi, Saigon and even Phnom Penh have had much of their charm undermined by modern development and frantic traffic conditions, there is a leisurely pace and a frozen-in-time quality of the Lao capital that makes it a pleasure to explore on foot. It helps, of course, that the Mekong is never far away. The river makes a splendid

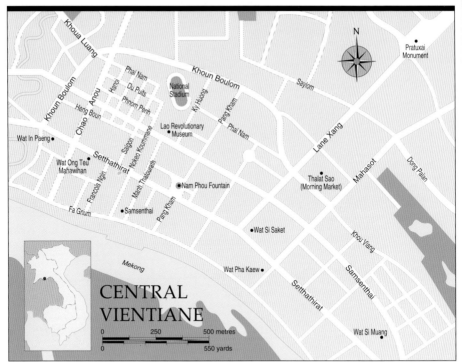

CENTRAL VIENTIANE

0   250   500 metres

0   550 yards

excuse for a sundowner at one of the river-side cafés. During the day, the galleries, markets and souvenir shops beckon, as do some fine wats.

Those looking for "sights" proper should probably put the temples and wats at the top of their list. The most important is dominated by the massive golden stupa of **Pha That Luang**, which towers over two monasteries and walled cloisters four kilometers (two and a half miles) north of the city center at the end of That Luang Street. The most revered Buddhist monument in Laos, King Setthathirat built That Luang on the site of a Khmer temple in the mid-sixteenth century, when Vientiane became the capital of the kingdom of Lane Xang. A statue of the founder sits atop a stone column in an enclosure in front of the huge, timber main gates. That Luang was virtually destroyed in 1828 by invading Thais, and the present structure is the result of a French restoration in 1900.

Each November, the complex becomes the focus of Vientiane's biggest religious festival. On the first day, a sacred white elephant is led to the stupa while ritual processions celebrate the event at temples all over the city. Hundreds of monks and novices pour in

from the provinces to take up a vigil in the cloisters around the stupa. At dawn on the second day, they're presented with alms and new robes. On the third day, thousands of faithful Buddhists walk to the stupa from the other temples, led by musicians and bearing offerings. Chanting and praying, they circle the stupa until the late hours of the night, many stopping to light candles and pray amidst the lively crowds.

Wat Si Saket is one of Vientiane's more splendid monasteries, and its oldest that is intact (it hasn't had to be rebuilt as have many of the older ones). It sits at the intersection of Lane Xang Road and Setthathirat Road. Built in 1818, its architecture shows a strong Thai influence, while the inner walls of the compound are packed with Laotian-style Buddha images. A Khmer image of Buddha seated under a canopy formed by a multi-headed cobra is one the hall's showpieces, along with statues that were damaged in the war. The wat's main hall, also Thai-style, is lined with Buddhist murals, and its ceiling is decorated with a floral design similar to those in the Thai temples of Ayutthaya.

The ornately decorated entrance to the main prayer hall at Wat Si Saket.

Wat Phra Keo, just opposite Wat Si Saket, was rebuilt in 1942 on the site of the former royal temple of the Lao kings. It's now a museum, with terraces and a main hall crowded with impressive Buddha images dating back to the sixth century, along with a gilded throne and, in a garden to the rear of the hall, a stone jar from the Plain of Jars.

Wat Ong Teu Mahawihan, on Setthathirat Road, near the intersection of Chao Anou Road, was also originally built in the sixteenth century, about the same time as That Luang, and was also destroyed in wars

of a huge procession two days before the That Luang Festival in November.

Wat Sok Pa Luang and nearby **Wat Si Amphon**, south of the city center near the Mongolian Embassy, both offer something more than the usual temple tour. They provide soothing herbal saunas, administered by nuns, and therapeutic massage. Although there is no charge, a donation of a few dollars is appreciated.

The architecture of the old French mansion in which the **Lao Revolutionary Museum** (open 8 to 11:30 AM and 2 to 4:30 PM,

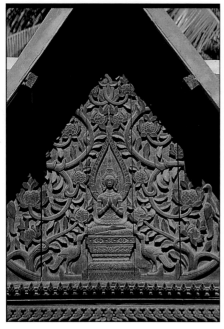

with the Siamese and later rebuilt. The name translates into "Temple of the Heavy Buddha," and it is dedicated to a massive bronze sixteenth-century Buddha image in its exquisitely decorated main hall. It is one of the most important wats in all of Laos. Built in 1566, **Wat Si Muang**, east of the city center at the confluence of Setthathirat and Samsenthai Roads, houses the foundation pillar of the city. The story goes that during the construction of the temple a pregnant woman named Nang Si was inspired to sacrifice her life, and jumped into the hole to be crushed by the pillar. She became known as the protector of Vientiane and is a revered inhabitant, with people coming to pay her homage. Wat Si Muang is the site

closed weekends) is housed on Samsenthai Road is one good reason for a visit. The museum is devoted to depictions of the Pathet Lao's struggle for power, with pictures and some weaponry. An exhibition of Khmer sculptures and Lao musical instruments can also be seen. The museum opens, sometimes, at 8 AM.

Vientiane's **Thalat Sao**, or **Morning Market**, is a sprawling marketplace just north of the city center, off Lane Xang Road. Today, much of the market has been moved into a series of huge pavilion-style buildings, and it's here that you'll find souvenir Soviet military watches and watch repairers. The main attraction is the enormous amount of Lao textiles, which fill literally hundreds of stalls.

Anyone even remotely interested in textiles will want to spend hours here, looking and examining the wares. To the left side are stalls selling skeins of hand-finished and dyed silk, all ready for working into the handlooms, while the creamy colored natural silks are ready for dyeing. The market is also a haunt of tribal women who come to buy new silk and bring in their handloomed textiles to sell. Ready-made silk clothing, table ware, fabrics and gift items are also available. Hill-tribe silver can also be found here, although the antiques have gone and much of the silver

la Cave, 345 Samsenthai Road). Stock up on baguettes together with some French cheeses and pâté at one of the burgeoning mini-marts (try **Phimphone Market**, 110 Samsenthai Road) and prepare a picnic or a day's jaunt into the countryside.

SHOPPING

It is easy to spend a day browsing the souvenir and textile showrooms — a visit to the Morning Market (Thalat Sao), with its myriad stalls, or the internationally famous salon of

is newly made. Beautifully crafted silver and gold belts are still readily available.

Just cruising around the city will introduce its special contrast of colonial French and traditional Buddhist architecture; its people, who have a friendly dignity; its lifeline, the Mekong River, the riverfront of which is a treat to stroll through, past a progression of bars and hotels that hug its western stretch; and its ricefields and farming communities along the southern road to Tha Deua and Buddha Park. The best way to do this is on a motorcycle, which you can rent for about US$5 a day (24 hours) from most hotels.

Above all Vientiane is a city to relax in — a city where a bottle of good French wine comes at a reasonable price (try **Vinotheque**

Laos

Carol Cassidy ((021) 212123 (appointments are required) are good places to start. Another is the **Art of Silk** ((021) 214308, supported by the Lao Women's Cooperative, UNICEF and SIDA, which has an extensive collection of antique handlooms in their museum above the showroom.

Kanchana ((021) 213467, in That Dam Street opposite the Ekalath Metropole Hotel, has a marvelous collection of antique textiles and beautiful new ones. In Samsenthai, the **Lao Cotton Showroom** has heavy handloomed cottons, perfect for furnishings, while **Doris Jewelry** ((021) 218821 in

OPPOSITE and ABOVE: Vientiane temple artistry. OVERLEAF: Wat Xieng Khuang (Buddha Park) is Vientiane's "Disneyland" of Buddhist lore.

the Lao Hotel Plaza has marvelous textiles, antiques and jewelry. Another jewelry shop not to miss is in the **Lane Xang Hotel** ℰ (021) 313223, owned by the knowledgeable Mr. Bounkhong Signavong.

ENVIRONS

The bizarre Buddha Park is actually called **Wat Xieng Khwan**, but bears special mention because it's not a temple at all but rather a showcase of Lao Buddhist and Hindu imagery. It is set in a pleasant tree-shaded park

on the banks of the Mekong, south of Vientiane, beyond the Tha Deua border post. Crowded with just about every sacred image possible from the two religions, and dominated by a huge reclining Buddha, it was designed and built in 1958 by a mystic named Luang Pu, who founded a cult based on a mixture of Buddhist and Hindu theology. After the 1975 revolution, he moved across the river to continue his teachings in Nong Khai. The Buddha Park is fascinating as a photo opportunity and is a pleasant place to spend an hour or two. Small stalls provide simple refreshments. You can take a car or *tuk tuk* for the 24-km (15-mile) ride, or go for the real adventure and take the local bus from Thalat Sao Bus Terminal.

WHERE TO STAY

Vientiane doesn't have the range of accommodation that other big Indochinese cities have, but it has enough to meet most budgets and tastes. Obviously, given that the city is pleasant to explore on foot, it is ideal to be based as centrally as possible.

Expensive

Vientiane's hotel scene has perked up considerably with the arrival of the first-class

233-room **Novotel Hotel** ℰ (021) 213570 FAX (021) 213572 E-MAIL novotlao@loxinfo .co.th, WEBSITE http://www.accorhotel.com, Unit 9 Samsenthai Road, with rooms from US$70 to US$450. While the location is a little further than walking distance from the main tourist drag, the hotel offers international standards, a 24-hour café, a gym, business center, tennis court, swimming pool, and one of the few discos in town allowed to play western music. The less-expensive rooms are extremely good value given the amenities they give guests access to.

Close to the town center is the glittering **Lao Hotel Plaza** ℰ (021) 218 800 FAX (021) 218808 E-MAIL lph@laoplazahotel.com WEB SITE http://www.laoplazahotel.com, 63 Samsenthai

Road. In the heart of Vientiane's tourist belt, the hotel includes a small shopping plaza containing some up-market art and book-shops. The big, cool lounge is a very pleasant place to for a drink, even for those staying elsewhere. Rooms cost from US$100 to US$400 a night.

Moderate

The **Lane Xang Hotel** ((021) 214100 FAX (021) 214108 E-MAIL clxhotel@yahoo.com, 1 Fa Ngum, overlooking the Mekong, is one of Laos's best travel deals, and has been for

but inside it has a good range of amenities, including a good business center, and the rooms are reliable if a little uninspired. Rates range from US$25 to US$50. The main drawback is that it is about one kilometer (half a mile) from the center of town.

The slightly seedy exterior belies the comfortable interior of the **Asia Pavilion Hotel** ((021) 213430 FAX (021) 213432, 379 Samsenthai Road. It has been expensively renovated since its pre-revolution days as the French Constellation Hotel, mentioned in John Le Carre's novel *The Honorable School-*

some years now. With competition from the big new hotels, Lane Xang has reduced its prices to US$25 per night, which, given its amenities, is a bargain. The hotel enjoys an excellent location within walking distance of Vientiane's best restaurants and shopping areas. Typical of government-run hotels, the relaxed and sprawling old hotel has several restaurants, a uniformed staff — all the men wear suits — massive gardens and a half Olympic-size pool in the grounds, not to mention billiard rooms and a health center.

Similar prices prevail at the **Mekong Hotel** ((021) 212938 FAX (021) 212822 E-MAIL mekonght@laotel.com, Luang Prabang Road. Granted, it is a monstrosity from the outside,

boy. It's central location makes it a popular place to stay. Rates range frosm US$28.

Inexpensive

For a budget hotel, the **Anou Hotel** ((021) 213630 FAX (021) 213632 E-MAIL anouhotel @laonet.net, 01–04 Heng Boun Street, has remarkably well-appointed rooms. There is a pleasant Old World atmosphere to this hotel, which enjoys a central location. Rates start at US$20, and are well worth the money.

The **Villa Sisavad** ((021) 212719 E-MAIL thongtsa@laotel.com, 93/12 Sisavad Road,

OPPOSITE: French bread alfresco and shoppers at the Morning Market. ABOVE: The Asia Pavilion Hotel (formerly the Constellation) in downtown Vientiane.

deserves a special mention. This centrally located small operation has bungalow-style rooms and a splendid swimming pool. Rates start at US$10.

WHERE TO EAT

.Like Phnom Penh, the NGO factor has led to an explosion of good restaurants around Vientiane. The result is not only excellent Lao and Vietnamese food, but also some very good international cuisine.

The alfresco garden restaurant and piano bar at **Le Parasol Blanc**, 263 Sibounheuang Road, is a pleasant place to relax in the expansive rattan chairs. The menu is diverse, ranging from baguette sandwiches and Lao specialties to authentic pizza. Prices are reasonable, at around US$5 per head.

French and Italian restaurants worth a try include the **Nam Phu Restaurant-Bar** ((021) 216248, Nam Phou Circle, opposite the fountain. The menu includes mostly French dishes, although they will provide Lao food on demand. Featuring excellent service, it is popular with visiting French tourists and diplomatic officials, along with resident expatriates. Costs are around US$10 and upwards.

Opposite Nam Phu, the very popular **L'Opera** ((021) 215099, an Italian restaurant with an Italian chef, is considered to be the best Italian in town, with good expresso coffee and a wide selection of Italian wines. Close by and also extremely popular is **Lo Stivale** ((021) 215651, 44 Setthathirat Road, which also has a resident Italian chef. It has an extensive range of homemade pasta dishes and a good wine list.

Also worth a visit is the **Le Bistrot** ((021) 215972, Francois Ngin Street, opposite the TaiPan Hotel, for *cuisine familiale* at very reasonable prices, along with popular French dishes and couscous. **Le Vendome** ((021) 216402, in the tiny Wat In Paeng Lane behind Wat In Paeng, features an intimate candle-lit atmosphere and a good range of French favorites. It's housed in a French villa littered with Asian bric-a-brac and antiques. A meal here costs around US$15.

Other European establishments include the old timer **Arawan** ((021) 215373, 478 Samsenthai Road, which also has a well-stocked

charcuterie and specializes in French favorites like *coq au vin* and French wine and cheeses. Prices are reasonable, and it is possible to dine for as little as US$5 per head providing you stay away from the wine list. **Souriya** ((021) 215887, 31 Pang Kham Road, sports a similarly homey menu, but serves up its dishes in more atmospheric French colonial style surroundings. Prices are around US$10 per head.

For Lao and Chinese food, there are a great many places to choose from. All the hotels do great Lao food for starters, as does the backpacker **Patuxai Café** on the Mekong — particularly popular at sunset. But for the best Lao cuisine in town — indeed some say the whole of Laos — go to **Kua** ((021) 214813, 111 Samsenthai Road. It's possible to spend the entire evening reading the menu, which seems to go on forever, but thankfully there are English-speaking staff members at hand to help out with recommendations. The setting in an old villa is excellent, and traditional live music features at night.

For Indian cuisine, **The Taj**, on Pang Kham Road, just north of the fountain square, is justly popular. The food is authentic and prices are very inexpensive, at around US$5 per head. **Just For Fun** ((021) 213642, opposite Lao Aviation on 51 Pang Kham Road, is a vegetarian restaurant with a range of herbal teas and meatless dishes.

For a meal on the run, baguettes are available all over town, and with a choice of fillings. The street food is worth a try too, though obviously you should check to see the environs are clean and the stand is doing regular business with locals.

Samsenthai has several restaurants, and a hole-in-the-wall establishment opposite the Asian Pavilion Hotel serves up excellent Vietnamese food — not the place for a fancy meal, but certainly the place for a satisfying dinner or lunch.

HOW TO GET THERE

Vientiane's international Wattay Airport is accessible from Singapore by Silk Air and Malaysian Air Services, which flies via Kuala Lumpur and Phnom Penh. From Phnom Penh, flights are by Royal Air Cambodge and Lao Aviation, and from Saigon

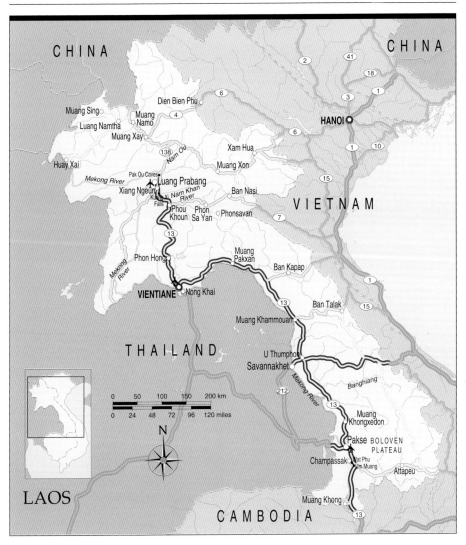

and Hanoi by Vietnam Airlines and Lao Aviation in a joint-venture deal. Thai International and Lao Aviation operate daily flights to Vientiane from Bangkok.

It is also possible to enter Laos by traveling by overnight train from Bangkok to Nong Khai, then driving across the Friendship Bridge into Laos, collecting a visa on arrival. If you're on a group or individual prepaid tour, you'll find a local tour agency mini-van or car waiting to take you the 20 km (12 miles) to Vientiane. If not, taxis are available and charge about US$5 to take you to town.

Lao Aviation operates all internal flights in Laos with a mixture of Russian and Chi-nese prop-driven aircraft, and some newer aircraft. Since Laos has opened up, it is possible to book reasonably priced flights all over the country.

LUANG PRABANG

To arrive in Luang Prabang by plane is to fly into one of Asia's most beautiful cities, a big tropical garden in the midst of a mountain-ringed valley. It is to see the waters of the Mekong and Nam Khan Rivers flashing amid the palms and other foliage, old French villas and civic buildings nestling here and there among the trees, and the gold-leafed spires of its many temples sparkling in the sun. For many years, Luang Prabang ranked with mythical Shangri-la as a fabled but virtually forbidden destination in Asia — protected by ramparts to the south, it was inaccessible by land and difficult to access by river. Even during the war it was difficult to get to, and out of reach completely during the revolutionary years. Only now is it wide open to foreigners — there is even a daily flight from Bangkok with Bangkok Airways.

From the ground Luang Prabang is even more idyllic. The road into town from the airstrip passes rows of neat timber shophouses, temples and weathered colonial buildings set among the trees, with the city's highest pagoda, That Chom Xi, atop a steep hill in the center of town, providing a dramatic backdrop all the way. To describe this royal town as a laid-back place would be an understatement: the people look as though they're enjoying a permanent siesta. The only real activity occurs in the early morning, when barefoot monks roam the misty streets, their saffron robes adding color to the gray dawn; they tread softly, in long orderly lines on their daily alms rounds.

Luang Prabang has been a designated UNESCO World Heritage Site since 1995. The organization cited Luang Prabang as the best-preserved historical town in Southeast Asia, recognizing its great historical and cultural significance, with 33 wats and 111 French-Lao buildings cited for specific conservation. No out-of-character buildings, advertising billboards, or big tourist hotels are allowed within the boundaries of the old city. (The downtown "business" district, where you'll find Lao Aviation, Inter-Laos Tourism, the General Post Office, the National Museum and the morning market, lies beyond the oldest quarter and is not protected). Within the protected area, power and telecommunication lines are buried out of sight and a number of ancient wats are being restored.

Luang Prabang is not a big place, and it is possible to cover most of it on foot or on bicycle. The people are friendly but also reserved: they nonchalantly accept foreigners in their midst, without getting excited, which makes it a pleasant place to explore.

As this is the Angkor Wat of Laos, it's very much part of a daily tourist conveyer belt that runs from Vientiane, with Lao Aviation operating daily flights full of tour groups and even pulling aircraft off other routes to provide extra services if the traffic gets too heavy.

In spite of being a popular destination, it is far from overcrowded. The slow pace, the evening chanting of the monks and the dawn alms parade through the cool streets make it a place that many travelers choose to linger in longer than they had planned. While organized tours to Luang Prabang are readily available, this is one town where a tour is not only unnecessary, but could be downright irritating. The town almost seems to be made to be explored at your own pace.

GENERAL INFORMATION

Most of Luang Prabang's tourist facilities, such as they are, are close to the Phousi Hotel on Setthathirath Road. The Lane Xang Bank is open weekdays from 8:30 AM to 3:30 PM can change cash and travelers' checks. The **National Tourism Office** ((071) 212092 is opposite the Phousi Hotel, though it offers little in the way of useful information for travelers. For car rental and Internet access, Luang Prabang's guesthouses and travelers' cafés are the best places to go.

WHAT TO SEE AND DO

The **National Museum** makes a good place to visit first. This former royal palace is an opulent French-Lao mansion that backs onto the Mekong. Originally constructed in 1904 as the official residence of King Sisavang Vong, father of the ill-fated last monarch, it is literally packed with precious Buddha statues of all descriptions and treasures from the dynastic era. The main hall, with its gold-painted walls, handloomed curtains from India and obvious opulence is only topped by the blood-red walls and mirrored decorations of the receiving room, where gasps of awe by impressed visitors can be heard at the entrance.

Some of the Buddha images appear to be priceless, including a reclining Buddha and a standing image made of marble. Other

Luang Prabang — "one big tropical garden."

images and treasures fill the large reception halls to the right and left of the entrance. To the right, the king's reception hall features busts of the various Laos monarchs, screens depicting the *Ramayana* and walls decorated with dramatic murals of traditional Laos life painted 70 years ago by the French artist Alix de Fautereau. Beyond, in another exhibition room, a large gold Buddha called the Pra Bang (from where Luang Prabang takes its name), presented to Fa Ngum by his Khmer benefactors when he conquered Luang Prabang, stands amid Buddhas fashioned from elephant tusks, a host of other sculptures, a temple frieze and three embroidered silk screens featuring Buddhist stories.

To the right of the entrance, next to the queen's reception hall, is a room crowded with exhibits of various official gifts given by foreign heads of state and VIPs over the years, the sort of fascinating kitsch that royalty and government leaders give each other, stuff that most people would probably keep in the attic or unload at a garage sale. Among all the wealth and finery, there is even a scale model of the Apollo moon vehicle *Columbia*, presented by Richard Nixon.

In the royal apartments to the rear of the throne and reception rooms are old sepia photographs of the royal family in happier times, including a misty Dietrich-style print of the queen. This human element counterbalances the moral and political issue of a royal entity who gave his royal blessing to the United States bombing and counter-insurgency operations in Laos during the war.

After all the finery of the receiving rooms, the bedrooms at the rear are surprisingly austere, devoid of any personal touches at all and much less luxurious than the average hotel room. No one outside the highest echelons of the government really knows what became of King Vatthana and his queen, but it's quietly whispered that after their exile to the Sam Neua Province, they were put to death in 1977 for refusing to support the revolutionary regime's policies.

Markets are always a focal point in smaller towns or rural areas. In Luang Prabang, they are populated by tribal populations coming in from the villages to sell their wares and produce. You will always see a few interestingly dressed folk around

the steps of the main market, the **Thalat Dala**, in the center of town, whose dim interior is filled with stalls selling textiles, hardware for use by the farming communities, silver jewelry and souvenirs, watches and a host of cookware and basic foodstuffs. The bustling morning market, **Thalat Sao**, at Wat Pasaman Road near Wat Phraphouthabat is perhaps the most colorful, and far less visited by tourists, no doubt because it is strictly a produce market supplying most of the town's needs. A small, but busy market fills the street leading up from the river to the Phousi Hotel, filled with vendors selling piles of fresh produce or bowls of steaming *pho* noodles.

Luang Prabang has so many temples that to visit the town and not see at least a few wats would be somewhat churlish. While one could spend a week or two visiting them all, several stand out as particularly interesting.

The commanding view of the town from **That Chom Xi**, on its high perch atop the peak of Phu Xi (or Phousi) is worth the climb alone. The That itself is relatively new, built in 1804. The panorama from the lower terrace of its stupa is wonderful at sunset, as the colors change across the city and the river stretches. Standing on a ridge close to the temple is an old revolving Russian anti-aircraft gun — a leftover from the early revolutionary days.

To the north of the peninsula, **Wat Xieng Thong** (Golden City Temple) is located on the confluence of the two rivers, and is considered to be the city's finest. The wat is best visited late in the afternoon, when the golden light shows off the temple to best advantage, the gilded carved doors glowing in the late afternoon sun. The large complex of shrines, pavilions and prayer halls features, among other things, brilliant and quite unusual mosaics and rare, gilded erotic carvings illustrating excerpts from the *Ramayana*. Among the other treasures at this 400-year-old site are a pavilion packed with Buddha images and a huge, gilded royal funeral chariot with dragon heads rearing from its prow, another containing a reclining Buddha dating back to the temple's

The beautiful National Museum, formerly the Royal Palace.

construction in 1560 and, at one corner of the complex, a royal barge.

The oldest temple site, **Wat Visoun**, located south of Wat Phou Xi near the Rama Hotel, dates back to 1513, shortly before the first Lao kingdom of Lane Xang was established here by the warlord Fa Ngum. The city's glory lasted only 12 years, until 1545, when the capital moved to Vientiane, but it remained a seat and power base of the Lao royalty right up until 1975, when the Pathet Lao hauled the last monarch, Savang Vattana, off to probable execution. Its main features are a collection of fifteenth-century ordination stones, a display of wooden Buddhas sculpted in the "Calling for Rain" posture. The dramatic white **That Pathum** (Lotus Stupa) in front of the main hall, is known more popularly as **That Mak Mo** (Watermelon Stupa) because of its bulbous shape. The collection of small gold and crystal Buddhas in the throne room of the National Museum is said to have been found in this stupa.

Wat Mai, close to the General Post Office off Luang Prabang's east–west main street, Phothiserat Street, is a relatively new temple, built in 1796. Its five-tiered roof and gilded, sculptured door panels depicting scenes from the life of Buddha and the *Ramayana* are among its key architectural features. The compound also houses two shallow-draft traditional barges, which lead celebrations on the rivers during the Lao New Year in April and the Water Festival in October. **Wat That Luang**, built in 1818 on a hill to the east of the city, has a central stupa containing the ashes of King Sisavang Vong.

Across the Mekong River from central Luang Prabang you'll find a complex of smaller temples that include **Wat Tham**, built into a limestone cave, and **Wat Chom Phet**, which provides another dramatic panorama of the town and river. Take a small boat from the bottom of the steps at Wat Xieng Thong.

WHERE TO STAY

Expensive

Probably the best address in Luang Prabang is **Villa Santi** ((071) 252157 FAX (071) 252158

E-MAIL info@villasantihotel.com WEB SITE www.villasantihotel.com, Sakkarine Street, previously known as Villa de la Princesse. It is set in a stylishly renovated former royal mansion, and is one of the gems of Luang Prabang's tourist industry. The rooms are deluxe by Lao standards, and the furnishings and decorations are said to have come from the royal collection. There is a quiet grassy courtyard for cocktails and buffets, an upstairs verandah bar and dining room with a view of the surrounding street life, and regular performances of traditional Lao court and tribal dancing.

The **Phou Vao Hotel** ((071) 212194 FAX (071) 212534 E-MAIL phouvao@hotmail .com, set on a hill to the east of the town, has a swimming pool and deluxe rooms

that start at US$85. It has superb views of Luang Prabang.

A converted villa guesthouse, the elegant and tiny **Auberge Calaos Hotel and Restaurant (** (071) 212100 FAX (071) 212085 E-MAIL calaoinn@laotel.com, close to Wat Xieng Thong, has just five spacious rooms. The villa has been beautifully restored, but asks a very steep US$200 and upwards for its rooms — substantial discounts are available through agencies and online booking sites.

Moderate

The sprawling **Phousi Hotel (** (071) 212717 FAX (071) 212719 E-MAIL phousi@laotel.com, Setthatirat Road, has a convenient location at the town's main intersection, at the corner of Phothisarat Street. The rooms are tastefully designed in a homey fashion and the hotel itself is set in tropical gardens reminiscent of Bali; the beer garden is a delightful place sit with a Beer Lao at the end of the day. Rooms range from US$35 to US$55.

Yet another charming hotel, but located at the other end of town, is the 24-room **Hotel Souvannaphoum (** (071) 212200 FAX (071) 212577, Phothisarat Street. It formerly belonged to Prince Souvanna Phouma. Room rates range from US$35 to US$75 per night. Rooms surround a sprawling garden, and the restaurant serves Lao and French cuisine.

A newer option is the 35-room **Muong Luang Hotel (** (071) 212790 FAX (071) 212790,

In Luang Prabang, the Mekong River at sunset.

Bounkhong Road, designed in traditional Lao style. The restaurant serves Luang Prabang and Lao dishes, and it is one of only two hotels with a swimming pool.

Inexpensive

The basic **Rama Hotel** ((071) 212247 has the advantage of being right in town and offers big, charmless but perfectly acceptable rooms for US$10 a night. It has Luang Prabang's only (very noisy) discotheque downstairs, which is the main drawback of the hotel.

WHERE TO EAT

As Luang Prabang blossoms into the most attractive destination in Indochina, the restaurant scene is also blossoming. The pick of the best includes the French **Auberge Duang Champa** ((071) 212420 overlooking the Khan River. Housed in an old French Villa, it is run by a Frenchman and his charming Lao wife, who offer a good French menu, starting at amazingly low prices of around US$2 for a set meal (à la carte costs more); there is also an acceptable wine list.

For a splash-out meal, the **L'Elephant Restaurant** ((071) 252482, Wat Nong, serves French and Lao cuisine at prices that by international standards are very reasonable.

Expect to pay around US$10 per head for a three-course meal.

ENVIRONS

The Buddhist grottoes of **Pak Ou Caves** lie 30 km (19 miles) along the Mekong River, and the trip there provides another insight into the beauty of this great waterway, especially in the dry season when the skilled boatmen effortlessly dodge the currents and whirlpools created by the low water. On the way, the squat, shallow-draft tour boats call into a small village that is famous for its traditional rice-wine stills. You can watch the fiery concoction being distilled and also enjoy a tipple or two, fortifying yourself for the rest of the trip ahead. Right in the midst of a sheer limestone cliff are the two Pak Ou Caves — an astonishing sight. A short climb brings you to the main cave and a sight that burns into the memory banks: hundreds and hundreds of **Buddha images** of all shapes, styles and sizes stand on terraces within the cave, held under the scrutiny of a local man who stands guard. There used to be a lot more statues, but Pak Ou was one of the prime targets of thievery and smuggling rackets which saw many of the treasures of Laos spirited out to the United States and the West during the war.

Beyond Pak Ou there's another spectacular limestone cliff, where the **Nam Ou River** joins the Mekong, and tour boats sometimes make a short trip along there before returning to Luang Prabang.

The small village of **Ban Phanom**, just a few kilometers east of the city, is Luang Prabang's favorite souvenir stop, where all tours, individual or group, inevitably end up, and it is well worth a visit. Although the clacking of handlooms has been more or less replaced by the quiet sounds of money changing hands as tourists make their purchases, the quality of the hand-loomed pieces is high, and prices are low. Ban Phanom is populated by Lu minority people, who were once responsible for

OPPOSITE: The prayer hall in Wat Xieng Thong. ABOVE: Poolside LEFT at the Luang Prabang Hotel. FOLLOWING PAGES: The gilded artistry of Wat Sen, typical of the Buddhist heritage of Luang Prabang.

weaving the fine textiles required by the royal family. Today it is famous for its quality **cotton and silk weaving,** and textiles are imported from other parts of the country to satisfy the ever growing market. You can still find the odd woman working on traditional looms, while others are busy haggling with the buyers in the busy market place that has sprung up in the center of the village. The village is part of a very sensible local government campaign to restore traditional arts and crafts. To get there take a jumbo from the main market, rent a bicycle

or just flag down a passing *tuk tuk*. It should cost just a few dollars to get there and back.

A pleasant drive 29 km (18 miles) south of Luang Prabang, brings you to the beautiful **Kuang Xi Falls** make a delightful excursion from the city. The lower falls have become a popular picnic spot while a second, less visited fall is accessible by a small trail.

HOW TO GET THERE

Improvements in the road between Vientiane and Luang Prabang mean that most travelers today rent a car for the journey or arrive by bus. It is also possible to fly, either from Vientiane with Lao Aviation or from Bangkok with Bangkok Airways.

Luang Prabang makes a triangle with Oudomxai and the Plain of Jars, so it is quite convenient to fly there before or after Luang Prabang.

From Thailand, a popular route is to enter Laos from Huay Xai in the very north and then travel by speedboat down the Mekong to Luang Prabang — it's something of a hair-raising trip, and operators require that passengers wear safety helmets. The journey takes around six hours.

NORTH OF LUANG PRABANG

As the remote north of Laos opens up to tourism, facilities are slowly improving. This is adventure territory — a land of rugged, jungled mountains peopled by hill tribes living in small villages. Getting around requires public transportation, a motorcycle or the services of a tour company, which is probably the best way to visit. A tour company like Diethelm or Intrepid will certainly maximize your experience and ensure that you get to visit interesting villages (see TAKING A TOUR, page 59 in YOUR CHOICE).

LUANG NAM THA

A flight slightly over an hour long from Luang Prabang over rugged mountain ranges brings you to the small airport of Luang Nam Tha, capital of Nam Tha Province, bordered by Myanmar to the northwest and China to the north. The province is home to 39 ethnic minority groups, who inhabit the remote mountain areas. While the town appears quite attractive, it is the villages outside of town, and particularly the old trading town of Muang Sing that are really worth the visit. That said, Luang Nam Tha has plenty of reasonable accommodation.

MUANG SING

A relatively new discovery on the tourist trail, the old trading settlement of Muang Sing dates back to the sixteenth century. Known for the numerous tribal people who inhabit the villages surrounding the broad rice plains of the Nam La River, Muang Sing was once the major opium market of the northern highlands, and is located just a few miles from the Chinese border. The main attraction is the colorful daily market attended by a mixed crowd of tourists and Tai Lu, Zao, Iko, Shan, Lao Sung, Hmong and Tai Daeng people who converge at the market for trade and pleasure, and by 10 AM its all over. Women set up stalls in the cold morning light doling out steaming bowls of turkey *pho* noodles — appreciated by both villagers and visitors. Other women sell fried donuts or approach tourists to sell hand-embroidered head wraps at bargain prices.

animist festival centers on a wat on a sacred hill to the south of town and starts a few days ahead of the full moon. Traditional dances, games and Lao pop music keep every one entertained.

MUANG XAY

Oudomxai Province sits between Luang Prabang and Luang Nam Tha, also sharing a border with China's Yunnan Province, and is home to 23 ethnic minorities including the Akha (Iko), T'ai Lu, T'ai Dam, and

Accommodation in Muang Sing is basic, costing around US$2 to US$3 a night, but for some a little discomfort is worth it for the adventure. No doubt more up-market rooms will become available as the tiny market town becomes better known. Outside the town it's possible to visit tribal villages, often a few kilometers' walk from the main road.

The best time of the year to visit is during the **Muang Sing Festival**, held on the full moon of the twelfth lunar month, which occurs around late October or early November, depending on the vagaries of the moon. During the festival, villagers come to town resplendent in their best costumes for several days of celebrations. This Buddhist-

T'ai Neua. Its burgeoning capital, Muang Xay, has a major Chinese feel to it, in part because imported skilled Chinese labor has contributed to major road-building projects to make it the northern commercial and trading hub, linking the town to surrounding provincial centers. As such, the brash town lacks the graciousness of other centers, and many of the hotels function as brothels for the Chinese workers. However, the market is good and the town is well located for trekking and hiking through remote mountain villages. It is possible that as canny tour operators become aware of

OPPOSITE: A Luang Prabang village hut.
ABOVE: Buddha images fill the sacred Pak Ou Caves downriver from Luang Prabang.

the potential, conditions will improve drastically. Muang Xay has flights to Luang Prabang and Vientiane.

XIENG KHOANG (PLAIN OF JARS)

One of Laos's more enigmatic destinations, the desolate Plain of Jars has caught the imagination of visitors since it was opened to tourism in the early 1990s. **Phonsavan**, the new capital of northern Xieng Khoang Province, was built after the former capital, Xieng Khoang, was virtually destroyed by bombing during the campaign against the Communist Pathet Lao in the Vietnam War. It's a sprawling and flat nondescript market town of cement and corrugated iron — a study in charmlessness that has little interest to visitors. The town lies at the center of a vast, defoliated, utterly devastated, dusty plain that still shows scars of some of the heaviest bombing of the war. In the dry season the winds that sweep across the area are distinctly cold in the daytime and bitter at night.

But Phonsavan is the gateway to a unique historical attraction, the large stone jars that lie scattered across the dry plains. Weighing as much as six tons, these mysterious vessels point to the sky like fat siege mortars, which more than one observer has cynically suggested the United States bomber pilots mistook them for. The ground is littered with UXO (unexploded ordnance) and is extremely dangerous, especially to children playing in the fields. Although it is being slowly cleared, visitors are cautioned to keep to the marked paths.

The jars are said to be many hundreds if not thousands of years old, but beyond that no one has really come up with the definite explanation for them, although theories of their origins abound. One suggests that they were wine fermentation jars put there by a sixth-century resistance hero to celebrate his victory over a despotic local ruler. Another suggests they were burial jars. Yet another explanation may well lie in the region's arid character during the winter months — were they, in fact, nothing more than water-storage vessels? Whatever

Sunset on the Mekong.

the answer, they tease the imagination, and they are one of those strange cultural attractions that draw visitors simply to be able to say they've seen it.

According to local reports, there were once several hundred jars at several sites across the region, but the smaller ones have been souvenired and others shattered, so that fewer than 100 now remain in the main site, in two groups scattered on a hillock and across the floor of a shallow valley. This main site **Thong Hai Vin** or Stone Jar Plain is 12 km (seven miles) from town.

Site Two, 23 km (14 miles) from town, has smaller jars scattered across two hillsides. Site Three is 28 km (17 miles) from town and reached by a delightful walk past a small wat and through ricefields. Here, strewn across a grassy hillock, is the most picturesque site, although the jars are smaller and less dramatic than at the main site. Other smaller sites are hidden in the hills but be warned — not all have been cleared of ordnance and could be dangerous.

The flight from Vientiane is certainly something not to be missed — it carries you over the rice-plains around Vientiane and then across beautiful mountain ranges featuring many rivers and literally dozens of potential whitewater rafting spots, as well as a vast reservoir (Ang Nam Ngum) and hydroelectric plant that not only serves domestic power needs but exports electricity to Thailand. Phonsavan itself, however, has little to offer aside from spectacular landscapes of lush rice terraces, especially in October and November after the wet season, and the mysterious novelty of the Plain of Jars. Most visitors find that one night is sufficient to explore the plains, with time enough to make it out to the old ruined capital of Xieng Khoang, where a lonely bombed Buddha surveys the surrounding land.

Those not on an organized tour will find getting around to be quite easy. Local tour guides meet every flight at the airport, drumming up business; they will take you on a hotel tour until you find one to your liking and then provide transport to the various sites. Jeeps and minibuses are available, and cost US$65 for the trip to the plains — significantly cheaper than a tour.

WHERE TO STAY AND EAT

Phonsavan's tourist facilities are basic, but there are a couple of more comfortable hotel options.

The simple **Auberge de la Plaine de Jarres** ((061) 212044, about one kilometer (half a mile) out of town and run by Sodetour, is where tour groups check-in. It is an excellent location from which to visit the jars. Rates run US$25 to US$50.

The large Communist-inspired **Phou Doi Travel Hotel** ((061) 212238, Phonsavan Road, can be recommended. It is an old hotel but well maintained, and the simple but large rooms start at US$10.

In "downtown" Phonsavan, near the market, the **Hayhin Hotel** (no phone), Route 7, has been given a bit of a facelift. It is a reliable budget hotel with rooms from US$5. Directly across the road, the **Phonesaysouron Restaurant** serves a fixed but wholesome Lao supper, and breakfasts of thick coffee and fried sesame buns. The nearby **Sangah Restaurant** offers simple but delicious Chinese, Laos and Thai-style dishes for just a few dollars.

PAKSE AND THE SOUTH

Pakse is the relatively prosperous administrative center of the Champassak Province and a lively market town. Lying in a balmy, subtropical landscape of rice paddies and groves of palms at the confluence of the Mekong and Se Don Rivers in southern Laos, it was built as recently as 1905 as the new capital of Champassak Province. While it has very little history of its own, it is the gateway to the former royal capital of Champassak and one of the most important religious sites in Southeast Asia — the pre-Khmer Hindu/Buddhist temple of Wat Phu. Pakse is also a key access point to one of the widest and most picturesque sections of the Mekong River and the 4,000 islands close to the Cambodian border. Until February 1998, Pakse market was a popular stop-off point for textile collectors who came in search of the handwoven silk *ikats*

TOP: The fabled Plain of Jars. BOTTOM: A market scene in Xieng Khuang.

from the surrounding villages. Unfortunately the market burned to the ground, leaving a lot of unhappy and poorer (although still alive) people in its wake.

It is possible to enter Laos from Ubon Ratchathani in Thailand, crossing by ferry at Chongmek, and thereby covering Pakse, Wat Phu and the southern islands before heading north and on to Vientiane.

PAKSE

Pakse itself is not a major sightseeing area, but it makes a convenient base for exploring the surrounding areas. To the north is the **Boloven Plateau**, home of tribal villagers, elephant workers, coffee plantations, the market town of Se Kong and the Se Kong River, waterfalls and the pleasant Thatlo Resort. To the south is **Champassak** and the pre-Angkor **Wat Phu**, the 4,000 Mekong Islands or **Si Phan Don**, and the remote and charming little town of **Attapeu**, which is close to the Ho Chi Minh Trail.

Pakse itself is the last post of civilization for the south, with some reasonable restaurants and hotels, a big and very lively market that shouldn't be missed and an interesting museum with an ethnological section exhibiting the tribal peculiarities of the southern minority people. Easy half-day trips can be made to the worthwhile weaving village of **Ban Saphay** 16 km (10 miles) north of town on the Mekong, where handloom silk is a specialty. You can rent a jumbo to get there. The **Taat Sae Waterfall** is off Road No. 13, south of Pakse.

Where to Stay

The **Auberge Sala Champa** ((031) 212273, just a two-minute walk from the busy market, may not be the best hotel in town, but it is the most pleasant to stay in. The air-conditioned rooms go for US$25 to US$35. Try one of the older, unrenovated rooms upstairs for a slightly seedy journey to the past, or the newer garden rooms with modern conveniences. This converted colonial villa offers comfort, charm, an air of antiquity and a powerful sense of what life must have been like in old Indochina — the woven bamboo walls and ceiling of its ground-floor bar, the sculptured stonework of its

patio, the vast wire-netted balcony restaurant upstairs, the geckos and the lazy ceiling fans. Reservations are required to eat here. The newer single-story annex built around the main house adds to the charm.

The former royal Boun Oum Palace, now known as the **Champassak Palace Hotel** ((031) 212263 FAX (031) 212781, Route 13, on the outskirts of town, is the best hotel in Pakse. Occupying a prominent position overlooking the Se Don River, it is certainly grand by Pakse standards but, for a palace, lacks atmosphere. Rooms start at US$40.

The **Souk Samlane Hotel** (/FAX (031) 212281 E-MAIL lxtrvel@laotel.com, 14 Ban Wat Luang, has a great location. Even if it looks like a dump from the outside, it is a perfectly acceptable lower mid-range hotel once you are inside. The 20 air-conditioned rooms start at US$20 and have balconies overlooking the street. A friendly ground-floor restaurant provides mainly Lao food along with a few Western dishes.

Two kilometers (a little over one mile) to the east, the **Champassak Residence Hotel** ((031) 212263 FAX (031) 212765, Route 13, is a well-managed hotel, with comfortable rooms and a pleasant garden setting. Rooms range from US$30 a night to US$50 for a suite. The restaurant serves Laos, French and Chinese food and the hotel rents boats and buses for trips out of town.

Where to Eat

With a large Chinese population, Pakse has several, if not glamorous, at least serviceable restaurants scattered around the town center. The **Champassak Palace Hotel** has good Lao, Chinese and Thai food and a fully stocked bar. The **Champassak Residence** has a cozy dining room and a bar, popular with expatriates staying in Pakse. Opposite the market, the **Sedone Restaurant** is relaxed and friendly with reasonable Laos and Chinese-style food.

CHAMPASSAK AND WAT PHU

The docking point for the journey to Wat Phu, Champassak has little to show of its former glory as a royal capital, but archeological teams are busy exploring the former city's ramparts. This sleepy little ghost town exhibits some striking examples of old French civic architecture, which stand virtually cheek-by-jowl with traditional and modern stilted, tin-roofed, wooden Lao homes. The town lies on either side of a red-dirt road that runs parallel with the river until it makes an abrupt right turn and becomes part of the triumphal approach to Wat Phu. Along the way you may see two gaudily decorated Buddha images almost hidden by the encroaching branches of Banyan trees. In the wide plain that lies before Wat Phu, another decrepit royal villa — a

summer pavilion — lies on the edge of a large lotus pool, left to fall into ruin since the last king of Laos, Savang Vatthana, and his queen disappeared into the murky gulag of socialist re-education.

The ruins of the ancient pre-Khmer temple Wat Phu lie 37 km (23 miles) from Pakse just past the town of Champassak — once the capital of the Champassak Kingdom and earlier part of the Khmer Angkor Empire. Situated on the lower eastern slope of the sacred mountain of Phu Kao, whose peak is said to resemble a lingam, it has been a holy site for millennia. The mountain is essential to Wat Phu's special status as a religious site — the monolith on top of it attracting Khmer Shivaites who built the

first temple there well before the rise of the Khmer Empire. In the sixth century a Chinese chronicle spoke of a temple on the site guarded by a thousand soldiers and dedicated to a spirit to whom the king offered a human sacrifice each year. Evidence suggests that it was also the principal temple of the capital of Chenla, Shreshthapura, which is believed to have been located on the site of present-day Champassak. As its name suggests, this in turn may previously have been part of the central Vietnam kingdom of Champa.

As possibly the oldest religious site used by the Khmer Hindus, Wat Phu is significant indeed. Its antiquity is all the more pronounced by the state it's in today. Of its two imposing main palaces, built on a terrace at the foot of the hill, only the outer walls are still standing, and their entrances, featuring elaborately sculptured gables, have all but collapsed — the huge stones tumbling as though struck by an earthquake. Beyond them, a series of steep stone stairways, also in a state of ruin, lead up the hillside to terraces where pavilions, a library and as many as six other buildings once stood. The main sanctuary, located on the highest terrace, is relatively well preserved, featuring an antechamber and side-naves with walls and lintels decorated with carved *devatas* and *dvarapalas*. Close by, against the foot of a cliff, there's a bas-relief carving of Shiva flanked by Brahma and Vishnu and, nearby, a huge flat stone with the outline of a crocodile carved deeply into it.

Guides will enthusiastically demonstrate how the outline neatly embraces the human body, and how a channel in the stone was put there to drain the blood — supporting the theory that this was in fact the altar upon which the early monarchs performed their human sacrifices.

The present ruins of Wat Phu are said to date back to the eleventh and twelfth centuries. Three Buddha images now stand in the sanctuary, and it is suggested that this may well be Southeast Asia's oldest Buddhist temple. But throughout the complex, much of the architecture and surviving decoration is definitely Hindu.

A Pakse woman prepares sticky rice.

The temple's key festival, staged in the three days leading up to the February full moon, coincides with the Buddhist Makha Puja, although unfortunately it has become a popular commercial venture in recent years, with local teenagers wandering about and loud music that manages to detract from the holy atmosphere one may be expecting. Another festival held each June climaxes with the sacrificial slaughter of a buffalo.

While Wat Phu is in less than perfect condition, it is well worth a visit for the at-

in her terrible aspect. But time and the elements, not to mention looters, have wreaked a violent toll, all but destroying the temple complex, except for the broken walls and traces of three towers of one of halls. Other relics — a lintel decorated with an image of Indra, and a stone lingam with four faces at its head — are scattered among the trees.

The standard tour of this region involves a boat trip to **Muang Thamo**, also known as Um Muang or Muang Tomo, a ruined Khmer temple constructed in about the

mosphere and the sense of history that pervades it. Nearby is a pavilion erected by a team of United Nations archeologists who are resurrecting the surrounding statuary.

The best way to get to Wat Phu is the languid trip by boat along the Mekong from Pakse. The trip, favored by the tour agencies, usually combines the temple tour with visits to the region's two other principal attractions; Champassak itself and another temple ruin, **Huei Thamo**. The site of this late ninth-century ruin lies in dense secondary forest close to a small riverside village about two and a half hours by boat beyond Champassak. It's known that the temple dates back to around AD 889, and was dedicated to Durga, consort of Shiva

same period as Wat Phu. The ruins include a broad causeway bordered by lingams and two carved stone sanctuaries that retain some degree of their original integrity. The return trip takes you back to Champassak where a car or mini-van is usually waiting to take you to Wat Phu. The tour takes a full day, and the return to Pakse is generally by road via a vehicular ferry that crosses the Mekong at Champassak. With these grand relics of the Khmer culture, the quiet charm of Champassak and the stunning vistas of the Mekong River and forested hills along the way, it's a day you'll remember for a long time.

It is also possible to rent a boat in Pakse or take a public boat from the boat jetty on Pakse's Se Don River and forget all about buses. Make the journey yourself, staying overnight in Champassak at the comfortable **Sala Wat Phu** for US$25 to US$30 per night. The knowledgeable and English-speaking manager is a fount of wisdom and advice on local matters. There is no need to book except at festival time. From Champassak to Wat Phu, a distance of a few kilometers, it is fun to take a local sidecar motorcycle or take a taxi from the ferry stop.

SI PHAN DON — THE 4,000 ISLANDS

Tours to the Mekong islands, Si Phan Don, further south, are also available from Pakse, or it is possible to see it on a do-it-yourself basis. Highlights include seeing the rare, fresh-water dolphins that come upriver to spawn in the dry season and several spectacular cascades near the Cambodian border. While making the river hardly navigable at this juncture, the cascades are extremely attractive. Guesthouses provide readily available accommodation, especially on the biggest island of **Don Khong** in the main village of Muang Khong, a former French settlement. The **Donekhong Hotel** ((031) 212077 on Khong Island at 3 Kanghong Street in Ban Khong Hong, has rates of around US$35, and is where the tour groups put up.

THATLO RESORT

About 88 km (60 miles) northeast of Pakse in Saravan is the delightful Thatlo Resort ((031) 212725 — a piece of natural wilderness on the edge of the Boloven Plateau. Small but comfortable chalets look out across a river and cascading waterfalls, a popular stopover on many tours of the south. Thatlo is in the midst of a coffee-growing area and hill-tribe region, with Katu and Alak villages worth exploring. Alternatively, it is rather pleasant spending time relaxing by the river. Thatlo Resort can be booked through **Sode Tours** ((031) 212122 in Pakse or through the main office in Vientiane at ((021) 213478 FAX (021) 216313. They can also organize transportation. Rooms cost from US$35.

HOW TO GET THERE

Lao Aviation operates daily flights to Pakse, and now that the new road is completed it is even possible to travel by road from Vientiane — a drive that takes about 14 hours (it's a horrendous journey). It is also certainly possible to depart by ferry and road to Ubon Ratchathani in Thailand, from where there are trains to Bangkok.

Several travel companies in Pakse can organize tours; try **Sodetour** ((031) 212122

in a French villa close to the boat jetty pier on Thasalakham Road. **Champa Residence** ((031) 212120 FAX (031) 212765 can also organize a tour or a car at reasonable prices for guests. The **National Tourism Authority of Laos** Champassak Office ((031) 212021 on Thasalakham Road (at the other end of the ferry pier) can rent cars for around US$80 per day.

OPPOSITE: Temple carvings at the Wat Phu Khmer ruins near Pakse. ABOVE: Transport on the Mekong River near Pakse.

Travelers'
Tips

GETTING THERE

Whether you are flying from North America, Europe or Australasia, the best way to approach Indochina, which is poorly served by international flights, is to fly to one of the regional hubs — Bangkok, Hong Kong or Singapore, in that order of preference — and connect to your first Indochina destination from there. Bangkok is the logical first choice, not only because it offers the widest choice of access to Indochina, but finishing up at Angkor Wat, which has direct flights back to Bangkok. But there are, a myriad of other ways to do it.

Regionally based carriers such as Cathay Pacific, Singapore Airlines, Silk Air, Malaysian Airlines, Royal Air Cambodge, Philippine Airlines, Thai International, Royal Brunei and Lao Aviation are among those that fly to Indochina.

Thai International has daily services from Bangkok to Saigon and Hanoi, and Cathay Pacific has daily flights from Hong Kong to Ho Chi Minh City and Hanoi. Both

also because, if you have a layover, it offers the best value for money of the three chief Asian air hubs. Moreover, for those thinking of overlanding, Thailand has land crossings to both Laos and Cambodia.

The permutations of flying into one of the three countries of Indochina from one of the three major Asian air hubs are so diverse that it would almost be an impossible task to list them all here. Best to choose your transit hub, decide the itinerary of your Indochina trip, and then talk to your travel agent about ticketing. The most logical route is to fly to Bangkok, transit to Vientiane (from where you can explore Laos), fly from Vientiane to Hanoi or Saigon and explore Vietnam, and then fly or overland from Saigon to Phnom Penh,

services are run in cooperation with Vietnam Airlines. Thai International also operates daily flights from Bangkok to Vientiane, and has three flights a day to Phnom Penh, again in cooperation with Lao Aviation and Royal Air Cambodge.

Within Indochina, the three national airlines operate daily services linking Hanoi, Saigon, Vientiane and Phnom Penh.

FLIGHTS TO INDOCHINA

Peak seasons are Christmas and New Year, Chinese New Year (late January to late

OPPOSITE: A fish market on the Cai River in Vietnam's historic Hoi An. ABOVE: Buddhist monks at Thien Mu Pagoda in Hue.

February, varying year to year) and summer, from June through September.

From the United States and Canada

All major airlines out of the United States and Canada have flights to Bangkok, Hong Kong or Singapore, with airlines such as Singapore, Cathay and United offering nonstop flights. Vancouver is the best-served Canadian city, with direct flights offered by both Canadian and Cathay. Cheaper airlines out of the United States will often involve a change in Seoul or Taipei.

The best deals are usually Apex tickets, which require you book and pay at least three weeks in advance, and stay at your destination at least seven days (but no longer than three months). Schedule changes (while sometimes possible) are frowned upon, and will sometimes involve further payments, or "penalties."

From Europe

There is a choice of many daily flights from Britain and other parts of Europe direct to Bangkok, Hong Kong or Singapore, though the cheaper tickets will involve a layover of varying length somewhere en-route. Local newspapers are the best place to check for bargains. British travelers looking for bargains might take a look at **www.cheap flights.co.uk**, which offers a staggering selection of discounted tickets to every conceivable Asian destination.

From Australia and New Zealand

Australia and New Zealand have a good range of flights to Bangkok, Hong Kong

and Singapore, as these destinations are all used as stopovers on the long-haul Europe flights. Royal Brunei has some very good deals, but Brunei — one of Asia's smallest and most expensive countries — is perhaps one of the least appealing stopovers in the region. Perth is the least expensive Australian location to fly from. Finding bargains out of New Zealand, on the other hand, is a challenge.

OVERLAND TO INDOCHINA

While most travelers still fly into Indochina from one of the Asian regional air hubs, an increasing number of travelers — particularly younger backpackers — are traveling by bus or train into the area. The best place to get organized for such a trip is Bangkok's Khao San Road, the backpacker capital of Southeast Asia. Any of the agencies here can organize the necessary visas and sell tickets for the first leg of the journey into either Laos or Cambodia.

The other route into Indochina is from China in the north, which allows travelers to start in Hong Kong and travel through China to Hanoi, either via Guangxi Province or Yunnan Province.

The main crossing from Thailand to Cambodia is from Aranyaprathet, around four hours by bus from Bangkok to Paoy Pet in Cambodia. From Paoy Pet there are connecting buses to Siem Reap that take anywhere between six and ten hours depending on the weather and the current condition of the road — appalling at the best of times. An alternative, less-used route is to travel to Trat, which is around seven hours east of Bangkok, and take a connecting ferry to the Cambodian island of Koh Kong. Connecting ferries go from there to Sihanoukville. At both border crossings, visas are available on the spot for 1,000 baht.

There are currently five border crossings between Thailand and Laos. The most commonly used is the crossing from Nong Khai in northern Thailand to Vientiane in Laos. Overnight trains run from Bangkok to Nong Khai. Also popular is the Chiang Khong crossing in the north of Thailand to Huay Xai in southwestern Laos. From Huay Xai, motorboats run down to Luang Prabang: a thrilling if somewhat dangerous trip.

The other Thai crossings to Laos — from northeastern Thailand or Isaan — are less used. The Mukdahan crossing to Savannakhet is an interesting option, as it allows for traveling overland from Savannakhet to Hue in Vietnam, though this is not a pleasant bus journey. The other two crossings are from Nakhon Phanom in northeastern Thailand to Muang Khammouan in Laos, and from Chong Mek in Thailand to Vang Tao and on to Pakse in Laos.

ARRIVING AND LEAVING

VISAS

Things have changed since the days when only overseas consulates provided visas to Vietnam, Laos and Cambodia. Vietnam now hands out two-month tourist visas from most Southeast Asian cities, including Vientiane, Phnom Penh, Bangkok, Hong Kong and Singapore. Alternatively, organize your Vietnam visa in or your own country's Vietnam embassy. Once inside Vietnam, you are free to travel where you want without restrictions.

Bear in mind, with Vietnam visas, that it is essential to plan in advance if you want to leave or enter the country by one of its overland border crossings, as this information has to be entered into the visa in order to actually make the crossing. If you have simply obtained a normal visa, it can be changed to accommodate a land crossing, but you will need to visit a Vietnam embassy or consulate and pay a US$5 fee to have the visa "corrected."

Cambodia grants one-month visas costing US$20 on arrival at all its border crossings, obviously including the main ones at the international airports of Phnom Penh and Siem Reap. One passport photograph is required. Extensions are reasonably easy to organize.

Lao visas are also much easier to arrange than before. Those flying into Vientiane or Luang Prabang, or taking the Friendship Bridge from Nong Khai to Vientiane, can get 30-day visas on arrival at a cost of US$30. Two passport photographs are required. Those traveling to Laos via one of the land crossings other than Nong Khai-Huay Xai will need to apply in advance for a visa. They are most easily obtained by a travel agency on Khao San Road in Bangkok, taking three working days. Bear in mind that Bangkok is the cheapest place to apply for Lao visas.

As visa requirements are regularly subject to change, it is always prudent to check regulations with the local embassies prior to your trip.

CUSTOMS

Customs regulations are different, of course, for each of the three Indochinese countries. Vietnam is the strictest of the three. Both Laos and Cambodia are fairly relaxed, and rarely check the luggage of foreigners crossing their borders. Vietnam's basic customs allowance is: 200 cigarettes, 50 cigars or 250 g of tobacco, one liter of wine, one liter of liquor and an unlimited amount of film. In the case of Cambodia, confusion reigns. It is almost impossible to determine what can and cannot be brought into the country and in what quantities. The best bet is

OPPOSITE: Schoolgirls in traditional *ao dais* in central Saigon. ABOVE: A village girl distills rice wine in the Luang Prabang region.

to use Vietnam's rules. Laos has the most liberal customs allowance, allowing for 500 cigarettes, one bottle of spirits and two bottles of wine.

DEPARTURE TAXES

Vietnam levies a departure tax of US$10 on all outgoing international flights. In Cambodia it is US$20 (US$4 for domestic flights), and in Laos it is US$10.

EMBASSIES AND CONSULATES

FOREIGN REPRESENTATION IN INDOCHINA

Vietnam
The following countries have embassies in Hanoi:
Australia ((04) 831-7755, Van Phuc Quarter.
Belgium ((04) 845-2263, 48 Nguyen Thai Hoc.
Cambodia ((04) 825-3788, 71A Tran Hung Dao Street.
Canada ((04) 823-5500, 31 Hung Vuong Street.
China ((04) 845-3736, 46 Hoang Dieu Street.
France ((04) 825-2719, 57 Tran Hung Street.
Germany ((04) 845-3836, 29 Thran Phu Street.
Italy ((04) 825-6246, 9 Le Phung Hieu Street.
Laos ((04) 825-4576, 22 Rue Tran Bing Trong.
Netherlands ((04) 843-0605, D1 Van Phuc Quarter.
New Zealand ((04) 824-1481, 32 Hang Bai.
Sweden ((04) 845-4824, Van Phuc Quarter.
Switzerland ((04) 934-6589, Central Building Office, 15th Floor, 44B Ly Thuong Kiet Street.
Thailand ((04) 823-5092, 63-65 Hoang Dieu Street.
United Kingdom ((04) 825-2510, Central Building, 31 Hai Ba Trung.
United States ((04) 843-1500, 7 Lang Ha Street.
    While foreign embassies are based in Hanoi, many foreign countries have consulates in Saigon. The main ones are:
Australia ((08) 829-6035, 5B Ton Duc Thang, District 1.
Cambodia ((08) 829-2751, 41 Phung Khac Khoan.
Canada ((08) 824-5025, 235 Dong Khoi, District 1.
China ((08) 829-2457, 39 Nguyen Thi Minh Khai, District 1.

France ((08) 829-7231, 27 Nguyen Thi Minh Khai, District 1.
Germany ((08) 829-1967, 126 Nguyen Dinh Chieu, District 3.
Laos ((08) 829-7667, 93 Pasteur, District 1.
Netherlands ((08) 823-5932, 29 Le Duan, District 1.
New Zealand ((08) 822-6907, 41 Nguyen Thi Minh Khai, District 1.
Switzerland ((08) 825-8780, 2 Ngo Duc Ke, District 1.
Thailand ((08) 932-7637, 77 Tran Quoc Tha, District 3.

United Kingdom ((08) 823-2604, 25 Le Duan, District 1.
United States ((08) 822-9434, 4 Le Duan, District 1.

Cambodia
The following countries have an embassy or consulate in Phnom Penh:
Australia ((023) 213470, 11 Street 254.
Belgium ((023) 360877, 1 Street 21.
Canada ((023) 213470, 11 Street 254.
China ((023) 720922, 256 Thanon Keomani.
France ((023) 430020, 1 Monivong Boulevard.
Germany ((023) 216381, 76 Street 214.
Laos ((02) 326441 FAX (02) 327454, 15-17 Thanon Keomani.
Thailand ((023) 363869, 4 Monivong Boulevard.

United Kingdom ((023) 427124, 27–29 Street 75.
United States ((023) 216436, 27 Street 240.
Vietnam ((023) 364741, 436 Monivong Boulevard.

Laos
The following countries are represented in Vientiane:
Australia ((021) 413600, on Nehru Road, Phone Xay.
Cambodia ((021) 314952, Thanon Saphan Thong Neua.
China ((021) 315103, Vat Nak Street.
France ((021) 215253, Setthatirath Road, BP 06.
Germany ((021) 312110, 26 Thanon Sok Pa Luang.
Thailand ((021) 214581, Route Phonekheng.
United Kingdom (c/o Australian Embassy).
United States ((021) 212581, 19 Bartholonie.
Vietnam ((021) 413400, 1 Thanon That Luang.

INDOCHINESE REPRESENTATION ABROAD

Vietnam
Australia ((02) 6286-6059 FAX (02) 6286-4534, 6 Timbarra Crescent, Malley Canberra, ACT 2606.
Canada ((613) 236-0772 FAX (613) 236-2704, 226 Maclaren Street, Ottawa, Ontario, Canada, K2P OL6.
United Kingdom ((020) 7937-33222 FAX (020) 7937-6108, 12-14 Victoria Road, London W8-5RD.
United States ((415) 922-1577 FAX (415) 922-1848, 1700 California Street, Suite 475, San Francisco, 94109; and ((202) 861-0737 FAX (202) 861-0917, 20th Street NW, Suite 400, Washington DC, 20036.

Laos
Australia ((02) 6286-4595 FAX (02) 6290-1910, 1 Dalman Crescent, O'Malley, Canberra, ACT 2606.
United States ((212) 832-2734 FAX (212) 332-4923, 317 East 51st Street, New York, New York 10022.

Cambodia
Australia ((02) 6273-1168 FAX (02) 6273-1053, 5 Canterbury Crescent, Deakin, ACT 2600, Canberra.
United States ((202) 726-7742 FAX (202) 726-8381, 4500 Sixteenth Street NW, 20011 Washington D.C.

TOURIST INFORMATION

Local tourist information offices are listed in each of the relevant destinations in this book, but it is worth noting that in Vietnam, Cambodia and Laos, government tourist offices are of little use. If they do anything at all it is generate hard currency through selling tours. In each of the countries of Indochina, travelers will find that the best sources of information are other travelers and the small cafés and guesthouses that have sprung up to cater to the needs of increasing numbers of young budget travelers who are visiting the region.

GETTING AROUND

BY AIR

The national carriers — Vietnam Airlines, Lao Aviation and Royal Air Cambodge — operate very efficient domestic networks in Indochina. They can also be quite flexible. Lao Aviation and Royal Air Cambodge add extra flights to their key cultural destinations, Luang Prabang and Angkor Wat, if the volume of tourists gets too big for scheduled services. In addition to these major carriers, a number of smaller airlines have come into existence in recent years, particularly in Cambodia, which in times past was particularly underserved domestically by its national airline.

Aircraft have also been upgraded in recent years, and travel today in Indochinese skies is presumably a lot safer than it was even half a decade ago.

Domestic airports across the region too are being modernized — witness the new airports at Phnom Penh and Siem Reap, which are impressive compared to the way they looked just a few years ago.

See the relevant destination sections for listings of local airlines.

BY ROAD

Modernization has been slow to come to the roads of Indochina. In all three countries the

The benign visage of a god king, Wat Thom Angkor.

roads are generally potholed, frequently washed out, and literally a pain in the posterior to travel on. That said, in many instances there is no alternative, and the one compensation is that throughout the region, the vehicles at least are improving. Luxury buses are no longer uncommon on the roads that run to destinations popular with foreign tourists — get off the beaten track, however, and you will be packed in with the off-to-market crowd, sharing your seat with caged chickens, in clapped-out vehicles that should have been put to rest years ago.

Rental cars, minibuses and limousines are available throughout the region, with everyone from budget guesthouse and cafés to five-star hotels and tour companies operating them. Prices vary very little throughout the region — around US$50 to US$80 a day, depending on the vehicle. This includes gas and the driver's accommodation if there's an overnight stay.

Private taxis are available in most cities, on call around the main hotels, but these generally involve a lot of haggling over the fare. But why cram yourself into a taxicab when you can roll along in the open air aboard a pedal-cyclo, which you'll find just about everywhere you go in Indochina, and will cost you about US$1 per hour (US$10 a day)? Otherwise, it's easy to rent motorcycles in Vientiane and Phnom Penh at about US$5 to US$10 per day (24 hours), and most cities rent bicycles if you want to get around a little more sedately.

BY BOAT

There are number of opportunities to travel by boat in Indochina, and it is generally a welcome relief from the roads. In Vietnam, the Mekong Delta region has become a popular destination, and travel both into the area from Saigon and around it can all be done on the water. In Laos, the most popular boat journey is from Huay Xai in the far southwest to Luang Prabang, an exhilarating, sometimes frightening journey at breakneck speeds down the Mekong. In Cambodia, most travelers who are not flying from Phnom Penh to Siem Reap take the daily boat services that connect the capital with Cambodia's most famous tourist

attraction — providing there are no breakdowns, and the boat is not dangerously overcrowded (unfortunately it happens), it's a very enjoyable journey, and faster than doing it by road.

BY RAIL

While Cambodia has a length of rail that connects Phnom Penh with the southern beach resort of Sihanoukville, travelers rarely use it — it was long considered too dangerous, and now the danger has been removed it is considered by most to be too slow. The only rail journey in Indochina that travelers use is Vietnam's *Reunification Express*, which links Saigon with Hanoi via the ancient capital of Hue.

ACCOMMODATION

Unless you get far off the tourist track, Indochina today has accommodation to suit all budgets and tastes. In all the major tourist destinations around the region, a frenzy of hotel and guesthouse construction over the last decade has led to a vibrant accommodation scene, and in some cases some very notable hotels.

In the 1990s investors throughout the region gambled on a tourist explosion that hasn't so much not happened as failed to meet their expectations, so that in most of the region today the supply of rooms exceeds demand. What this means for visitors is substantial discounts. They are seldom available for those who walk in off the street, though at cheaper hotels some negotiation on rates is acceptable. However, for those who plan ahead and book online or through an agency, discounts of 50 percent or more are not uncommon. Websites for online booking are included throughout this book in all the WHERE TO STAY sections of the destinations chapters.

Hotel rates are fairly consistent throughout the region. Hotels that are listed under the **very expensive** category will be US$180 and upwards, while those in the **expensive** category will be between US$100 and US$180.

Travelers between Saigon and Hanoi, can choose between the Reunification Train ABOVE or the arduous public bus system BELOW.

Moderate hotels are those that cost between US$35 and US$100, while **inexpensive** hotels are US$35 and less.

RESTAURANTS

Dining in Indochina is something of mixed bag, and surprises abound. One of the biggest is the explosion of excellent and inexpensive international restaurants in destinations like Siem Reap in Cambodia and Luang Prabang in Laos. Phnom Penh, too, astounds many first-time visitors with

its abundance of excellent Khmer and European restaurants.

Not so long ago, even in the big cities of Indochina, dining out offered little in the way of variety. Those days are gone. In Hanoi, Saigon, Hue, Phnom Penh and Vientiane, it's possible to dine almost as well as you could in Bangkok or Hong Kong — and at a lot more reasonable prices too.

The arrival of so many excellent international restaurants makes it easy to neglect the local cuisines, which of course is a great pity. In this book we have tried to present the best of both worlds, balancing the newer, often trendier arrivals serving French or Continental cuisine (the big favorites in these former French colonies) with restaurants that offer the best in local cuisine.

BASICS

BUSINESS AND BANKING HOURS

Business hours throughout Vietnam, Cambodia and Laos follow a similar pattern.

Businesses and government offices tend to open early, between 7:30 and 8 AM, and then close for a long, siesta-like lunch from around 11:30 AM to 1:30 or 2 PM. Closing times are usually either 5 or 5:30 PM. These hours extend to banks and to most tourist attractions, such as museums.

CURRENCY

The three currencies of Indochina are: in Vietnam the *dong;* in Cambodia the *riel;* and in Laos the *kip.* While you will find that United States dollars can be used to a greater or lesser extent throughout the region (everywhere in Cambodia, some places in Laos and Vietnam), and that the Thai *baht* will be accepted in the Thai border areas of Laos and Cambodia, the dong, riel and kip are of no use outside their respective borders. Exchange rates for each of the three currencies are unstable — check for the latest before leaving and continue to check on a daily basis as you travel through the region.

In Vietnam, the newish 50,000-dong note makes it considerably easier to carry local currency without feeling as though you've robbed a bank (or that someone might rob you). In Vientiane and Phnom Penh, you can pay for a meal in a restaurant with United States dollars and request your change in a mixture of dollars and the local currency — and get it all at the exact exchange rates.

As for currency exchange, most local and foreign joint-venture banks in Vietnam, along with the better-class hotels, will convert the main international currencies at a cost — it is always better to stick to money changers when possible; most banks take forever to change.

Virtually all major hotels and restaurants in Laos and Cambodia accept credit cards and can often cash traveler's checks as well.

ELECTRICITY

Vietnam works on two currents, 110 volts and 220 volts, depending what city you're in, with two-pin round-prong outlets for 110 volts and two-pin United States-type outlets for 220 volts. If you're taking a hairdryer, electric shaver or Handycam battery charger with you, make sure it's multi-system: 110 to 220 volts.

Laos and Cambodia are a lot simpler — both have 220-volts two-pin United States-type outlets wherever you go, though the antiquated wiring may have you wondering about overloads and short-circuits. In Phnom Penh particularly, blackouts occur quite regularly, and most older hotels will provide candles in the rooms. Of course, it also means no air-conditioning when the power fails.

NATIONAL HOLIDAYS

Vietnam

The following national holidays are observed in Vietnam:

January 1 Solar New Year
January 23 Eve of Tet
January 24–26 Vietnamese New Year, Tet Nguyen Dan
February 3 Anniversary of the Founding of the Communist Party
March 8 Women's Day
March 26 Youth Day
April 30 Liberation of Ho Chi Minh City (Saigon), Reunification Day
May 1 International Labor Day
May 19 Ho Chi Minh's Birthday
June 1 Children's Day
July 27 Memorial Day for War Martyrs
August 19 Revolution of 1945
September 2 National Day
November 20 Teacher's Day
December 22 Army Day

Cambodia

At the time of writing there was some uncertainty as to the future of some Cambodian national holidays, so it would be sensible to check on the latest information before leaving for Cambodia.

January 1 New Year
January 7–8 Victory over Genocide Regime
March 8 Women's Day
April Cambodian New Year (dates vary according to lunar calendar)
May 1 Labor Day
May 7 Visaka Bochea
May 11 Royal Plowing Ceremony
June 11 International Children's Day
June 18 Birthday of Her Majesty the Queen

September 24 Constitution Day and Coronation Day
October 23 Paris Peace Agreement Day
October 30-November 1 Birthday of His Majesty the King
November 9 Independence Day
December 10 International Human Rights Day

Laos

The following national holidays are observed in Laos:

January 1 New Year

January 6 Pathet Lao Day
January 20 Day of the Army
March 8 Women's Day
March 22 Day of the People's Party
May 1 Labor Day
June 1 Children's Day
August 13 Lao Issara, Day of the Free Laos
October 12 Liberation Day
December 2 Independence Day

TIME

Vietnam, Cambodia and Laos are all seven hours ahead of Greenwich Mean Time. In other words, when it is midday in Hanoi (and Phnom Penh and Vientiane) it is 5 AM in London, midnight in New York, 9 PM in Los Angeles and 4 PM in Sydney.

TIPPING

Tipping is not expected anywhere in Indochina, but it is always appreciated. It should

OPPOSITE: Plowing with water buffalo in ricelands near Nha Trang. ABOVE: Farming near Da Nang.

be reserved for occasions when especially good service is rendered.

COMMUNICATION AND MEDIA

TELEPHONES, FAX AND INTERNET

International dial-direct telephones and fax services are now fairly common in the up-market hotels in Vietnam and Cambodia, though an incoming or outgoing fax will often take up to 24 hours to get through in Vietnam. This is generally the

access too, though it is not as widespread in Laos as it is in Vietnam and Cambodia.

To call the numbers listed in this book from outside their respective countries, dial the international direct-dial prefix followed by the country code and then the area code without the initial zero. Country codes are as follows: Vietnam (84), Laos (856) and Cambodia (855). International direct-dial prefixes in Indochina are: Vietnam (00), Laos (14) and Cambodia (00). The zero in the local area code must be dialed when a number is called from within the country.

time it takes for scrutinizers in the Post Office to translate it before passing it on. However, there's no such petty censorship in Phnom Penh. If your hotel has no communication facilities, then up-market hotels will let you use their Business Center, quite often for a very reasonable fee. Internet cafés are ubiquitous throughout the region, and can be found wherever there are backpackers.

Phnom Penh, likewise, has international telephone and fax services, with most hotels hooked up; but rates are as extortionate as Vietnam. Telephone calls are remarkably cheap in Laos, compared to the high rates charged in Vietnam and Cambodia. The situation has improved vastly with Internet

MEDIA

Vietnam is well covered by news media, most of which is based in Hanoi. There are two English-language newspapers run by foreign journalists, with a high degree of input by local journalists. The fortnightly *Vietnam Economic Times* is probably the most responsible at reporting local news, with the older *Vietnam Investment Review* also giving excellent coverage, with a slant, not surprisingly, towards investment. Both are worth grabbing on arrival in Vietnam. They also both run excellent monthly entertainment guides. Saigon's best magazine stall is opposite the Rex Hotel, where copies of current papers and magazines gleaned from incoming planes are sold, as well as current *Newsweek* and *Time* magazines. You can dig through the piles on display and find marvelous back issues with articles that you missed the first time round.

Media in Phnom Penh consists of the fortnightly *Phnom Penh Post*, started during the days of UNTAC by a group of intrepid journalists, and the *Cambodia Daily*.

News publications available in Laos include the *Bangkok Post*. *Time* and *Newsweek* are available at hotel bookstores, and Vientiane's Raintree (in Laos Plaza Hotel Lobby) has a decent array of books.

What all this amounts to is that it is always best to keep smiling and feel your way through any problems that arise. The same goes for haggling over prices. Smile and be prepared to be flexible about your "bottom line" and you will get far better results than if you simply state your price and stick aggressively to your guns.

More specific to this part of the world, are etiquette issues that are related to Buddhism. When touring a Buddhist temple for example, remember that it's a mark of respect to dress for the occasion — shirts and

ETIQUETTE

Etiquette does vary from one country to the next in Indochina, but there are certain broad rules travelers less familiar with Southeast Asia should bear in mind while traveling through the region. Perhaps foremost among these is that in most situations, directness will not earn you any points. Throughout Southeast Asia (and China and Japan for that matter), directness is only seen as a last resort, and in the short-term is seen as confrontational. In a confrontation, such thinking runs, someone is going to have to step down, which results in a loss of face, something that in Asia is to be avoided at all costs.

slacks (or jeans) rather than shorts and tank-tops, and women should cover their arms and legs. Monks and novices are forbidden to accept anything directly, hand-to-hand, from women. In Laos and Cambodia, it's very disrespectful to sit with your feet pointing at other people (be careful too when crossing your legs), and the local people will naturally contort themselves (when sitting on a boat or wherever) so as not to point their foot.

It's also bad form to touch or pat people on the head, the head is a holy place and even a friendly pat on the head for a child is best avoided.

OPPOSITE: The Century Hotel and typical river life in Hue. ABOVE: The Lan Xang Hotel in Vientiane.

HEALTH

Although standards of hygiene throughout Indochina are low compared to Western countries, and indeed compared to neighboring Thailand, international standard medical services for tourists are available in all the capital cities (see the GENERAL INFORMATION sections of the relevant sections). In the meantime, a few sensible and basic precautions should help to guard against any problem bigger than an occasional case

of upset stomach. First of all, stick to bottled water, which is readily available throughout the region, and if you are new to Asia it's probably best to avoid ice too. Secondly, when eating out, a good precaution against becoming ill (though by no means a failsafe one) is to look for restaurants or food stalls that are doing a steady business — this at least ensures a healthy turnover of ingredients in the kitchen. If the place is popular with locals, it probably has reputable hygiene standards.

Hepatitis is the most prevalent disease to guard against, and no one should travel the region without prior vaccination. Although most older hotels have mosquito nets, malaria and encephalitis are common

enough that you'll need encephalitis shots before traveling and a course of malaria pills while you're on the road. At least take a good repellant and keep it handy. The cooler dry season in the northern winter months has noticeably fewer mosquitoes. Try not to be too paranoid, however. The odds are stacked high against you contracting either of these diseases in Indochina, as they are only really a serious problem in certain areas.

To put all this into perspective, these are the sort of health precautions that one would expect to take in any developing region. With prudence, the worst thing you'll have to safeguard yourself from is an upset stomach and accompanying diarrhea.

SECURITY

Indochina requires the sort of precautions you'd take against theft anywhere else in the world — put anything of particular value in the hotel safe-deposit, don't carry a lot of money on you in the streets, and keep your camera close to you at all times. Laos has a very low crime rate, and so have Phnom Penh and Angkor Wat, but Saigon requires extra care day and night. Resident expatriates seem to accept it as part of the price they pay for living there. Thieves are extremely accomplished and very fast. Be warned and come prepared. Theft from hotel rooms is not unknown, particularly in Saigon's older, more down-market hotels, and there have been several quite serious hotel thefts in Da Nang.

WOMEN ALONE

Women traveling alone should find few difficulties in predominantly Buddhist Indochina. Dress modestly — a dress or long shorts or trousers, rather than short shorts and halter tops — and behave in a respectable and respectful fashion, and there is no reason why the trip should not prove to be delightful. One good ploy to adopt for single women is an imaginary husband and a child or two; as most Asians find it almost inconceivable that a woman could be traveling alone, and to be without a family is to be a subject of pity.

GAY AND LESBIAN TRAVELERS

It would be unwise to expect the countries of Indochina to be as sexually open as most of those in the West. In rural Indochina, displays of affection between the sexes are frowned upon, and to be overtly gay or lesbian would shock most locals in Vietnam, Laos or Cambodia. Naturally, gay communities do exist, and the best places to make contact with them will probably be in late-night bars. In Phnom Penh, the Heart of

underdeveloped. This is not to say that traveling in the region with a disability is impossible, simply that it will present certain difficulties: sidewalks, where they exist, are often potholed and cluttered with roadside stalls and parked mopeds; disabled access ramps are non-existent; and in many parts of the region getting from one place to another involves a certain amount of push and shove. The best advice for disabled travelers is to travel with a companion, or hire a guide who can help with any problems that may arise.

Darkness bar attracts some gay travelers and locals, and the same is true of Apocalypse Now in Saigon. It would pay to be discreet.

A good Vietnam resource for gay travelers is Vietnam Gay Resources and Travel Tips by Utopia www.utopia-asia.com/tipsviet.htm. The same Website also has some gay and lesbian travel tips for Laos and Cambodia.

DISABLED TRAVELERS

Vietnam, Laos and Cambodia are difficult countries to get around in for travelers with any form of disability. Outside the five-star hotels in the major tourist destinations, travelers will find tourist facilities still highly

WHEN TO GO

Although Indochina lies in the subtropical zone, the climate has distinct variations and when you go depends largely on what weather you prefer. The northern areas of Vietnam and Laos catch the tail end of the northern monsoons from China and Central Asia, which in the winter months bring cold and wet weather and temperatures that drop as low as 8°C (46°F) to 15°C (59°F). It can get particularly cold in the Lao mountains, in Muang Sing and on the barren Xieng Khoang Plateau and the Plain of Jars,

OPPOSITE: A monk in a woolly hat in Luang Prabang's early morning chill. ABOVE: The tranquility of Indochina — the Mekong in Luang Prabang.

where an icy wind cuts through to your bones. Northern Vietnam, in the mountain areas of Sa Pa and Dien Bien Phu, is similarly chilly. Hanoi and Luang Prabang too can be cold and gray in the winter, but after a week, the sun can shine through and the weather becomes unseasonably warm.

For the most part, there are really only two seasons to Indochina: hot and wet and hot and dry. In the summer, Hanoi gets extremely hot and humid, with temperatures often above 30°C (86°F), and the heat and humidity intensify as you head south. The southern monsoon brings a great deal of rain, but it's a fairly benign season. In Vietnam, Laos and Cambodia you generally get one refreshing cloudburst a day, usually in the late afternoon, with fine weather either side of it. However, Vietnam lies at the end of the path of the Asia-Pacific typhoons, which often dash themselves along its central and northern coasts in the summer months, bringing powerful gales, torrential rain and flooding.

The dry season, from October to early April, is the best time to travel through the region. The days are warm to hot and the nights cool, though you can get an occasional day of chilly fog and rain. As an added bonus, the countryside turns lush and green after the raining season. Whatever the season, heat and the risk of dehydration — especially if you travel around on motorcycles or open cyclos — should be kept in mind at all times.

WHAT TO TAKE

Light cotton tropical clothing is most suitable for travel in southern Indochina, though if you're traveling north in the winter months prepare for cold conditions. Dress in layers that can be added and removed with the temperature fluctuations. A warm jacket, several changes of socks and a hat do not go amiss. Even in the summer months, a pullover or light jacket should be carried if you're going to destinations such as Da Lat in Vietnam's Central Highlands or Sa Pa in the north. The mountains of Laos, too, can get chilly at night. A thick jacket can be welcome in Hanoi in February, while Vientiane in the same month can be very warm.

Essentially, however, there is no need to panic unduly about forgetting anything important. In all the major cities of Indochina it is possible to pick up almost anything you may have forgotten to bring with you — the worst that might happen is that it may be a little more expensive than it would have been at home.

LANGUAGE BASICS

Picking up some of the local lingo in Indochina is complicated by the fact that the three major languages spoken here have very little in common, in addition to each being very difficult for speakers of European languages to learn. Vietnamese and Lao, for a start, are tonal languages, which

means that, like Chinese, the meaning of a sound is based not only on how it is pronounced, but also on how it is pitched. This is something that average Westerners who tackle one of these languages take several years to master, if in fact they ever do. Khmer, at least, is non-tonal, but it's not an easy language to pick up in hurry, as its sounds are very difficult to learn in a short period of time.

This is not the place to attempt a crash course in three difficult unrelated languages, and anyone who likes to have some fun with one of them — or perhaps all three — while on the road is advised to pick up a phrasebook or three. Providing you can accept the occasional howls of laughter from the locals with a grin, you will not regret the effort.

Anyone who has studied any Thai will find many similarities between what they have learned and what they hear in Laos. If you have learned enough Thai to have a basic conversation, you will probably find that most Lao people will be able to understand what you are saying, even if you cannot understand what they are saying back to you — the two languages are very closely related.

The most important word to learn in Laos is *sabadee*, which is a gracious and all-purpose greeting that shows respect and friendliness, just as *sawadee* does in Thailand. It can be used for all ages and classes of people and almost guarantees a pleasant

Hmong girls walk their way to Sa Pa town.

response. The other important word is thank you, which translates as *kopp chai lai lai* — also guaranteed to bring a smile to the face of the recipient.

The ubiquitous noodle soup translates as *pho* (pronounced "fuh") while chicken is *kai* and the spicy Laos salad is pronounced *laap*. For counting to ten: 1 — *neung*, 2 — *sorng*, 3 — *saam*, 4 — *sii*, 5 — *haa*, 6 — *hok*, 7 — *chet*, 8 — *pet*, 9 — *kao*, 10 — *sip*.

In Vietnam, with their system of honorifics and titles, there is no all-purpose greeting except for *chiow* — which no one really seems to use much. With the extremely complex tonal system of Vietnamese language, one word like *ga* can mean, among other things, "chicken" or "railway station," which clearly provides ample room for some serious miscommunication — as in stopping people on the street to ask, "Excuse me, where is the chicken?"

Rice is *com* and the noodle soups are known as *pho*. Beef is *bo* and white rice noodles are *bun*. Spring rolls are *cha gio*, pronounced as "chah yio." Numbers from one to ten are: 1 — *mot*, 2 — *hai*, 3 — *ba*, 4 — *bon*, 5 — *nam*, 6 — *sau*, 7 — *bay*, 8 — *tam*, 9 — *chin*, 10 — *muoi* or *chuc*.

Once you have mastered Lao and Vietnamese, you can set your sights on Khmer. The numbers from one to ten are: 1 — *mouy*, 2 — *pee*, 3 — *bay*, 4 — *boun*, 5 — *bram*, 6 — *bram-mouy*, 7 — *bram-pee*, 8 — *bram-bei*, 9 — *bram-boun*, 10 — *duop*. Chicken is *maan*, fish is *trey*, noodles *mee* or *moum banjook*, and a pagoda or monastery is called a *wat*. Good luck.

RECOMMENDED WEB SITES

Many web sites with information about Vietnam are of a commercial nature, recommending tours or selling rooms in hotels, and those that are not seem to be infrequently updated. One exception to this rule is the portal-style Vietnam Online **www.vietnamonline.net**, which has sections on everything from breaking news to information on travel destinations, with a lot in between. A site with links to other Vietnam sites is Travel Resources for Vietnam and Asia **www.veloasia.com/resource .html**, though some of the links are now out of date. A good listing of websites on a host of subjects related to Indochina can be found at **http://rectravel.com/khlavn/ khlavn.htm**. It brings together a host of informal travel writing on the region, much of which will interest those planning a more adventurous unguided journey through the region.

Groovy Saigon **www.groovysaigon.com** can be particularly recommended for those visiting the city. As the name suggests, it includes listings and reviews of practically everything of interest in the city. Far less ambitious is **www.hanoitravel.com**, a modest site with information on things to do in Vietnam's northern capital.

Cambodia's most comprehensive site can be found at **www.cambodia-web.net/ directory**. Also worth referring to for the latest on Cambodia is **www.kampuchea.com**. While aimed mostly at expatriate Cambodians it also has information of value to anyone planning to visit the country. The Cambodian Information Center (CIC) **www cambodia.org** is also worth taking a look at, though it is less practical and mostly of interest to those who are planning a lengthy stay in the country.

For the latest political developments in Laos try **www.lan-xang.com**, which also includes some softer feature stories on the country from time to time. A more specifically travel-related site is Laos-Travel.net **http://laos-travel.net/index.htm**, which is well designed and has both practical information and travel features on the country.

RECOMMENDED READING

The best recent introduction to the region can be found in Milton Osborne's *The Mekong: Turbulent Past, Uncertain Future* (Atlantic Monthly, 2000). Osborne traces the history of the Mekong through the cultures and civilizations that have flourished on its banks. It is particularly strong on the histories of Laos and Cambodia, less so on Vietnam. New Yorker contributor, Stan Sesser, meanwhile, has written a book with two memorable chapters on Indochina (one on Laos and the other on Cambodia) in *Lands of Charm and Cruelty: Travels in Southeast Asia* (Picador, 1987).

A more standard history of Laos — and essential reading for anyone who truly wants to understand the country — can be found in *A History of Laos* by Martin Stuart-Fox (Cambridge University Press, 1997), which is regarded as the most authoritative book on the subject. A more colorful history worth looking for (while not widely available, Amazon stocks it), is Christopher Kremmer's *Stalking the Elephant Kings: In Search of Laos* (University of Hawaii, 1977). Part travelogue, part mystery story, the book attempts to answer the question of what happened to the Lao royal family.

The Vietnam War has produced many books. The best round-up, however, can be found in Stanley Karnow's *Vietnam: A History* (Penguin, 1997), companion to a PBS television series, and an essential history of how the war came to take place and how it played out. Also highly recommended is *A Bright Shining Lie: John Paul Vann and America in Vietnam* by Neil Sheehan (Vintage, 1989). Lieutenant Colonel John Paul Vann's disillusionment with the way America was fighting its war in Vietnam led him to leak classified information to reporters, and this book about his involvement with Vietnam is a passionate exposé of the reasons for the United States failure in Southeast Asia. Meanwhile, for a sense of the war as it was experienced by those who fought it and reported it, the book to read is *Dispatches* by Michael Herr (Picador, 1968),

The Mekong Delta floating markets are one of the region's "must sees."

which presents the lives of the foot soldiers and reporters in transcendent prose. Jon Swain's *The River of Time* (St. Martin's Press, 1997) is mostly memoir with a particular focus on the fall of Phnom Penh to the Khmer Rouge, but it also evokes the author's love of the region.

Perhaps the Vietnam War classic is a novel that actually predates the American involvement: *The Quiet American* (Penguin, 1954) by Graham Greene, which predicts the Quixotic nature of the United States' fears of the domino effect in Southeast Asia,

left as a boy. *Gecko Tails: A Journey Through Cambodia* (Weidenfield & Nicholson, 1996) by Carol Livingston is an interesting account of a woman's sojourn in contemporary Cambodia. Amit Gilboa's *Off the Rails in Phnom Penh: Into the Dark Heart of Guns, Girls and Ganja* (Mass Market, 1998), is a racy account of the seedier side of expatriate life in Cambodia. Meanwhile, Paul Theroux's *The Great Railway Bazaar* (Penguin, 1975) has an interesting account of his journey on Vietnam's *Reunification Express* before reunification took place.

against the backdrop of an unconventional love story set in French colonial Vietnam. A more recent novel on the Vietnam War is Tim O'Brien's *The Things They Carried* (Broadway Books, 1989), a superbly written and evocative sequence of stories set mostly in Vietnam. For a Vietnamese perspective on the war, Bao Ninh's *The Sorrow of War* (Secker and Warburg, 1993) is widely available in English translation in Vietnam.

Since the region opened up, several worthwhile travelogues have come out. The most recent, and probably the best, is Andrew X Pham's *Catfish and Mandala: A Two-Wheeled Voyage Through the Landscape and Memory of Vietnam* (Picador, 1998), which describes Pham's return to the country he

For anyone who wants a better understanding of the textiles of Laos, look out for Mary F Connors' *Lao Textiles and Traditions* (Oxford University Press, 1996). The same author has also written a worthwhile book on Vietnam's minority cultures called *Ethnic Minorities in Vietnam* (Hanoi Foreign Languages Publishing House, 1984). For a better understanding of the food of the region *The Foods of Vietnam* (Stewart Tabori & Chang) by Nicole Routhier and Martin Jacobs is a beautifully illustrated recipe guide to the best in Vietnamese cuisine.

The colonial architecture of the Grand Hotel faces Nha Trang's Beach Boulevard and the broad beach.

Quick Reference A–Z Guide
to Places and Topics of Interest

A | **accommodation, general information**
colonial-era hotels 38
room rates in Cambodia 37, 266
room rates in Laos 266
room rates in Vietnam 36, 266
accommodation, where to stay in Cambodia
Angkor 39, 215, 216
Phnom Penh 39, 198, 201
Siem Reap 39, 215, 216
Sihanoukville 207, 209
accommodation, where to stay in Laos
Champassak 257
Luang Nam Tha 248
Luang Prabang 242, 245
Muang Sing 249
Pakse 254
Phonsavan 251
Saravan 30
Si Phan Don 257
Vientiane 234, 236
accommodation, where to stay in Vietnam
Bai Chai 124
Can Tho 184
Chau Doc 184
Con Dau Islands 187
Cuc Phuong National Park 121
Da Lat 38, 154
Da Nang 142
Dien Bien Phu 125
Doi Son 122
Duong Dong 186
Ha Long Bay 124
Hai Phong 122
Hanoi 38, 108, 114, 116
Hoi An 146, 147
Hue 132
Long Xuyen 184
My Tho 180
Nha Trang 40, 151
Phan Thiet 176
Phu Quoc Island 186
Qui Nhon 149
Sa Pa 15, 126
Saigon 170, 173
Vung Tau 178, 179
airline offices
Hanoi (Vietnam) 104
Hue (Vietnam) 130
Phnom Penh (Cambodia) 192
Saigon (Vietnam) 161
Siem Reap (Cambodia) 212
Vientiane (Laos) 224
airports
Da Lat Airport (Vietnam) 155
Da Nang Airport (Vietnam) 142
Hanoi Airport (Vietnam) 120
Ho Chi Minh City Heliport (Saigon, Vietnam) 187
Luang Nam Tha Airport (Laos) 248
Nha Trang Airport (Vietnam) 152

Phu Bai Airport (Hue/Vietnam) 135
Phu Cat Airport (Qui Nhon, Vietnam) 149
Phu Quoc Island Airport (Vietnam) 186
Pochentong Airport (Phnom Penh, Cambodia) 191
Pochentong Airport (Phnom Penh/Cambodia) 205
Siem Reap International Airport (Cambodia) 219
Tan Son Nhat Airport (Saigon/Vietnam) 175
Wattay International Airport (Vientiane, Laos) 236
An Bang (Vietnam) 132
Angkor (Cambodia) 25, 37, 54, 59, 66, 76, 191, 209, 212–215. *See also* Siem Reap
Angkor Thom (Angkor, Cambodia) 76, 214
Angkor Wat (Angkor, Cambodia) 11–12, 42, 76, 143, 214
Apocalypse Now bar and nightclub (Saigon, Vietnam) 165, 175
Army Museum (Hanoi, Vietnam) 45, 114
Art of Silk Museum (Vientiane, Laos) 231
Attapeu (Laos) 254

B | **Ba Be Lake (Vietnam)** 26, 27
Ba Dinh Square (Hanoi, Vietnam) 112
Ba Pagoda. *See* Ngia An Hoi Quan Pagoda
Ba VI Lake (Vietnam) 26
Bac Ha (Vietnam) 14, 32, 126
Bac Ninh Province (Vietnam) 50
Bach Dang (Da Nang, Vietnam) 141
Bach Ma National Park (Vietnam) 26, 29
backpacking in Cambodia
accommodation 37, 201, 209, 216
destinations 207, 216
general information 37
nightlife 205
restaurants 204
transportation 37, 219
backpacking in Laos
accommodation 37, 235
general information 37
restaurants 37, 236
transportation 37
backpacking in Vietnam
accommodation 36, 108, 116, 122, 126, 132, 135, 142, 147, 149, 151, 155, 173
destinations 125, 147, 148
general information 33
restaurants 36, 108, 147, 152
tours 108
transportation 33
Bai Chai (Vietnam) 124
Bai Sau (Vung Tau, Vietnam) 178
Bai Truoc (Vung Tau, Vietnam) 178
Bamboo Island. *See* Hon Tre
Ban Phanom (Laos) 48, 245
Ban Saphay (Laos) 254
Bangkok (Thailand) 130
Banteay Samre (Angkor, Cambodia) 212, 215
Banteay Srei (Angkor, Cambodia) 20, 22, 212, 214, 215
Bao Dai Villas (Nha Trang, Vietnam) 150, 151

Bao Dai's Summer Palace (Da Lat, Vietnam) 153
Baphuon (Angkor, Cambodia) 76, 212
bargaining 105, 271
Bassac River (Cambodia) 98
Bay Mau Lake (Hanoi, Vietnam) 105
Bayon Temple (Angkor, Cambodia) 11, 54, 76,
    212, 214
Ben Binh (Vietnam) 18, 19
Ben Duoc (Vietnam) 18, 19
Ben Thanh (Saigon, Vietnam) 161, 165
Bhan It (Vietnam) 148
bicycle and motorcycle rental
    Da Lat (Vietnam) 153
    Hanoi (Vietnam) 106
    Hue (Vietnam) 138
    Nha Trang (Vietnam) 151
    Phnom Penh (Cambodia) 192, 266
    Saigon (Vietnam) 162
    Vientiane (Laos) 224, 231, 266
Bien Hoa (Vietnam) 167
Binh Tay Market (Saigon, Vietnam) 170
boat races 50, 53
Boloven Plateau (Laos) 26, 30, 254, 257
Buddha Park (Tha Deua, Laos) 231, 234
Buddhism 95, 96, 179, 206, 271
bullfighting 50
Buon Ma Thuot (Vietnam) 26
business and banking hours 268

C Cai Luong Theatre (Hanoi, Vietnam) 118
Cai River (Vietnam) 150
Cambodia 189–220
Can Tho (Vietnam) 15, 38, 180–184
Can Tien (Vietnam) 148
canoeing in Vietnam
    Ha Long Bay 30
Cao Daism 96, 141, 179
car and motorcycle rental, general information 32
car rental
    Champassak (Laos) 257
    Da Lat (Vietnam) 153
    Hanoi (Vietnam) 104, 125
    Hue (Vietnam) 138
    Nha Trang (Vietnam) 151
    Saigon (Vietnam) 162
Cat Ba (Vietnam) 25, 124
Cat Ba Archipelago (Vietnam) 26, 121, 124
Cat Ba Island (Vietnam) 25
Cat Ba Island National Park (Vietnam) 25, 26, 27
Cat Cat (Vietnam) 17
Cat Island. See Hon Mieu
Cat's Tooth Mountain (Vietnam) 143
Catholic churches
    Long Xuyen (Vietnam) 184
    My Tho (Vietnam) 180
    Tra Kieu (Vietnam) 143
Catholicism 95, 96
Cavern Pagoda (Chau Doc, Vietnam) 184
Cay Dua (Vietnam) 186
central markets
    Can Tho (Vietnam) 184
    Da Lat (Vietnam) 152, 153
    Hai Phong (Vietnam) 122
    My Tho (Vietnam) 180
    Phnom Penh (Cambodia) 14, 49, 193, 196
    Saigon (Vietnam) 161, 162, 165
Central Saigon Mosque (Saigon, Vietnam) 165

Cha Ban (Vietnam) 148
Cham Island (Vietnam) 145
Cham museums
    Da Nang (Vietnam) 45, 140, 141, 143
    My Son (Vietnam) 70, 143
    Tra Kieu (Vietnam) 143
Cham ruins (Qui Nhon, Vietnam) 148
Cham Tower (Phan Thiet, Vietnam) 176
Champassak (Laos) 20, 76, 251, 254, 255, 256
Champassak Province (Laos) 251
Chau Doc (Vietnam) 38, 88, 184, 186
Chau Van Liem Boulevard (Saigon, Vietnam) 170
Chicken Village (Da Lat, Vietnam) 155
children, traveling with
    attractions 118
    general information 41
Chinatown (Saigon, Vietnam). See Cholon
    (Saigon, Vietnam)
Chinese All Community House (Hoi An,
    Vietnam) 145
Choeung Ek (Cambodia) 206
Cholon (Saigon, Vietnam) 78, 96, 159, 161, 168
Christianity 95, 179
Chua Cao Dai (Da Nang, Vietnam) 141
Chua Huong Pagoda (Vietnam) 121
Chua Mot Cot. See One Pillar Pagoda
Chua Tram Gian (Vietnam) 120
Citadel (Hue, Vietnam) 130, 131
City Hall (Saigon, Vietnam) 162, 164
climate
    Cambodia 274
    Laos 273, 274
    Vietnam 273, 274
Con Dau Island (Vietnam) 26
Con Dau Islands (Vietnam) 186
Con Son Island (Vietnam) 186
Con Thien Firebase (Vietnam) 138
Confucianism 95, 112, 121, 179
Crazy House (Da Lat, Vietnam) 153
credit cards 104, 192, 268
Cu Chi Tunnels (Vietnam) 18, 19, 179
Cua Dai Beach (Hoi An/Vietnam) 145
Cuc Phuong National Park (Vietnam) 26, 28,
    121, 122
currency
    Cambodia 192, 268
    Laos 268
    Vietnam 268
customs 263
cycling in Vietnam
    Hanoi to Saigon 31
cyclos 105, 159, 162, 266, 274

D Da Lat (Vietnam) 25, 29, 31, 38, 58, 150, 152–155
Da Lat Cathedral (Da Lat, Vietnam) 153
Da Lat University (Da Lat, Vietnam) 153
Da Nang (Vietnam) 45, 66, 70, 78, 83, 98, 130, 140–
    142, 143, 144, 148
Dai Giac Pagoda (Saigon, Vietnam) 168
dance
    Cambodia 12, 17, 18, 41, 42, 53, 66, 195, 216
    Laos 41, 42, 43, 66, 249
    Vietnam 41, 42, 43, 66
Datanla Falls (Da Lat, Vietnam) 155
departure tax 264
Dien Bien Phu (Vietnam) 32, 82, 124–125
Dien Bien Phu Victory Museum 125

Din Bin Pass (Vietnam)   125
disabled travelers   273
diving in Cambodia
  Sihanoukville   207
diving in Vietnam
  Ha Long Bay   31
  Nha Trang   54, 149, 150
Do Son (Vietnam)   122
Doc Let Beach (Vietnam)   152
Doc Lic (Vietnam)   32
Domaine de Marie Convent
  (Da Lat, Vietnam)   153
Don Khong Island (Laos)   257
Dong Du (Vietnam)   19
Dong Khoi Street
  (Saigon, Vietnam)   158, 161, 162, 165
Dong Son (Vietnam)   127
Dong Xuan Market
  (Hanoi, Vietnam)   105, 110, 111
Dray Sap Waterfall (Vietnam)   26
Du Hang Pagoda (Hai Phong, Vietnam)   122
Duang Dong (Vietnam)   186
Duong Xuan Thuong Village (Vietnam)   132

E eating and drinking   54, 58.
See also restaurants, general information
Ebony Island. See Hon Mun
electricity   268
Elephant Terrace. See Terrace of the Elephants
embassies and consulates
  Cambodian representation abroad   265
  foreign representation in Hanoi and Saigon
    (Vietnam)   264
  foreign representation in Phnom Penh
    (Cambodia)   264
  foreign representation in Vientiane (Laos)   265
  Lao representation abroad   265
  Vietnamese representation abroad   265
Emerald Buddha Pagoda. See Wat Preah Keo
Emperor of Jade Pagoda (Saigon, Vietnam)   168
Endangered Primate Rescue Center
  (Vietnam)   29, 121
etiquette   271

F Fai Fo. See Hoi An
Fang Xi Pan. See Mount Fansipan
FAX services   270
festivals and special events in Cambodia
  Bonn Chaul Chnam, April   51
  Bonn Dak Ben and Pchoum Ben, May 6, 51
  Boun Kathen, October   53
  Genocide Day, May 9, 51
  Independence Day, November 9, 53
  King's Birthday, October 30 and November 1, 53
  Labor Day, May 1, 51
  National Day, January 7, 50
  national holidays   269
  New Year, January 1, 50
  Ramayana Festival, November (Angkor)   18, 41, 53
  Tet, Lunar New Year, January/February   50
  Vesak Day, May   51
  Water Festival, November 25, 53
  Women's Day, March 8, 50
festivals and special events in Laos
  Boun Awk Phansaa, October   53
  Boun Bang Fai, May   51
  Boun Kao Padap Dinh, August   53

  Boun Khao Phansaa, July   53
  Boun Khoun Khao, January   50
  Boun Nam Water Festival, October   53
  Boun Pha Wet, December/January   50
  Boun Pi Mai, April
    (Luang Prabang and countrywide)   50
  Boun Suang Heua, October   53
  Boun That Luang, November
    (Vientiane)   53, 96, 228
  Boun Visahhabousa, May   51
  Elephant Processions, April (Luang Prabang)   96
  Labor Day, May 1, 51
  Lai Hua Fai, October   53
  Lao National Day, December 2, 53
  Lao New Year, April (Luang Prabang and
    countrywide)   242
  Magha Puja, February (Wat Phu)   50
  Muang Sing Festival, October/November
    (Muang Sing)   249
  national holidays   269
  New Year, January 1, 50
  Tet, Lunar New Year, January/February   50
  Wat Phu Temple Festivals, February and June   256
  Wat Si Muang Procession, November
    (Vientiane)   230
  Water Festival, October (Luang Prabang)   242
festivals and special events in Vietnam
  Chua Huong Pagoda Pilgrimages, February to April
    (Chua Huong Pagoda)   121
  Ho Chi Minh's Birthday, May 19, 53
  Labor Day, May 1, 51
  Lim Festival, February (Lim Village)   50
  National Day, September 2, 53
  national holidays   269
  New Year, January 1, 50
  Tet, Lunar New Year, January/February   50
  Thay Pagoda Festival, March/April (Hanoi)   121
  Vesak Day, May   51
fine arts museums
  Hanoi (Vietnam)   45, 112
  Saigon (Vietnam)   45, 167
Fine Arts School (Phnom Penh, Cambodia)   195
Floating Market (Phung Hiep, Vietnam)   15
Friendship Bridge (Laos)   91, 223, 237

G gay and lesbian scene   273
General Post Office
  (Saigon, Vietnam)   66, 161, 162
geography   98
Giac Lam Pagoda (Saigon, Vietnam)   168
Giac Vien Pagoda (Saigon, Vietnam)   168
golf in Vietnam
  Da Lat   31, 153
  Phan Thiet   31, 176
Government Guesthouse (Hanoi, Vietnam)   110
Grand Hotel d'Angkor
  (Siem Reap, Cambodia)   18
Great Temple (Tay Ninh, Vietnam)   98, 179

H Ha Long Bay (Vietnam)   27, 30, 66, 98, 108,
  121, 123–124
Ha Son Binh Province (Vietnam)   121
Hai Ba Trung Street (Hanoi, Vietnam)   105
Hai Ba Trung Temple (Hanoi, Vietnam)   113
Hai Phong (Vietnam)   27, 58, 80, 121–123, 124
Hai Van Pass (Vietnam)   140
Halls of the Mandarins (Hue, Vietnam)   131

Ham Nghi Market (Saigon, Vietnam) 165
Hang Kenh Communal House
  (Hai Phong, Vietnam) 122
Hang Kenh Tapestry Factory
  (Hai Phong, Vietnam) 122
Hanoi (Vietnam) 32, 38, 40, 43, 45, 47, 50, 54, 56,
  58, 78, 79, 80, 96, 103–120, 122, 142
Hanoi Hilton. See Hoa Lo Prison Museum
Hanoi Opera (Hanoi, Vietnam) 66, 109, 118
health
  eating out 272
  vaccinations 272
  water 41, 272
Hero Square. See Me Linh Square
hiking in Laos
  Muang Xay 251
hiking in Vietnam
  Da Lat 155
  Hoang Liem Nature Reserve 26, 126
  Mount Fansipan 15, 26
  Sa Pa 17, 126
Hinduism 95, 255
history
  battles against China 70, 78, 121, 125
  Cambodia independence 82
  Champa Kingdom 70, 72, 74, 75, 76, 78, 89, 95,
    142, 144, 149, 176
  Demilitarized Zone 98, 138, 140
  Democratic Republic of Vietnam 80
  Dien Bien Phu 82
  First Indochina War 80, 125, 127, 150
  French colonialism 78, 79, 80
  Funan Kingdom 70, 72, 75
  Ho Chi Minh Trail 103, 138, 179, 254
  Javanese invaders 75
  Khmer Empire 72, 74, 75, 76, 95, 212, 255
  Khmer Rouge 17, 51, 80, 82, 85, 86, 87, 94, 96, 98,
    179, 184, 191, 195, 198, 206, 212
  Lane Xang Kingdom 74, 76, 228, 242
  Laos independence 82
  mountain tribes 72
  Nguyen Dynasty 22, 78, 130, 150
  Nixon's Cambodia invasion 84, 85, 86
  Pathet Lao 82, 85, 94, 230, 242, 251
  Red Khmer. See Khmer Rouge
  Second Indochina War. See Vietnam War
  Thai impact 76, 77
  Viet Cong 84, 85, 98, 130, 168, 179
  Viet Minh 80, 82, 125, 150
  Vietnam divided 82
  Vietnam independence 82
  Vietnam War 18, 66, 82, 84, 85, 98, 103, 111,
    114, 122, 127, 130, 138, 140, 142, 148, 164,
    166, 179, 251
history museums
  Dien Bien Phu (Vietnam) 125
  Hanoi (Vietnam) 110
  Saigon (Vietnam) 45, 166
Ho Chi Minh City. See Saigon
Ho Chi Minh Mausoleum
  (Hanoi, Vietnam) 105, 112
Ho Chi Minh Museum
  (Can Tho, Vietnam) 180
Ho Chi Minh Square (Saigon, Vietnam) 164
Ho Chi Minh Trail 138, 179, 254
Ho Tay. See West Lake
Ho Thien Quang Lake (Hanoi, Vietnam) 113

Ho Truc Bach (Hanoi, Vietnam) 111
Hoa Bin (Vietnam) 32
Hoa Haoism 184
Hoa Lo Prison Museum
  (Hanoi, Vietnam) 80, 114
Hoa Lu (Vietnam) 121
Hoan Kiem District. See Old Quarter
Hoan Kiem Lake
  (Hanoi, Vietnam) 47, 104, 105, 108, 114
Hoang Liem Nature Reserve (Vietnam) 26
Hoi An (Vietnam) 32, 58, 140, 143, 144–148
Hon Mieu (Vietnam) 150
Hon Mun (Vietnam) 149
Hon Tam (Vietnam) 150
Hon Tre (Vietnam) 149
Hon Yen (Vietnam) 149
Hong Gai (Vietnam) 121, 124
hospitals
  Hanoi (Vietnam) 104
  Hue (Vietnam) 130
  Phnom Penh (Cambodia) 192
  Saigon (Vietnam) 161
  Vientiane (Laos) 224
Hôtel de Ville. See City Hall
Huay Xai (Laos) 20, 248
Hue (Vietnam) 14, 22, 23, 32, 40, 43, 58, 79, 96, 98,
  127–138, 148
Huei Thamo (Laos) 256
Hung Vuong Boulevard (Saigon, Vietnam) 170
Huong Giang. See Perfume River
Huong Tich Mountain (Vietnam) 121
Huy Van Pass (Vietnam) 32

I Imperial Library (Hue, Vietnam) 131
Imperial Museum (Hue, Vietnam) 131
Independence Beach (Sihanoukville,
  Cambodia) 207
Independence Museum (Hanoi, Vietnam) 114
Internet access
  general information 270
  Hoi An (Vietnam) 147
  Phnom Penh (Cambodia) 192
  Sihanoukville (Cambodia) 209
Islam 179

J Jade Mountain Temple. See Ngoc Son
Japanese Covered Bridge (Hoi An, Vietnam)
  58, 145

K Khe Sanh (Vietnam) 138
Kien Giang Province (Vietnam) 70
Killing Fields (Cambodia) 86, 198, 206
Kim Lien Village (Vietnam) 127
Kirirom National Park (Cambodia) 30
Koh Dach (Cambodia) 207
Kon Tum (Vietnam) 148
Krong Bong Waterfall (Vietnam) 26
Kuang Xi Falls (Laos) 26, 248

L Lai Chau (Vietnam) 32, 125
Lak (Vietnam) 26
Lake of Impeccable Clarity (Hue, Vietnam) 132
Lane Xang Road (Vientiane, Laos) 224
Lang Bian Mountain (Vietnam) 155
Lang Co (Da Nang, Vietnam) 140
Lang Son (Vietnam) 121
languages 274, 276

Lao Cai (Vietnam)   17, 32, 125, 126
Lao Revolutionary Museum
   (Vientiane, Laos)   47, 66, 230
Lat (Vietnam)   155
Le Van Duyet Temple (Saigon, Vietnam)   96
Lim Village (Vietnam)   50
Long Bien Bridge (Hanoi, Vietnam)   105, 110
Long Hoa (Vietnam)   179
Long Son Pagoda (Nha Trang, Vietnam)   150
Long Xuyen (Vietnam)   184
Luang Nam Tha (Laos)   248
Luang Prabang (Laos)   14, 20, 26, 32, 40, 42, 47, 48,
   51, 53, 57, 66, 74, 76, 79, 96, 237–245, 248

M Majestic Hotel (Saigon, Vietnam)   166
Marble Mountains (Vietnam)   142, 144
markets. *See also* central markets
   Binh Tay Market (Saigon, Vietnam)   170
   Dong Xuan Market (Hanoi, Vietnam)   105, 109,
      110, 111
   Ham Nghi Market (Saigon, Vietnam)   165
   Morning Market (Luang Prabang, Laos)   240
   Morning Market (Vientiane, Laos)   49, 230, 231
   Muang Sing Market (Laos)   249
   Pakse Market (Laos)   254
   Russian Market (Phnom Penh, Cambodia)   49, 198
   Saturday market (Sa Pa/Vietnam)   125
   Sunday market (Bac Ha, Vietnam)   32
   Sunday market (Bac Ha/Vietnam)   126
   Thalat Dala (Luang Prabang, Laos)   240
mausoleums
   Khai Dinh (Hue, Vietnam)   23, 132
   Minh Mang (Hue, Vietnam)   23, 132
   of Ho Chi Minh (Hanoi, Vietnam)   105, 112
   Tu Duc (Hue, Vietnam)   131
Me Linh Square (Saigon, Vietnam)   165
medical care
   Hanoi (Vietnam)   104
   Phnom Penh (Cambodia)   192
   Vientiane (Laos)   224
Mekong Delta (Vietnam)   15, 29, 33, 38, 66, 72, 77,
   98, 179–186, 192, 266
Mekong Islands. *See* Si Phan Don
Mekong River   19, 20, 53, 91, 98, 179, 192, 223, 224,
   231, 234, 237, 245, 251, 256
Minh Lau Pavilion (Hue, Vietnam)   132
minorities
   Cambodia   89
   Laos   20, 89, 245, 248, 249, 257
   Vietnam   14, 17, 88, 113, 121, 124, 125, 126, 127,
      148, 155, 168
Moc Bai (Vietnam)   175
money exchange
   Cambodia   192, 198, 212, 268
   Laos   268
   Vietnam   104, 268
Monkey Island (Vietnam)   152
Mount Fansipan (Vietnam)   15, 26, 126
Mountain Church (Tra Kieu/Vietnam)   144
Muang Khong (Laos)   257
Muang Sing (Laos)   14, 248, 249
Muang Thamo (Laos)   256
Muang Tomo. *See* Muang Thamo
Muang Xay (Laos)   249
Mui Ne Beach (Phan Thiet, Vietnam)   176
Municipal Theatre Hanoi. *See* Hanoi Opera
Municipal Theatre Saigon. *See* Saigon Opera

Municipal Water Puppet Theater
   (Hanoi, Vietnam)   118
Municipal Water Puppet Theater
   (Hanoi/Vietnam)   43
Munirangsyaram Pagoda
   (Can Tho, Vietnam)   184
Museum of Ho Chi Minh City
   (Saigon, Vietnam)   166
music
   Cambodia   18, 43, 216
   Laos   40, 42, 43, 236, 245, 249
   Vietnam   43, 66, 117, 131, 147, 173
My Son (Vietnam)   70, 142, 143
My Tho (Vietnam)   180

N Nam Cat Thien National Park (Vietnam)   26, 29
Nam Khan River (Laos)   53, 237
Nam O (Da Nang, Vietnam)   140
Nam Ou River (Laos)   245
Nam Phou Fountain (Vientiane, Laos)   224
Nam Tha Province (Laos)   248
Napoleon III Pavilion (Phnom Penh,
   Cambodia)   195
National Biodiversity Conservation Areas
   (Laos)   30
National Cambodian Dance Company   42
National Highway 1 (Vietnam)   32, 140
national museums
   Luang Prabang (Laos)   239, 240
   Phnom Penh (Cambodia)   45, 195
newspapers and magazines   270
Nghe Tinh Province (Vietnam)   127
Nghia An Hoi Quan Pagoda
   (Saigon, Vietnam)   168
Ngo Quyen Street (Hanoi, Vietnam)   105
Ngoc Son (Hanoi, Vietnam)   109
Nguyen Thieu (Vietnam)   148
Nha Trang (Vietnam)   31, 32, 40, 54, 148, 149–152,
   155, 178
Nha Trang Cathedral (Nha Trang, Vietnam)   150
Niet Ban Tinh Xa Temple
   (Vung Tau, Vietnam)   178
nightlife
   Do Son (Vietnam)   122
   Hanoi (Vietnam)   118
   Nha Trang (Vietnam)   152
   Phnom Penh (Cambodia)   204, 205
   Saigon (Vietnam)   159, 165, 175
Ninh Binh (Vietnam)   121, 127
Ninh Hoa (Vietnam)   152
Nong Khai (Thailand)   91, 234, 237
Notre Dame Cathedral (Hue, Vietnam)   96, 132
Notre Dame Cathedral (Saigon, Vietnam)   96, 159,
   161, 162

O Oceanographic Institute
   (Nha Trang, Vietnam)   150
Ochheuteal Beach (Sihanoukville,
   Cambodia)   207, 208
Odong (Cambodia)   78, 96, 206
Old Quarter (Hanoi, Vietnam)   56, 105, 108
One Pillar Pagoda (Hanoi, Vietnam)   112
opera houses
   Hanoi (Vietnam)   43, 66, 109
   Saigon (Vietnam)   43, 158, 162
Orchid Farm (Saigon, Vietnam)   167
Oudomxai Province (Laos)   89, 249

P painters and paintings 59
Pak Ou Caves (Laos) 20, 245
Pakse (Laos) 20, 30, 76, 91, 95, 251, 254, 255, 257
Paksong (Laos) 26
Pasteur Institute (Nha Trang, Vietnam) 150
people
  Bao Dai 150
  Fa Ngum 74, 240, 242
  Gia Long 78
  Greene, Graham 163
  Ho Chi Minh 43, 80, 82, 103, 112, 127
  Hun Sen 87, 91, 94, 204
  Jayavarman VII 76
  Le Loi 109
  Lon Nol 85
  Ly Thai Tho 72
  Ngo Dinh Diem 82, 95
  Nguyen Cao Ky 84, 166, 167
  Nguyen Van Thieu 84, 150, 166, 167
  Pol Pot 85, 87, 191, 198
  Sihanouk, Norodom 29, 82, 85, 86, 94, 194
  Snow, Edgar 117
  Souvanna Phouma 82, 85
  Souvanna Vong 82, 85
  Tran Hung Dao 72, 109, 165
  Trung Sisters 71, 113
Perfume Pagoda. See Chua Huong Pagoda
Perfume River (Vietnam) 15, 22, 23, 96, 130, 131, 132
Pha That Luang (Vientiane, Laos) 96, 228
Phan Rang (Vietnam) 70
Phan Thiet (Vietnam) 31, 88, 176, 178
Phap Lam Pagoda (Da Nang, Vietnam) 141
Phimeanakas (Angkor, Cambodia) 212
Phnom Chiso (Cambodia) 206
Phnom Penh (Cambodia) 14, 17, 32, 37, 39, 45, 58, 76, 77, 85, 96, 98, 191–206
Pho Da Pagoda (Da Nang, Vietnam) 142
Pho Dinh Tien Hoang (Hanoi, Vietnam) 105
Phong Tho (Vietnam) 125
Phonsavan (Laos) 15, 251
Phu Kao (Laos) 255
Phu Quoc Island (Vietnam) 26, 186
Phung Hiep (Vietnam) 15
Phung Island (Vietnam) 180
Phung Son Tu Pagoda (Saigon, Vietnam) 168
Phuok Kien Assembly Hall (Hoi An, Vietnam) 145
Plain of Jars (Laos) 15, 25, 66, 98, 251
Play Cu (Vietnam) 148
Po Nagar (Nha Trang, Vietnam) 150
population
  Cambodia 89
  Laos 89
  Vietnam 88, 96
Port of Saigon (Saigon, Vietnam) 166
Pratuxai Monument (Vientiane, Laos) 224
Presidential Palace (Hanoi, Vietnam) 113
Psar Thmei (Phnom Penh, Cambodia) 14, 196
Psar Tuol Tom Pong. See Russian Market (Phnom Penh, Cambodia)
Purple Forbidden City (Hue, Vietnam) 131

Q Quan Am (Saigon, Vietnam) 168
Quan Cong Temple (Hoi An/Vietnam) 145
Quan Thanh Pagoda (Hanoi, Vietnam) 96, 112

Quang Dong Communal House (Hoi An, Vietnam) 145
Quang Tri (Vietnam) 98
Qui Nhon (Vietnam) 148, 149
rafting in Laos
  Plain of Jars 251

R Ramayana 195
Red River (Vietnam) 104, 111
Red River Delta (Vietnam) 70, 71, 79, 95, 98, 122
religion
  Cambodia 94, 95, 96
  Laos 94, 96
  Vietnam 95, 96
restaurants, general information
  bread and coffee 55
  imperial Hue cooking 23
  international restaurants 268
  Khmer cooking 57
  Lao cooking 56
  regional specialities in Indochina 55, 56
  regional specialities in Laos 57
  regional specialities in Vietnam 55, 56
  street food 55
  tipping 269
  top restaurants 40
  Vietnamese cooking 54
restaurants, what to eat in Cambodia
  Chinese cuisine (Phnom Penh) 204
  Chinese cuisine (Siem Reap) 217
  Continental cuisine (Siem Reap) 219
  European cuisine (Siem Reap) 217
  French cuisine (Phnom Penh) 204
  French cuisine (Siem Reap) 216, 217
  international cuisine (Phnom Penh) 204
  Khmer cuisine (Phnom Penh) 204
  Khmer cuisine (Siem Reap) 216, 219
  Malaysian cuisine (Siem Reap) 217
  pizzas (Phnom Penh) 204
  seafood (Sihanoukville) 209
  Thai cuisine (Phnom Penh) 204
restaurants, what to eat in Laos
  Chinese cuisine (Pakse) 254
  Chinese cuisine (Phonsavan) 251
  Chinese cuisine (Vientiane) 236
  French cuisine (Luang Prabang) 243, 245
  French cuisine (Pakse) 254
  French cuisine (Vientiane) 236
  Indian cuisine (Vientiane) 236
  Italian cuisine (Vientiane) 236
  Lao cuisine (Luang Prabang) 243, 245
  Lao cuisine (Pakse) 254
  Lao cuisine (Phonsavan) 251
  Lao cuisine (Vientiane) 236
  Luang Prabang cuisine (Luang Prabang) 57
  pizzas (Vientiane) 236
  Thai cuisine (Luang Prabang) 40, 245
  Thai cuisine (Pakse) 254
  Thai cuisine (Phonsavan) 251
  Vietnamese cuisine (Vientiane) 236
  Western cuisine (Pakse) 254
restaurants, what to eat in Vietnam
  breakfast (Saigon) 55, 174
  Chinese cuisine (Da Lat) 155
  Chinese cuisine (Da Nang) 142
  Chinese cuisine (Hai Phong) 122
  Chinese cuisine (Hoi An) 148

Chinese cuisine (Saigon)   173
Continental cuisine (Hanoi)   115
Continental cuisine (Saigon)   173
European cuisine (Hoi An)   148
French cuisine (Da Lat)   155
French cuisine (Hanoi)   40, 117
French cuisine (Saigon)   173
imperial cuisine (Hue)   40, 135
Indian cuisine (Saigon)   174
international cuisine (Saigon)   174
Italian cuisine (Da Nang)   142
Italian cuisine (Hanoi)   117
Italian cuisine (Nha Trang)   152
Italian cuisine (Saigon)   173
Mediterranean cuisine (Hanoi)   117
pastries (Saigon)   173
pizzas (Da Nang)   142
pizzas (Hanoi)   117
pizzas (Nha Trang)   152
pizzas (Saigon)   173
seafood (Hanoi)   56
seafood (Hon Mieu)   150
seafood (Hue)   135
seafood (Nha Trang)   151, 152
seafood (Qui Nhon)   149
seafood (Vung Tau)   179
Southeast Asian cuisine (Da Lat)   155
Southeast Asian cuisine (Nha Trang)   152
Thai cuisine (Hanoi)   117
vegetarian cuisine (Nha Trang)   152
vegetarian cuisine (Saigon)   174
Vietnamese cuisine (Da Lat)   155
Vietnamese cuisine (Da Nang)   142
Vietnamese cuisine (Hai Phong)   122
Vietnamese cuisine (Hanoi)   117
Vietnamese cuisine (Hoi An)   147
Vietnamese cuisine (Hue)   135
Vietnamese cuisine (Nha Trang)   152
Vietnamese cuisine (Qui Nhon)   149
Vietnamese cuisine (Saigon)   173, 174
Western cuisine (Da Lat)   155
Western cuisine (Hai Phong)   122
Western cuisine (Saigon)   173
restaurants, where to eat in Cambodia
Angkor   217, 219
Phnom Penh   58, 201, 204
Siem Reap   58, 217, 219
Sihanoukville   209
restaurants, where to eat in Laos
Luang Prabang   40, 57, 243, 245
Pakse   254
Phonsavan   251
Vientiane   236
restaurants, where to eat in Vietnam
Bai Chai   124
Da Lat   155
Da Nang   142
Ha Long Bay   124
Hai Phong   122
Hanoi   40, 56, 108, 115, 116
Hoi An   147
Hon Mieu   150
Hue   40
Nha Trang   151
Qui Nhon   149
Sa Pa   126
Saigon   40, 55, 159, 173

Song Cau   149
Vung Tau   179
Reunification Express (Vietnam)   12, 13, 118, 152, 176, 266
Reunification Palace (Saigon, Vietnam)   45, 167
Revolution Museum (Hanoi, Vietnam)   114
Revolutionary Museum
    (Con Son Island, Vietnam)   187
Rex Hotel (Saigon, Vietnam)   159, 162, 164, 171
Rockpile (Vietnam)   138
Royal Palace (Phnom Penh, Cambodia)   96, 193
Royal Palace Museum (Luang Prabang, Laos)   47
Royal Theatre (Hue, Vietnam)   131
Russian Market
    (Phnom Penh, Cambodia)   49, 198

S   Sa Pa (Vietnam)   14, 15, 26, 32, 108, 125–126
safety
    Cambodia   25, 37, 198, 266, 272
    Laos   25, 251, 272
    Vietnam   162, 272
Saigon (Vietnam)   32, 40, 45, 47, 58, 66, 78, 80, 96, 98, 120, 142, 150, 158–176
Saigon Business Center (Saigon, Vietnam)   165
Saigon Opera (Saigon, Vietnam)   158, 162, 164
Saigon Racecourse (Saigon, Vietnam)   170
Saigon River (Vietnam)   159, 162, 165
Saint Joseph's Cathedral (Hanoi, Vietnam)   96, 110
Sam Mountain (Chau Doc, Vietnam)   184
Sam Neua Province (Laos)   240
Saravan (Laos)   30, 257
Savannakhet (Laos)   98
School of Fine Arts (Phnom Penh, Cambodia)   17
Se Don River (Laos)   251
Se Kong (Laos)   254
shadow puppet shows   18, 43
shopping, general information
    bargaining   13, 271
    country markets   13, 15
shopping, what to buy in Cambodia
    antiques   198
    CD's   198
    ceramics   198
    clothes   198
    gems   196
    handicrafts   49
    jewelry   196
    Khmer scarves   14, 49, 196
    porcelain   49
    silk   49, 59, 196, 198, 207
    textiles   49
    T-shirts   198
    watches   196
shopping, what to buy in Laos
    antiques   49
    cotton weavings   231, 248
    hand-embroidered head wraps   249
    hill-tribe silver   230
    jewelry   234, 240
    old Chinese ceramics and porcelain   48
    silk   59, 230, 248, 254
    silver and gold belts   231
    Soviet military watches   230
    textiles   48, 49, 59, 230, 231, 240, 248
    tribal basketware   48
    watches   240
shopping, what to buy in Vietnam

arts and crafts   114
bamboo crafts   108
basketware   149
carpets and tapestries   122
Celadon ceramics   47
clothing   114, 146, 165
Da Lat jam   153
electronics   105, 110, 165
embroidered costumes   14
embroidered linen   108
handicrafts   14, 48, 114
handmade glassware   47
handmade paper   108
jewelry   108, 165
lacquer ware   130
lacquer-covered bamboo platters   47
lacquered idols and statues   47
linen   110
luggage   165
paintings   114
silk   114, 184
souvenirs   15, 114
Soviet military watches   108
tribal costumes and textiles   15, 47
watches   165
weavings   155
shopping, where to shop in Cambodia
  Koh Dach   207
  Phnom Penh   14, 49, 196, 198
shopping, where to shop in Laos
  Ban Phanom   48, 245
  Ban Saphay   254
  Luang Prabang   14, 48, 240
  Muang Sing   14, 249
  Vientiane   48, 49, 230, 234
shopping, where to shop in Vietnam
  Bac Ha   14
  Da Lat   153, 155
  Hai Phong   122
  Hanoi   47, 48, 105, 108, 110, 114
  Hoi An   146
  Hue   14, 130
  Phung Hiep   15
  Sa Pa   14, 15
  Saigon   47, 165
  Song Cau   149
  Tan Chau   184
Si Phan Don (Laos)   252, 254, 257
Siem Reap (Cambodia)   18, 32, 37, 39, 42, 53, 54, 66, 191, 209–219. *See also* Angkor (Cambodia)
Sihanoukville (Cambodia)   37, 205, 207–209
Silk Street (Hanoi, Vietnam)   105
Silver Pagoda (Phnom Penh, Cambodia)   194
snorkeling in Vietnam
  Nha Trang   149, 150
Sofitel Da Lat Palace (Da Lat, Vietnam)   153
Sofitel Da Lat Palace (Da Lat/Vietnam)   38
Sokha Beach (Sihanoukville, Cambodia)   207
Son La (Vietnam)   32
Song Cau (Vietnam)   149
Song Hong River. *See* Red River
South China Sea   71
spectator sports in Vietnam
  horse racing   170
sports in Cambodia
  diving   207
sports in Laos

hiking   251
rafting   251
sports in Vietnam
  canoeing   30
  cycling   31
  diving   31, 54, 149, 150
  golf   31, 153, 176
  hiking   15, 17, 26, 126, 155
  snorkeling   149, 150
  surfing   54
Spratley Islands   71
Sung An Temple (Hue, Vietnam)   132
Supreme Harmony Palace. *See* Thai Hoa Palace
surfing in Vietnam
  Nha Trang   54
Swift Island. *See* Hon Yen

T   Ta Keo (Angkor, Cambodia)   215
Ta Phrom (Angkor, Cambodia)   11, 215
Ta Promh Tonle Bati (Cambodia)   206
Taat Sae Waterfall (Laos)   254
Tad Phan Falls (Laos)   26
Tam Bao Pagoda (Da Nang, Vietnam)   141
Tam Dao (Vietnam)   121
Tam Nong Reserve (Vietnam)   29
Tan Chau (Vietnam)   184
Taoism   95, 179
Tay An Pagoda (Chau Doc, Vietnam)   184
Tay Ninh (Vietnam)   96 179
Tay Ninh Province (Vietnam)   98, 141, 179
Tay Phuong Pagoda (Vietnam)   120
Tay Trang (Vietnam)   124
telephones   270
Temple of Literature (Hanoi, Vietnam)   58, 112
Terrace of the Elephants (Angkor, Cambodia)   76, 212, 215
Terrace of the Leper King (Angkor, Cambodia)   212, 215
Tha Deua (Laos)   231
Thai Hoa Palace (Hue, Vietnam)   131
Thalat Dala (Luang Prabang, Laos)   240
Thalat Sao (Luang Prabang, Laos)   240
Thalat Sao (Vientiane, Laos)   49, 230, 231
Than Long Island (Vietnam)   180
Thanh Hoa (Vietnam)   127
Thap Bac. *See* Bhan It
Thap Doi (Vietnam)   148
Thap Duong Long (Vietnam)   148, 149
Thar Thap Pagoda (Vietnam)   148
That Chom Xi (Luang Prabang, Laos)   238, 240
That Lo Falls (Laos)   26
That Mak Mo (Luang Prabang, Laos)   242
That Pathum (Luang Prabang, Laos)   242
Thatlo Resort (Laos)   26, 254, 257
Thay Pagoda (Vietnam)   120
The Huc (Hanoi, Vietnam)   109
Thien Hau Pagoda (Saigon, Vietnam)   96, 168
Thien Mu Pagoda (Hue, Vietnam)   23, 96, 130, 132
Thien Quang Lake (Hanoi, Vietnam)   105
Thieng Vuong Pagoda (Da Lat, Vietnam)   153
Thirty-six Streets (Hanoi, Vietnam)   104, 108
Thoi Son Island (Vietnam)   180
Thong Hai Vin (Laos)   15, 251
time   269
tipping   269
Tombs of the Nguyen Dynasty (Hue, Vietnam)   58

Ton Le Sap Lake (Cambodia)   89, 98
tour operators
    in Australia   60
    in Canada   61
    in Indochina   61
    in Thailand   61
    in the United Kindom   61
    in the United States   60
tourist information in Cambodia
    Angkor   212
    Phnom Penh   192
    Siem Reap   212
tourist information in Laos
    Luang Prabang   239
    Vientiane   224
tourist information in Vietnam
    Hanoi   104
    Hue   130
    Saigon   159
tourist information, general information   265
tours in Indochina
    Legends of Indochina tours   38
tours in Laos
    Mekong River cruises   20
tours in Vietnam
    Cham Ruins tours   149
    cycling tours   31
    Demilitarized Zone tours   140
    diving and snorkeling trips   31, 151
    Ha Long Bay tours   124
    Mekong Delta cruises   38
    Perfume River tours   23, 131
Tra Kieu (Vietnam)   143
train stations
    Hai Phong (Vietnam)   121
    Saigon (Vietnam)   176
Tram Chim Reserve (Vietnam)   29
Tran Hung Dao Statue (Saigon, Vietnam)   72,
    109, 165
Tran Hung Dao Temple (Saigon, Vietnam)   168
Tran Quoc Pagoda (Hanoi, Vietnam)   96, 111
Trang Tien Street (Hanoi, Vietnam)   105
Transportation in Cambodia
    by boat   32, 206, 219, 266
    by bus   205, 265
    by car or motorcycle   32, 266
    by plane   219, 265
    by train   266
Transportation in Laos
    by boat   32, 248, 266
    by bus   37, 265
    by car   266
    by plane   265
Transportation in Vietnam
    by boat   266
    by bus   32, 33, 118, 130, 176, 265
    by car or motorcycle   32, 266
    by plane   32, 265
    by train   12, 13, 32, 118, 176, 266
Transportation to Indochina
    by plane from Australia and the New Zealand   262
    by plane from Canada and the United States   262
    by plane from Europe   262
    general information   261
    overland from China to Vietnam   262
    overland from Thailand to Cambodia   262
    overland from Thailand to Laos   262, 263

Transportation, urban
    Hanoi (Vietnam)   105, 106, 120
    Hue (Vietnam)   135
    Phnom Penh (Cambodia)   193, 205
    Saigon (Vietnam)   162, 175
    Vientiane (Laos)   224
traveler's checks   268
trekking. See hiking
tribal groups. See minorities
Truong Son Martyr Cemetery (Vietnam)   138
Truong Son Mountains (Vietnam)   140
Truong Song Trail. See Ho Chi Minh Trail
Tuol Sleng Museum (Phnom Penh,
    Cambodia)   198, 206
Tuol Sleng Museum
    (Phnom Penh/Cambodia)   86

[U] Um Muang. See Muang Thamo

[V] Valley of Love (Da Lat, Vietnam)   25, 153
Van Mieu   112. See Temple of Literature
Victory Beach (Sihanoukville, Cambodia)   207
Victory Monument (Phnom Penh,
    Cambodia)   193, 196
Vientiane (Laos)   20, 32, 42, 47, 49, 53, 58, 66, 74,
    76, 96, 98, 223–237, 242, 248, 265
Vietnam Museum of Ethnology
    (Hanoi/Vietnam)   45, 113
Vijaya. See Cha Ban
Vinh (Vietnam)   127
Vinh Moc Tunnels (Vietnam)   138
Vinh Nghiem Pagoda (Saigon, Vietnam)   168
Vinh Phu Province (Vietnam)   121
Vinh Trang Pagoda (My Tho, Vietnam)   180
Vinotheque la Cave (Vientiane, Laos)   231
visas
    Cambodia   262, 263
    Laos   237, 263
    Vietnam   263
Vung Tau (Vietnam)   176–179, 186

[W] War Remnants Museum
    (Saigon, Vietnam)   45, 80, 166
Wat Chom Phet (Luang Prabang, Laos)   242
Wat Koh (Phnom Penh, Cambodia)   196
Wat Lang Ka (Phnom Penh, Cambodia)   196
Wat Mai (Luang Prabang, Laos)   242
Wat Moha Montrei
    (Phnom Penh, Cambodia)   196
Wat Ong Teu Mahawihan (Vientiane, Laos)   230
Wat Ounalom (Phnom Penh, Cambodia)   196
Wat Phnom (Phnom Penh, Cambodia)   192, 195
Wat Phra Keo (Vientiane, Laos)   230
Wat Phu (Laos)   20, 66, 95, 251, 254, 255–256
Wat Preah Keo (Phnom Penh, Cambodia)   195
Wat Si Amphon (Vientiane, Laos)   230
Wat Si Muang (Vientiane, Laos)   53, 230
Wat Si Saket (Vientiane, Laos)   228
Wat Sok Pa Luang (Vientiane, Laos)   230
Wat Tham (Luang Prabang, Laos)   242
Wat That Luang (Luang Prabang, Laos)   242
Wat That Luang (Vientiane, Laos)   53
Wat Visoun (Luang Prabang, Laos)   242
Wat Xieng Khwan. See Buddha Park
Wat Xieng Thong (Luang Prabang, Laos)   240
water, drinking   41, 272
water puppetry   43, 118, 121

web sites
   Cambodia information
     www.cambodia-web.net/directory/ or
     www.kampuchea.com. or www.cambodia.org 276
   events in Saigon
     www.vneconomy.com.vn and
     www.groovysaigon.com   161
   gay and lesbian scene
     www.utopia-asia.com/tipsviet.htm   273
   Hanoi information
     www.hanoitravel.com/, 276
   Indochina links
     http://rectravel.com/khlavn/khlavn.htm   276
   Laos information
     www.lan-xang.com   276
   Laos travel
     http://laos-travel.net/index.htm   276
   lunar calendar dates
     www.flash.net/~pburch/lunarcal.html   50
   Vietnam information
     www.vietnamonline.net   276
   Vietnam links
     www.veloasia.com/resource.html   276
West Lake (Hanoi, Vietnam)   *96, 105, 111*
wildlife
   Cambodia   30
   Laos   30
   Vietnam   27, 29, 121, 127, 187
women, traveling alone   272
World Heritage Sites
   Angkor Wat (Cambodia)   209
   Hoi An (Vietnam)   145
   Luang Prabang (Laos)   53, 238

   X Xa Loi Pagoda (Saigon, Vietnam)   *168*
      Xieng Khoang Province (Laos)   *15, 25, 98, 251*
      Xuan Huong Lake (Da Lat, Vietnam)   *152*

Photography Credits

All photographs are by **Alain Evrard** with the exception of the following:

Jill Gocher: pages 10–14, 16, 17, 19–31, 33–42, 44–46, 48–57, 59, 60, 125, 126, 131, 151, 171, 181 *top*, 187, 198, 207, 214, 243, 264, 275, 277, 278.

Nick Wheeler: pages 7 *left and right*, 96, 97, 104 *left and right*, 113, 116, 127, 132–133, 134, 136–137, 143, 168, 202–203, 220–222, 224–227, 229–235, 238–239, 241, 244–251, 253 *top and bottom*, 255–259, 271-273.

Tim Hall: page 64.